Conversations with Stanley Kauffmann

Literary Conversations Series
Peggy Whitman Prenshaw,
General Editor

Photo credit: Courtesy of Stanley Kauffmann, photo by Jerzy Kosinski

Conversations
with Stanley Kauffmann

Edited by
Bert Cardullo

University Press of Mississippi
Jackson

www.upress.state.ms.us

The University Press of Mississippi is a member of the Association of American University Presses.

11   10   09   08   07   06   05   04   03   4   3   2   1
∞
Library of Congress Cataloging-in-Publication Data
Conversations with Stanley Kauffmann / edited by Bert Cardullo.
      p.   cm.—(Literary conversations series)
   Includes index.
   ISBN 1-57806-565-8 (alk. paper)—ISBN 1-57806-566-6 (pbk. : alk. paper)
   1. Kauffmann, Stanley, 1916– —Interviews. 2. Criticism—United States—
History—20th century. 3. Authors, American—20th century—Interviews. 4. Critics—
United States—Interviews. I. Cardullo, Bert. II. Kauffmann, Stanley, 1916– III. Series.
PS3521.A7255Z64   2003
809—dc21   2003043270

British Library Cataloging-in-Publication Data available

Books by Stanley Kauffmann

Plays

The Red Handkerchief Man: A Play in Three Acts. New York: Samuel French, 1933.
"The Mayor's Hose" in *Second Yearbook of Short Plays.* Evanston, Ill.: Row, Peterson, & Co., 1934.
The Prince Who Shouldn't Have Shaved: A Frolic in One Act. Rock Island, Ill.: Ingram, 1934.
How She Managed Her Marriage; A Little Play in One Act. New York: Samuel French, 1935.
The Singer in Search of a King; A Play in One Act. New York: Samuel French, 1935.
The True Adventure; A Comedy in Three Acts. New York: Samuel French, 1935.
Altogether Reformed. New York: Samuel French, 1936.
"A Million Stars" in *Ladies Night: A Collection of Sketches for Women, by Various Authors.* By Arthur LeRoy Kaser and others. Franklin, OH: Eldridge Entertainment House, 1936.
Cyrano of the Long Nose. Franklin, OH: Eldridge Entertainment House, 1937.
"The Marooning of Marilla" in *Tournament Plays: Thirteen One-Act Plays Never Before Published.* New York: Samuel French, 1937.
Come Again: A South Seas Vignette in One Act. New York: Dramatists' Play Service, 1937.
Coming of Age: A One-Act Comedy. New York: Samuel French, 1937.
Eleanor on the Hill: A One-Act Fantasia on Comic Themes. New York: Samuel French, 1937.
Mr. Flemington Sits Down. New York: Samuel French, 1938.
"The More the Merrier" in *One-Act Play Magazine and Radio Drama Review.* Ed. William Kollenko. Boston: One Act Play Magazine, Inc., 1939.
Consider Lily. Produced but not published, 1939.
"Overhead" in *Sixth Yearbook of Short Plays.* Evanston, Ill.: Row, Peterson, & Co., 1940.
The Salvation of Mr. Song. Rock Island, Ill.: Ingram, 1940.
The Victors. Produced but not published, 1940.
Bobino, His Adventures, in Two Acts. Evanston, Ill.: Row, Peterson, & Co., 1941.
Food for Freedom: A United Nations Play for Elementary School Children in One Act. Boston: Baker's Plays, 1944.

Essays and Criticism

A World on Film: Criticism and Comment. New York: Harper & Row, 1966.
Figures of Light: Film Criticism and Comment. New York: Harper & Row, 1971.
American Film Criticism: From the Beginnings to "Citizen Kane"; Reviews of Significant Films at the Time They First Appeared [Editor, with Bruce Henstell]. New York: Liveright, 1972.
Living Images: Film Comment and Criticism. New York: Harper & Row, 1975.
Persons of the Drama: Theater Criticism and Comment. New York: Harper & Row, 1976.
Before My Eyes: Film Criticism and Comment. New York: Harper & Row, 1980.
Albums of Early Life. New Haven: Ticknor & Fields, 1980.
Theater Criticisms. New York: Performing Arts Journal Publications, 1983.
Field of View: Film Criticism and Comment. New York: Performing Arts Journal Publications, 1986.

Distinguishing Features: Film Criticism and Comment. Baltimore: Johns Hopkins University Press, 1994.
Regarding Film: Criticism and Comment. Baltimore: Johns Hopkins University Press, 2001.

Fiction

The King of Proxy Street, a Story. [Published as *The Bad Samaritan* in England.] New York: The John Day Company, 1941.
This Time Forever, a Romance. Garden City, NY: Doubleday, Doran, and Company, Inc., 1945.
The Hidden Hero, a Story. New York: Rinehart, 1949.
The Tightrope. [Published as *The Philanderer* in England]. New York: Simon and Schuster, 1952.
A Change of Climate. New York: Rinehart, 1954.
Man of the World. [Published as *The Very Man* in England.] New York: Rinehart, 1956.
If It Be Love. London: M. Joseph, 1960.

Contents

Introduction

Wolcott Gibbs, late of *The New Yorker,* once wrote the following of his experience as a film critic: "It is my indignant opinion that ninety per cent of the moving pictures exhibited in America are so vulgar, witless, and dull that it is preposterous to write about them in any publication not intended to be read while chewing gum." Gibbs vowed that he would never review another movie, and he kept his vow.

As it happens, he quit movie reviewing just before it was discovered that there was a market for European films in the United States. It was the 1946 box-office triumph in New York of Rossellini's *Open City* that opened the way for many low-budget Italian and French pictures. Even better ones began coming here, from Asia as well as Europe, after the 1950 success of Kurosawa's *Rashomon.* These foreign films increasingly exposed the tinsel and cardboard of the indigenous product, but—more to the present point—they made the reviewing of movies a rewarding activity.

Stanley Kauffmann's career as film critic for *The New Republic* began not long afterward, in February of 1958. Significantly, this was also the year in which *Agee on Film* was published, and thus a year that marks the beginning of a change in general attitudes toward serious film criticism in America. Indeed, the 1960s and early 1970s were heady times for such criticism. In colleges and universities, in cafés, bars, theater lobbies, and their surrounding sidewalks, movies were the subject of heated debates. (As one member of the Film Generation—a phrase coined by Kauffmann, incidentally—who moved through college and on to graduate school in the late sixties and early seventies, I can vouch that the best dorm-room arguments were never about people or politics or even Vietnam: they were about movies.) Neither moviegoing nor movie reviewing was new, as Kauffmann points out in the interview titled "Film to Me Is Another Art," and as his own *American Film Criticism: From the Beginnings to "Citizen Kane"* proved. But youthful hordes, uncomfortable with literature and not yet enslaved by television, now found something to get excited about in the cinema. More than ever before and perhaps ever since, they looked to critics to stimulate, shape, or confirm their opinions, and they gravitated toward the critics who best satisfied their individual bents.

By "critics" I mean journalistic ones (*critics,* as opposed to newspaper reviewers), not academics or scholars. It was the former group which led the fight to give film stature as art, and by the first few years of the 1970s that battle had been won. Virtually every college and university in America by then was offering film courses, and many had degree programs or were in the process of developing them. Yet with every new course, program, and treatise, ironically, the less relevant the writing of the pioneering journalistic critics became to the professors. Was this a case of film education outdistancing the journalists, who had advanced to establishment middle age or beyond and had therefore ceased to grow intellectually? Or had the demands to achieve academic respectability killed off the love of movies in those film scholars, who, once drawn to motion pictures out of passion, were now burying them in mounds of hopelessly "scientific," theoretical garbage? (For a detailed discussion of this matter, see the start of my conversation with Kauffmann reprinted from *South Atlantic Quarterly.*)

The split between the academics or scholars and the journalistic critics can best be understood, I think, in terms of classical and romantic temperaments: one deductive, starting with general principles and moving to specific examples, the other inductive, relying on each "text" to stimulate insights appropriate to it. And because of the strong French influence on academic thinking about film, it was unlikely then, just as it is now, that American journalistic critics would adopt any of the academy's viewpoints. For those viewpoints go against a longstanding American tradition. Leslie Fiedler put this issue best when he said something to the effect that no matter what they try to do, the French keep reinventing neoclassicism while the Americans keep reinventing romanticism. And Stanley Kauffmann said something similar to me in "The Film Generation and After": "The academic critics think of me as an impressionist, because I deal experientially with film, deal with it analytically in terms of a highly personal set of standards. I could not possibly codify for you what my beliefs are about film; it's a matter of instances rather than precepts." It seems, then, that for the foreseeable future journalistic criticism will be at odds with academic film study. But the journalists still need to be read, especially in universities, if only to keep alive the romantic enthusiasm that brought professors to the cinema in the first place.

Where does Stanley Kauffmann stand among the journalistic critics? Though precise terminology is elusive, there were, at the time he became prominent, two kinds of critics: the eggheads, who preferred what were loosely called art films, and the populists, who grooved on Hollywood movies and their foreign counterparts where they could find them. Both groups are treated, under different names, in this volume's very first interview, originally published in *The Seventh Art*. The eggheads were Stanley Kauffmann, Dwight Macdonald, Vernon Young, and John Simon, with relatively few adherents. The populists were Andrew Sarris, Pauline Kael, and Manny Farber, with their legions of followers. In between, and antecedent to both groups, were good souls like James Agee, Robert Warshow, and Otis Ferguson.

Of the egghead critics, Kauffmann was, and is, the least dogmatic and the least elitist. For over forty years, he has been writing about film in *The New Republic* and elsewhere—a fact celebrated by Charlie Rose in this book's final interview. And, since 1968, Kauffmann has also been teaching film as well as theater and writing courses at the Yale Drama School, Hunter College, the City University of New York Graduate Center, and beyond. His own writing style is civilized and easygoing, not chattily egocentric like Kael's, cultishly soul-baring like Sarris's, or olympianly ironic like Macdonald's. He is a man at home in film history, conversant with culture and the arts, informative without being preachy, using his writing to think about his subject and pleased to take us into his confidence.

The internal consistency of Kauffmann's evaluations makes clear that he says what he thinks, though his insights are neither gratuitously shocking nor necessarily innovative, and he does not make a show of himself or battle on behalf of his own reputation. Here, then, is a critic who takes films more seriously than he takes himself. His stance was, and continues to be, anything but a commonplace one among his fellow critics. Indeed, much film criticism appears to be written by persons who have no other life. By contrast, Kauffmann appears to be a man of large interests, great knowledge, and supreme responsibility, as especially evidenced by his 1981 interview in *Contemporary Authors*.

A particular value of his work is his willingness to go against critical consensus. Kauffmann has never been intimidated, for example, by precious, arty analyses and endorsements of films that included the *Cahiers du cinéma* cachet among their number. Nor has he ever been overawed by films that won their fame because of their "difficulty," or because they claimed to be "advanced." Just because a film was labeled *nouvelle vague* or was by Jean-Luc Godard, François Truffaut, Philippe de Broca, Agnès Varda, even Jean Cocteau or Robert Bresson, Kauffmann did not cast aside his responsibility as a critic to take on the mantle of a cinéaste. No matter how big or idolized the director, Kauffmann has always striven to separate brouhaha from artistry.

Witness his disliking of *The Serpent's Egg* despite the fact that he is an Ingmar Bergman fan; his not hesitating to explain why *Perceval* fails even though he is otherwise an admirer of Eric Rohmer; or, in the *Salmagundi* interview, his extended critique of Woody Allen's urbane realism. Witness also the following comeuppances Kauffmann delivered to Luis Buñuel in his very first collection of film criticism, *A World on Film*: "He is a master technician with the outlook of a collegiate idealist who has just discovered venality and lust." . . . "Buñuel, the swami of sadism, has now reached the point of self-parody." . . . "Buñuel remains, for me, a highly resourceful technician and a highly neurotic adolescent." Buñuel may have been too old and too far gone for change by this time (1966), but these harsh words surely gave some "Buñuel-can-do-no-wrong" devotees a prod toward reevaluating their master.

All the pieces on Buñuel in *A World on Film* are grouped together, which is not as trivial an editorial choice as it may sound. Rather, it is symptomatic of Kauffmann's longtime concern with continuity—one that continues in his latest collection, *Regarding Film*. When, in *Before My Eyes,* you read his review of *Family Plot,* you also register the important point that, for all the encomia about Alfred Hitchcock's style, a Hitchcock film has always stood or stumbled by virtue of its script. An extended piece on *8½* discusses not just that film but its relation to Fellini's life and its place in the cinematic pantheon as well as the artistic pantheon generally. Writing on the much-awarded *Tree of Wooden Clogs,* Kauffmann once again swims against the critical tide by asserting that it is far from top-drawer Olmi, and proceeds to explain why by citing much earlier, better films by this director like *Il Posto* and *The Fiancés.*

Breadth of range is another Kauffmann virtue. What other critic would begin a review of Robert Altman's *A Wedding* by relating the film to latter-day European naturalism; in another piece, compare Ingmar Bergman to Eugene O'Neill; or, in still another, detail the ways in which young German filmmakers of the 1970s utilized American popular culture? Who other than Kauffmann would lay out Lina Wertmüller's options for portraying the Holocaust in *Seven Beauties* . . . and then explain why she decided on comedy; call *Close Encounters of the Third Kind* not simply the best science-fiction movie ever made but "an event in the history of faith"; notice in Warren Beatty's *Bulworth* an unacknowledged debt not only to Frank Capra's *Meet*

John Doe but also to a Finnish *and* a Ukrainian film; or discuss, during a single conversation (with Studs Terkel) about the theater, the subjects of Pinter and acting, Beckett and Bert Lahr, Brecht and Berlin, and Dickens and performance?

Perhaps even better, Kauffmann's elegy to Jean Renoir in *Before My Eyes* beautifully (and concisely) details the man's style, influence, and achievement, then goes on to fix him in the context of twentieth-century culture: "First, the length of his life—of *his* life, not just anyone who happens to survive for eighty-four years—gives him a unique place. He connected *La Belle Epoque,* from his father the painter, to the present day. He was an exponent of a view of art that doesn't promise to be generated again: art as community, from which one can make every bitter expedition into blackness, as Renoir certainly did, but which supports the expedition and strengthens its unsentimental insistence."

In this era of fake profundity, and from the perspective of his more than four decades as a critic, over thirty years as a teacher, and many more years as an editor, playwright, and novelist, Stanley Kauffmann clearly continues to see films in the broad cultural and historical context that eludes the tunnel-vision reviewers whose only reference points are Hollywood and old movies, and the box office. He is particularly sensitive to the parasitic relationship that middle-brow movies too often have with genuine art. "He's the film equivalent of the advertising-agency art director who haunts the galleries to keep his eye fresh," Kauffmann wrote of Robert Altman in *Before My Eyes*. "The future may judge our age culturally by its high estimate of Robert Altman. Indeed, the Altman nonsense is already coming undone."

Reviewing Kauffmann's *Living Images* a number of years ago, one reviewer writer suggested that his most salient quality as a critic was that of "raffish dignity." That raffishness is as lively as ever, as in this understatedly but effectively witty comment about *Fargo,* from *Regarding Film*: "The hot news about Joel and Ethan Coen is that they have made a tolerable film." Or, from the same collection, these slicing words about *Touch of Evil*: "Heston's attempts to be a dashing young man were painful even when he was young." Often Kauffmann's opening lines are as amusingly provocative as Pauline Kael's. Witness the following three from *Before My Eyes*: "When François Truffaut has an idea, he makes a film. And sometimes when he doesn't have an idea, he makes a film anyway." . . . "Heaven has blessed Paddy Chayefsky. He was born with just enough of everything." . . . "One way to pass the time while watching a turkey with big people in it is to wonder why they agreed to do it."

Sometimes, however, Kauffmann's amusing provocativeness or dignified raffishness turns to harsh dismissal. This may be the result of an impatience with stars or directors who keep flourishing despite his low opinion of them, but Kauffmann has seemed less willing since the 1980s to be gentlemanly. Thus his bugbear Robert Altman was (and continues to be) seen as "a walking death sentence on the prospects of American film" and "a public embarrassment," his *Quintet* "paralyzingly stupid." *Shampoo* struck Kauffmann at the time as "disgusting," while Liza Minnelli in *New York, New York* resembled a "giant rodent en route to a costume ball." Perhaps for a critic so concerned with film's relationship to larger culture, the many opportunities lost, bungled, or cheapened had come to seem unbearable.

Even so, as early as 1959, Kauffmann was able to toss off this line in dismissal of Gregory Peck: "[He] embodies Gordon Craig's deal of an actor: an *Übermarionette,* wooden to the core." Only two years later he had this to say about the performance of Jackie Gleason in *The Hustler*: "It is the best use of a manikin by a director since Kazan photographed Burl Ives as Big Daddy [in *Cat on a Hot Tin Roof*]." And, in 1963 in an interview published by the magazine *Seventh Art,* he dismissed *la politique des auteurs* with the following words: "I think it is utterly boring . . . [something] for irresponsible children. It bores me even to say as much as I've said."

Whether harsh or generous, Kauffmann is most certainly a master of the felicitous phrase and memorable characterization. So, in *Regarding Film,* he describes Emma Thompson as the "first film actress since Katharine Hepburn to make intelligence sexy"; he finds in *Amistad* "a sense of presence in the past" he has not experienced since Bergman's *Virgin Spring*; and he notes that Oliver Stone "in appalling measure" succeeds in *Natural Born Killers.* Kauffmann is acute about a lesser but related film, *Pulp Fiction,* which "nourishes, abets, cultural slumming [with] calculated grunginess." And, ever sensitive to cinematography, he writes of *Stalingrad* that "the colors don't glamorize, they confirm," while in the camera work of *Sister My Sister,* he finds "the everyday put before us as evidence of strangeness." In *Carrington,* for its part, "appurtenances of class and of conscious bohemianism are integral to the characters themselves, not imposed as décor. Setting and story are unified."

As they were not, for instance, in *Barry Lyndon.* At a time—the last quarter of the twentieth century and beyond—when gorgeous cinematography has all but overwhelmed intelligent screenwriting, Kauffmann's senses never overpower his sensibility. Of *Barry Lyndon,* whose visual splendor blinded many critics to its intellectual emptiness, he wrote in *Before My Eyes*: "Stanley Kubrick began professional life as a photographer and has lately been reverting to his first career. His new film . . . very nearly accommodates Zeno's paradox of motion: it seems to remain . . . in one place while actually it is moving ahead. Kubrick has produced three hours and four minutes of pictures." Unlike *auteurists* and other aesthetes, Kauffmann understands that "films begin where most reviews don't: the screenplay."

Which is not to say that he is the kind of film critic who can easily be dismissed as "literary"—though the editors of *The Creative Expression* may not have helped his cause by titling their interview with him "Literary Criticism"! In fact, Kauffmann reserves his greatest scorn for screenwriters whose prose never equals their literary aspirations, deftly puncturing the pretensions of, among others, James Toback (*The Gambler*) and Thomas McGuane (*The Missouri Breaks*). He is also mercilessly attentive to the sort of detail that is usually overlooked in hyperbolic reviews. Reviewing *The Godfather, Part II* in 1975, for example, he patiently noted four gigantic plot holes before adding casually, "And, by the way, the ship on which young Vito is said to be arriving in New York from Sicily is actually leaving New York, sailing south past the Statue of Liberty."

One of the subconscious advantages of being a critic on a "little" magazine like *The New Republic* may be that one feels sufficiently free to tout small films, or neglected art, in addition to covering major releases like *The Godfather.* Kauffmann has always shown this predilection for unheralded work, perhaps never more strongly than in *Before My Eyes.* There Elaine May's barely acknowledged *Mikey and Nicky* is praised as "an implicitly large film" and "an odd, biting, grinning, sideways-scuttling rodent of a picture" that is the best film by an American woman to date. *Go Tell the Spartans,* to Kauffmann's eyes, is the finest film about Vietnam, far above *Coming Home*—a point that he expands upon during his interview in *South Atlantic Quarterly* with reference to *Platoon* and *Full Metal Jacket.* The flaws in *Go Tell the Spartans* are pointed out, but so are the wider accomplishments. And so is the acting.

I give you Kauffmann on the acting of Jane Fonda—someone whose career he has watched from the beginning, as he explains in both the *Film Heritage* and Dick Cavett interviews. He deftly locates the mediocrity of 1978's *Coming Home* as the source of Fonda's "crimped" performance: "[Her] performance seems . . . crimped by the role's careful sterilization. There's nothing much more than Jane Wyman pertness at the start, to which is later added some Elissa Landi soul. I choose '30s references because, under the '68 trappings, a perennial movie-movie is what *Coming Home* is." Such a comment is typical of Stanley Kauffmann's criticism and serves as evidence, together with the following nuggets, that he remains the only American film critic who has a thorough, incisive appreciation of the performance side of cinema.

From *A World on Film,* sample these remarks comparing Frank Sinatra with Marlon Brando: "[T]he emotion displayed by Sinatra, one feels, is always Sinatra's emotion, not the character's. . . . If it were possible to see Sinatra in Brando's role in *On the Waterfront,* that would clarify the difference between mere simulation and creative acting." Here is Kauffmann on the creative acting of Paul Newman, from the interview "Film to Me Is Another Art":

> He's much more subtle than he's given credit for. . . . If I could take clips from [*Sometimes a Great Notion* and *Pocket Money*] and show them to you side by side, figuratively, I think I could demonstrate what I mean about subtlety of imagination working its way out through vocal inflection, physical attitudes, personality aura, and . . . other factors. [Newman] *thinks* differently in his pictures. . . . It's not a question of a stock company actor putting on hook nose and beard and becoming "somebody else"—that's easy. He works from a core outward, differently. And you would find, I believe, that his whole system of timing was different in *Pocket Money* from what it was in the logging picture.

Finally, consider this analysis, from *Regarding Film,* of the two stars who have played Humbert Humbert in *Lolita*: "James Mason is the ideal Humbert. He gives us a doomed man, conscious of it, accepting it. [Jeremy] Irons in the role [gives] it his customary vestments of intelligence and sensitive reticence, but at his deepest he is no more than melancholy. Mason suggested a tragic fall." As for the difference between a comic performer and a comic actor, Kauffmann replies in *A World on Film*: "A performer is a person who does things to make you laugh; an actor creates a character at whose actions and utterances you laugh." To Kauffmann, Peter Ustinov and Peter Sellers are comic performers; Alec Guinness and Jack Lemmon are comic actors.

Probably most important in any consideration of Stanley Kauffmann's critical virtues is that, while many of his fellow reviewers have been carried away on their own waves of hyperbole during the past few decades—particularly in their undiscriminating remarks about film acting—he has not forgotten the real duty or responsibility of a critic. Which is to exercise his judgment in the service of art, as he argues in his conversation with *Salmagundi*'s Robert Boyers, not to try desperately to substitute rhetorical fireworks for the experience of art, or to attempt to create masterpieces by fiat rather than discover them by careful observation. To be sure, Kauffmann is not afraid to generalize from his detailed observations, though he is always careful to avoid the thesis-mongering that too often passes these days for cultural criticism.

For his part he avoids such axe-grinding, making no dichotomy between his aesthetics and his morality. Letting one flow into the other, Kauffmann thus explores movies in order to search out the universality of their subject matter, the artistry of their technique, and the moral force that makes some art objects greater than others. He wonderfully does all three in a review of that difficult yet impressive film *Last Year at Marienbad,* where, neither blinded by its technique nor alienated by its innovation, he could lucidly and sympathetically find its artistic impulse at the same time as he had to conclude, "After *Marienbad,* I knew more about Resnais and Resnais's search for reality; but after *La notte* and *L'avventura* I knew more about myself."

Kauffmann's description of Harry Alan Potamkin, in a thoughtful appreciation of the late Marxist critic, could equally apply to himself: "He judged film by its own criteria certainly . . . but criteria no more lax or unbuttoned than those that any good critic would apply to any other art." Unfortunately, as Kauffmann noted in this piece from *Before My Eyes,* "The assumption, then and now, is that such an approach precludes appreciation of good popular film. . . . Or that such an approach marks the 'literary' film critic." Perhaps this was too sour a view of the scene in the late 1970s. But it is none too sour a view from the vantage point of 2002. If anyone is beleaguered these days, it is critics with taste and intelligence—like Stanley Kauffmann.

Still, Kauffmann feels considerably less beleaguered than most of his fellow film critics; and, as he pointed out in his 1992 interview with me, "The serious critic . . . who can't enjoy what to him is a good entertainment film, is lacking in full capacity for enjoying the best film, I think." As Kauffmann himself would agree, the fact that an Ozu film doesn't run very long in the nation's biggest city does not prove any more about the status of the art and its audience than the fact that Athol Fugard's drama *Boesman and Lena* didn't break the *Hello, Dolly!* attendance record or that John Berryman's

Dream Songs didn't outsell the poetry of Rod McKuen. It is not so much that Kauffmann is sanguine about the current state of cinema; rather, he knows that masterpieces in any form in any age are few and far between, and that a responsible critic must exercise the same judgment in the valleys as on the peaks. In the meantime, he is hardly waiting around for the next great work of art to appear, or for an old master miraculously to regain his powers.

Indeed, Kauffmann's powers of discernment are perhaps most evident in his writing about films that are far from being total successes; he is capable of simultaneously appreciating their virtues (often limited) and deploring their shortcomings (often considerable). "*Julia* is irresistible," he confessed in 1977. "Tears must flow. Mine certainly did. But this is not to say that it's really good. In fact, if it were *really* good, tears might flow less, perhaps not at all. . . . *Julia* is first-class middle-brow beautified film-making." Or consider, from 1978, this vintage-Kauffmann criticism of Terrence Malick's *Days of Heaven*: "He brought over Nestor Almendros for this film . . . [and] . . . has proved, by doing this, the last thing he wanted to prove: there is no such thing as an artist-cinematographer, there are only good cinematographers who sometimes work for artists. . . . And when the director is weak, as Malick is here, he tends to lean more and more on the good cinematographer's ability, and so swamps the film in pretty pictures."

In the end, Stanley Kauffmann's film writing creates the kind of evocative and sensitive critical world that recharges a work of art while searching out and probing its parts. He does not merely mediate between his readers and the artwork; he allows the play of his intelligence to respond to the force of that work, using language to capture the thrust of a film and test it against its own possibilities. At his best, Kauffmann responds to the cinema, in Henry James's phrase, with perception at the pitch of passion. Agreement with him matters less than recognition of his ability to summon up the memory of films enjoyed; to evoke the pleasure of, and build up the appetite for, films unseen; and, on privileged occasions, to change our long-held but nonetheless obsolete critical estimates, or to make us reflect for the first time on the magic of being born at a time when the arrival of film could transform one's life. Without the movies, writes Kauffmann in *Regarding Film,* "Josef von Sternberg might have spent his life in the lace business; Howard Hawks might have remained an engineer; David Lean might have browned out his life as a London accountant." So too did Kauffmann discover film criticism at the right time, to his and everybody's gain.

He continues to write film criticism, moreover, at the age of eighty-six.

Kauffmann was also a frontline drama critic for a time, and some remarks on this role of his—among his others as a playwright, a novelist, a book publisher's editor, a book reviewer, and a university professor—are in order. In 1963 the Public Broadcasting television station in New York, Channel 13, invited him to review plays once a week. In January of 1966 Kauffmann became the drama critic for *The New York Times,* a post he held until September of the same year. And from 1969 to 1979 he was the theater as well as the film critic of *The New Republic,* serving finally, from 1979 to 1985, as the theater critic for *The Saturday Review.* Two collections of dramatic criticism came out of all this activity: *Persons of the Drama* (1976) and *Theater Criticisms* (1983).

Unlike Kauffmann's collections of film criticism, which, among other uses, serve as guides to movies that are "revived" in theaters, on television, or on videotape, collections of theater criticism have no precisely parallel use. When one of the plays discussed is revived, the new production must in some way alter it. For this very reason, collections of theater criticism like Stanley Kauffmann's have, I think, a special importance that more than compensates for their lack of "utility." In a sense, one part of the past—like the "unknown" plays of Shaw treated in Jane Ann Crum's interview with Kauffmann—would not exist without them. Collections of performance criticism, then, are books of *witness.* Surely, like other critics, performance critics can help to illuminate works, can test, revise, and extend criteria, can capture qualities and pose questions (if not posit answers). But the unique reward of performance criticism is in its immediacy and the distillation of that immediacy, in the salvaging of pertinences.

Those pertinences, for Kauffmann, always include acting (as well as directing and design), just as they do in his film criticism. But the pertinences also include the play as a piece of literature; and, in his combining of telling performance or theatrical criticism with keen dramatic evaluation, Kauffmann has to know he is emulating his acknowledged hero, Bernard Shaw. As Kauffmann himself wrote of the arrival of Shaw the critic, in an essay in *Yale/Theatre* later adapted for *Persons of the Drama,* "Through the nineteenth century, English-language criticism concentrated on acting and was often good on the subject; it was weak on new scripts. This fitted a theatre that was strong on acting, particularly of old plays, and whose new plays were patterned to a pietistic society. . . . There was bound to be a change because of changes in social attitudes, literary standards, and consequent theatre ambitions. The change is first importantly apparent in the criticism of Bernard Shaw."

Only a few theater critics are worth reading; still fewer are worth reading twice. That Stanley Kauffmann, along with Shaw, belongs in the second group is evidenced, in *Theater Criticisms,* by some eighty reviews and a handful of essays spanning the seasons between *Travesties* (1975) and *'night, Mother* (1983). As it happens, these two plays, as plays, were deliriously received by most critics, while Kauffmann had grave reservations about their dramatic art. He has had grave reservations about many of the productions, playwrights, and performers applauded by his colleagues. But Kauffmann is no mere naysayer. He has reasons for his nays; he presents them with clarity; and he tries to create a critical environment in which good things in the theater can get recognized at the expense of what is bad. Discussing *Travesties,* for example, he shows how its playwright, Tom Stoppard, "plunges into promising situations and then breaks their promises, too shortwinded to fulfill them artistically and intellectually." Marsha Norman's *'night, Mother,* he writes, is "a stunt," and his analysis of the play's plot and characters leads inescapably to his conclusion that "if the play were true—to Norman's characters as she wants us to think of them—it wouldn't exist."

Kauffmann's value as a drama critic resides in his values as a critic generally, which he does not hesitate to declare in the *Prompt, Village Voice,* or *Performing Arts Journal* interviews about contemporary American theater and playwriting. After decades of going to the theater, he still expects excellence (as in his most recent review, of the Roundabout production of *Major Barbara,* for the May 2002 issue of *Performing Arts Journal*) and he is brilliant at explaining why he has or has not found it. That he stopped writing regular theater criticism in 1985, while he continues as a film critic, deserves some comment, however. For theater criticism once attracted a number of writers of the caliber of Stanley Kauffmann: Eric Bentley, Richard Gilman, Susan Sontag, Mary McCarthy, Kenneth Tynan, John Simon (not to speak of George Jean Nathan and Stark Young before them)—writers, in short, who could be expected to analyze a play or production intelligently, and to correct the misjudgments of the daily press. Today, this kind of corrective has practically disappeared (one notable exception: Robert Brustein), as the dissenting critics have departed or shifted to other fields like music. Most intellectual journals have long since stopped carrying theater chronicles.

And John Simon's own virtually single-handed crusade, in *New York* magazine, to preserve high standards became vitiated by his uncontrolled savagery, his excessively punning style, his peculiar prejudices, his personal attacks on the physical appearance of actors, his obsessive campaign against real or imagined homosexuality on the stage, and, lastly, his turning of his critical fury into its own mode of performance for the amusement of television talk-show audiences eager to see the bad man in person. Simon's "progress" (now finally ended, though he continues to write film criticism) may suggest why so many other serious writers, like Stanley Kauffmann, have abandoned the writing of all but occasional theater criticism, for it shows what may happen to a person of intelligence and discrimination when he observes too long the execrable products of the American theatrical scene (unmitigated, as in the case of film, by international imports in sufficient numbers).

Stanley Kauffmann comments on the crisis of theater-and-film-criticism in more than one of the interviews in this book, as he does on such subjects as the function of criticism, the qualifications of a critic, the influence or power of critics, newspaper reviewing versus magazine criticism versus academic scholarship, critical theory as opposed to critical practice, and the film criticism of the New York "school." Other topics touched on in the following conversations include the relationship between theater and film, particularly the difference between stage and screen acting; the relationship between novels and the movies made from them; Shakespeare and the cinema; Shaw, criticism, and theater (a kind of leitmotif that weaves its way through a number of the following interviews); sex, realism, taste, and violence in the cinema; various national cinemas along with the best films to come out of them; the phenomenon of film festivals; and the issue of government subsidy for the arts.

Broadway, Off-Broadway, Off-Off Broadway, and regional theater in the United States are treated at length in *Conversations with Stanley Kauffmann,* as are such American playwrights as Tennessee Williams, Edward Albee, Arthur Miller, and Sam Shepard. Similarly, Kauffmann talks about the relationship between Hollywood and independent American film, on the one hand, and between popular American movies and international art-house cinema, on the other, at the same time as he discusses the work of directors like Federico Fellini, Michelangelo Antonioni, Charlie Chaplin, Martin Scorsese, Margarethe von Trotta, and Bertrand Blier. The work of such actors as Laurence Olivier, Toshiro Mifune, Maggie Smith, Vanessa Redgrave, Barbra Streisand, and Robert Duvall is also analyzed.

My deep thanks to Stanley Kauffmann for being the critic (not to mention the interviewee) many of us aspire to be, as well as for championing criticism in two art forms—theater and film—more hostile to it than any others. My thanks to him also for his cooperation in putting this volume together; and my gratitude goes out equally to all the journals that had the good sense to publish these "dialogues" in the first place. For Kauffmann's sake, I am so pleased at the extent to which all the interviews reveal his sense of cultural mission, his application to drama and film of the highest standards, his predilection for certain artists and themes, his love of good art in any form. Speaking to this love, I would like to close with these words, written by Lionel Trilling about a great artist, F. Scott Fitzgerald, but equally applicable to Stanley Kauffmann, the *critic* as artist: "We feel of him, as we cannot feel of all moralists, that he did not attach himself to the good because this attachment would sanction his fierceness toward the bad—his first impulse was to love the good."

BC
2002

Chronology

1916   Born 24 April, the son of Joseph H. Kauffmann, a dentist, and Jeanette (Steiner) Kauffmann.

1931   Graduates from DeWitt Clinton High School, New York City. Actor and Stage Manager, Washington Square Players, New York City, until 1941.

1935   Graduates from the College of Fine Arts, New York University, with a Bachelor of Fine Arts degree in drama.

1943   Married 5 February to Laura Cohen; no children.

1945   Writer, producer, and director of a weekly radio serial for the Mutual Broadcasting Company, until 1946.

1949   Associate Editor, Bantam Books, until 1952.

1952   Editor-in-Chief, Ballantine Books, until 1956.

1957   Consulting Editor, Ballantine Books, until 1958.

1958   Film Critic, *The New Republic,* until 1965.

1959   Editor, Alfred A. Knopf, until 1960.

1961   Freelance book reviewer and cultural commentator, up to the present, for numerous magazines, among them *Horizon, Harper's, Commentary, The American Scholar, The Kenyon Review, The Atlantic, The Yale Review, Salmagundi, American Film, The New York Times Book Review,* and *The London Times Literary Supplement.*

1963   Drama Critic, WNET-TV (Channel 13), New York City, until 1965; resumed, 1966–1967. Host of the weekly series "The Art of Film," WNET-TV, New York City, until 1968 (Emmy, 1963–1964).

1964   Ford Foundation Fellow for Study Abroad. Elected Honorary Fellow of Morse College, Yale University.

1966   Drama Critic, *The New York Times.* Member of the National Society of Film Critics, until 1971. Associate Literary Editor, *The New Republic,* until 1967.

1967 Film Critic, *The New Republic,* up to the present.

1968 Visiting Professor of Drama, Yale University, until 1973.

1969 Theatre Critic, *The New Republic,* until 1979. Juror, National Book Awards.

1971 Ford Foundation Fellow for Study Abroad.

1972 Member, Theatre Advisory Panel of the National Endowment for the Arts, until 1976.

1973 Distinguished Professor of English, York College of the City University of New York, until 1976.

1974 George Jean Nathan Award for Dramatic Criticism.

1975 Juror, National Book Awards.

1976 Visiting Professor of Drama, City University of New York Graduate Center, until 1992.

1977 Visiting Professor of Drama, Yale University, until 1986. Member, Theatre Advisory Panel of the New York State Council on the Arts.

1978 Rockefeller Fellow, Villa Serbelloni, Bellagio, Italy.

1979 Theatre Critic, *Saturday Review,* until 1985. Guggenheim Fellow, 1979–1980.

1982 George Polk Award for Film Criticism.

1986 Birmingham Film Festival Award for Criticism. Edwin Booth Award from the City University of New York Graduate Center. Travel grant from the Japan Foundation for interest in and support of Japanese films. Publication of *Before His Eyes: Essays in Honor of Stanley Kauffmann.*

1992 Distinguished Visiting Professor of Theater and Film, Adelphi University, until 1996.

1993 Visiting Professor of Drama, Hunter College of the City University of New York, up to the present.

1995 Fellow of the New York Institute for the Humanities of New York University. Outstanding Teacher Award from the Association for Theatre in Higher Education.

1999 Telluride Film Festival Award for Criticism.

2002 "Film Culture: Past and Present," a Symposium in Honor of Stanley Kauffmann, sponsored by the Center for the Humanities at the City University of New York Graduate Center.

Conversations with Stanley Kauffmann

Something about Film Makes People Nuttier than Other Arts
Seventh Art / 1963

From *Seventh Art* 1, no. 4 (Fall 1963): 7, 8, 24.

Q: Pauline Kael wrote in a recent *Film Quarterly:* "The role of the critic is to help people see what is in a work, what is in it that shouldn't be, what is not in it that could be. He is a good critic if he helps people understand more about the work than they could see themselves." Would you agree with this definition of the role of the critic?

A: Yes, there's nothing about it to disagree with. My own root definition of criticism is T. S. Eliot's. It sounds priggish and schoolmasterish, but I think it contains the nub of what serious critics try to do. He said that the purpose of criticism is the elucidation of works of art and the improvement of taste. If you're not afraid of facing matters harshly, I think that is the truth of the matter. Miss Kael doesn't disagree with it, of course; she is just saying it in a different way—not quite as austerely.

Q: What do you think of the *politique des auteurs?*

A: It's just boring. Really, I think it is utterly boring. I talked with Miss Kael when she was here in New York a few weeks ago about her article, which was excellent, and with which I agree absolutely. My only criticism of it is that she used a cannon to kill what to me is only a flea. It is sort of self-preening emotional exercise by people who have no real interest in what I call criticism, who are interested only in using a specific work (in this case, a film) as an occasion for rhapsody. There is less of this kind of criticism in other arts—of course, there is some—*Art News* is full of it—but relatively less because they can get away with less. Film's a baby art and it has a much less well developed aesthetic. There are damn few films that can in soberness be called masterpieces, although the words "masterpiece" and "classic" are used as commonly as "pass the salt," particularly in auteur criticism. I think it's for irresponsible children. It bores me even to say as much as I've said.

Q: What do you think of Kael's suggestion that auteur criticism is related to pop art, that their fascination with the slick commercial product is much the same thing as painting a Campbell soup can?

3

A: Like the thing she quotes about the Raoul Walsh picture and the way they sit around in France and talk about the plastic vividness of the way the gangster squeezed the trigger? I don't know, maybe there is a relation. There's a Russian term—"sheer upside-downness"—one shows one's perception by saying white when everyone else says black—when everyone is praising, let us say, Antonioni or Bergman, you praise Samuel G. Fuller. You thereby show that you are neither one of the herd nor are you unperceptive.

Q: Dwight Macdonald wrote in a recent *Esquire* that what film needs at the moment are some critics who "cast a cold eye" on film. He compares this with Max Beerbohm's attitude when he undertook theatre criticism. What do you think of this comment?

A: What I presume Macdonald means by "cast a cold eye" is the opposite of auteur criticism. But the example of Beerbohm is a poor one because I think Beerbohm is the granddaddy of *New Yorker*-ish drama criticism. He is absolutely the source of most things that are wrong with drama criticism. His predecessor, Shaw, was a great critic. They brought in Beerbohm for no other reason than that he was an elegant man-about-town who wrote exquisitely, who said, I think—if not in his first, in very nearly his first review—that the theatre bored him. Never understood it. Never claimed to understand it. However, he wrote about it very amusingly and was in direct contrast not with Shaw because there isn't any comparison (one was a giant, the other was a butterfly) but with other drama critics of his day who were earnest men with third rate minds and who wrote abominably. From Beerbohm derived such critics as the late Wolcott Gibbs who was, of course, a complete critical nonentity, such as John McCarten, and from him derived the worst elements in an otherwise good critic, Kenneth Tynan. So Macdonald has really made a good statement and given what to my mind is a bad example.

Q: Do you think some confusion exists to some degree between the film critic and the film fan?

A: I think that confusion exists to some degree in the auteur critics, who are looking neither for art nor for the opportunity to criticize art, but for orgasmic substitutes.

Q: What qualifications do you think that the critic should bring to his job?

A: I couldn't limit them. After I name twenty, someone else could name twenty more. Some things that are desirable are—some experience in the art itself. I get occasional letters from young people in college who want to be film critics. I try to get across to them that one ought not to proceed at once to judgment. One ought to sweep a stage or carry coffee for a film director—some experience in how the art is made—before one proceeds to judge it. Given two people of equal critical ability, the one who has had some "making" experience is bound to give you the more rewarding criticism. What is most obvious about most young people who write criticism—I say young because obviously we're talking about people going into criticism and not those past salvation like me—is that they know just staggering amounts about films, incredibly detailed data, but they don't know anything else. Every time they see a picture with shadows in it they say it is Doestoyevskian. They have no "roundedness" of cultural background or interest in life, one might say. There's something about films that makes people nuttier than other arts, nuttier in the sense of being absolutely concentrated and unbalanced, in the educational sense.

Obviously, if you're going to be a critic you have to know something about writing. As James Agate once said—a statement that needs to be taken very carefully or it can lead to auteur excesses—it is part of the function of the critic to help recreate in the reader some of the feeling that the author created in him. Now, this can be done in excess. An example that comes to mind is Romain Rolland's book on Beethoven which consists mostly of trying to make you go up in the air the way Beethoven made him—it's a ridiculous book. But to go back to the matter of writing, if a man can't convey how he felt as well as how he thought about a film, he's had it, he's handicapped. I suppose the basic difference between the competent critic and the intelligent cultivated member of the audience is that both know what happened to them when they were watching, let us say, a film, but the critic, when he thinks about it, can tell *why,* or should be able to.

I would go further and disagree with those who say that this is where the function of the critic ends, this is only a matter of subjective reaction and judgment. I think when he thinks he knows why and how it fails, or where it could have been done better, it is his province, not his duty, but his province to say so. Other critics disagree—they say it is not the critic's function to say how it might have been improved or how such and such an actor could have been better, or how such and such a director would have done this or that.

Q: Does film make different demands on the critic than literature or the other arts?

A: Obviously, since it is a different art. Film lays booby traps for critics in certain ways because it is the youngest, it is the newest of the arts. It is very difficult, even if it were desirable, to come to film criticism without other frames of reference. What's the vocabulary of films? It's very hard to write three sentences about a picture without using terms that are equally applicable to literature or to the theatre. Film has almost no vocabulary of its own—*montage*—once you've used the word *montage* you're through. The critic who wants to do his job must be aware of the relationship between film and the other arts, and of obligations in the sense of inheritance. But one should also do one's damnedest to judge film as film in its own language, in its own medium, with its own possiblities and its own beauties. A nice question, for example, is whether filmmaking isn't too easy, whether it isn't more difficult to create a beautiful image in a line of poetry than just point your camera at something, through a mist, and take a misty picture of a girl leaning against a tree. One must not judge the image in terms of whether it would be more difficult to do it in poetry than it is with a camera. And one must be careful not to make the film equate with a poem.

Still, if film does make its own specific demands, nevertheless, because of its position in the history of society and the history of art, it cannot be independent of all the other arts that have happened around it. Film has developed so quickly—after all, it is only fifty years since the development of the camera in 1891 to *Citizen Kane*—it's staggering. Because it has happened so quickly, we forget that we're ahead of ourselves. It's like making a fast jet trip, getting there in four hours and taking two days to adjust to the fact that your're there. The movies have gone ahead like a jet. Whole concepts of aesthetics, of cultural foundation are yet to come—a tradition has yet to come.

Q: Do you think that film criticism has any effect on film?

A: On filmmakers, I would say very slight. You're talking, of course, about serious film criticism, not newspaper reviewing. Commercially speaking, newspaper reviewing has a very large effect, particularly in New York on foreign films—it can make or break them—no foreign film can survive bad reviews in the New York papers, although many Hollywood pictures do. Artistically speaking, film criticism has, my guess would be, no effect on filmmakers. Somerset Maugham said years ago that in his experience authors give you books to read for your criticism but what they really give them to you for is your praise. It's very difficult for filmmakers to take criticism.

Negative film criticism, even if it is constructive, is taken to be non-understanding. Sound criticism is very hard for the maker of the thing to take inside himself and use from the inside out again.

Q: Do you think that there is a potentially large audience in this country for the "art" film?

A: Yes, most distinctly. Without being Pollyanna-ish about it and unduly sanguine, I think that although the line in this country in most arts is either static or down, the one point where it seems to be going up is in films— maybe it's because film isn't old enough to be jaded. This seems to me to be the one place in the arts where there are really avid appetites for good things. I talk at colleges a little and there is tremendous, one might almost say, faith in the film. I'm not talking about American film or whatever film but just *the* film. There seems to me to be a feeling—to use blanket expressions—that the novel isn't speaking, the theatre hasn't said anything for a long time except now and then occasionally in a whisper, painting is knotted up in its own problems rather than communicating. The film is live and getting more so.

To the Theatre with Love: A Polemic

Prompt / 1967

From *Prompt,* no. 12 (1967): 20–29.

Q: Mr. Kauffmann, we'll begin by asking you a few questions about your own field, professional criticism. What kind of background or experience helps to make a good critic of theatre?

A: Well, I have to begin by assuming innocently that you mean me. I can't prescribe rules for anyone; I can only talk about my own personal background, as it leads into what I'm doing now. I trained for the theatre. I went to the New York University Department of Dramatic Art to train to be an actor and possibly a director, and at that time I was doing a lot of writing as well. I wrote a lot of poetry and actually had a great deal published. I very nearly had a volume of poetry published while I was an undergraduate in college. It was during the Depression, and three publishers wrote me that they would have published it if it hadn't been 1933 or so. The head of the Dramatic Art Department, Randolph Somerville, read my poetry and liked it, and said to me, as my teacher and mentor, that this was the kind of impulse in writing and thought that the theatre needed, and had I ever thought of writing plays? I had not really, so I began to write plays while I was an undergraduate. I can say quite objectively that I was much too facile, much too skillful, too quickly. I used to write one-act plays between classes and sell them too Samuel French and people like that. I published thirty-five or forty one-act plays under a variety of names while I was still an undergraduate.

Q: We'd probably still find them in Samuel French catalogues.

A: Some of them. Many of them have been dropped; some of them you wouldn't know, because they're under pen names. Except possibly for two or three of the whole lot, I hope that no one ever connects them to me.

But while I was still an undergraduate, I was invited by Randolph Somerville to join a group called the Washington Square Players. This takes a bit of explanation. He was the director of that company; some members of the company taught in the Dramatic Art Department. We played in two university theatres and also at a theatre we subsequently built in Cooperstown, New York. It was not, however, a college group. It had very few undergraduates working in the company. I was kind of specially tapped when I was a freshman. It was largely a Shakespearean repertory company, and the intent was to build a permanent repertory theatre. I first played with them about late 1931. The company lasted ten years until the outbreak of the war, but the war didn't really break it up; this happened for a variety of internal reasons. Most of the repertory was Shakespeare. There was some Shaw and one or two other things. I also wrote a couple of plays for them that they produced. One was a children's play, *Bobino,* which I wrote because we used to play frequently at high schools, we had these Shakespearean costumes, and we wanted a way to make the bus fare do double-duty. So we'd go out a little earlier, perform my children's play in the costumes for, let's say *As You Like It,* and then that night do *As You Like It.*

All this is just by way of explaining my theatre training. I had my four years as an undergraduate, majoring in Dramatic Art, and I worked with the Washington Square Players a total of ten years. I was a small-part actor; the company was too good for me to be a large-part actor. It was really quite a serious company. I worked as a stage manager, I did a lot of their lighting, and was in charge of their music, almost all of which was recorded. I would select it and play it during the performances, so I had ten solid years of all kinds of theatrical experience from selling tickets and putting up posters to acting in and writing plays.

The basics. Aristotle and posters. After the company broke up, or just about the time it was breaking up, I became disenchanted for a time with the theatre and with trying to write plays, and I began to write novels. I had my first one published in 1941, the year the company did break up. Subsequently I had seven or eight novels published, as well as stories and articles, over a period of almost twenty years.

About four or five years after I left the company, I went into radio. That would have been about 1945. Some radio people read some of my published one-act plays, and the Mutual Broadcasting Company invited me to go into radio. I wrote several weekly radio serials and produced and directed them. That lasted about a year and a half. It wasn't terribly interesting to me, although it was very lucrative. I concentrated only on writing for a few years after that and then I got a chance to go into book publishing. On and off I was in publishing for about eleven years as an editor. While I was doing this, through a series of coincidences, beginning with my serving on a jury at a trial that lasted nine weeks, I became a film critic. Another member of the

jury was a film critic; we talked a lot about films, and through him an opportunity arose for me to write film criticism; that's how I became a film critic.

Q: Was he acquitted?

A: The critic . . . ? No, the criminal wasn't acquitted; he was found guilty.
So I became a film critic. I'd always been crazy about films, and it was
through an extended series of lunches with this other film critic on the jury,
I don't mean this in any snide way, but it was by talking to him that I realized
how much I knew about films. I hadn't really examined this before; I had
just loved going to see them. And I knew that if I were able to write about
film, I would do so.

Q: It's nice to be in agreement with the authorities.

A: Sometimes. But just about that time I got an offer to write about films
for a magazine; that didn't last very long, only about three or four articles.
Then I went to the *New Republic,* and I wrote about films for them for eight
years. Loved it! Loved every moment of it! It was the happiest experience of
my writing life, and being back with them now is again a happy experience.

All this long exposition is just to explain how I came to be writing criticism
in three fields: literature, theatre, and films. There are other ways to arrive at
writing criticism, some of them fortuitous, some of them planned. Almost
every critic has a different story to tell. Mine is one that grows out of specific
training and background in those three fields.

Q: You've moved easily back and forth between film and theatre criticism:
is this difficult, or is a good film critic also a good theatre critic?

A: No, I don't think that necessarily follows at all. It's possible to be a
very enlightening film critic without being a good theatre critic, because there
are cinema values, about which one can be acute and tasteful, which are of
no relevance to the theatre. It's more likely, I would hazard the guess, that a
good theatre critic would be a good critic of films, than that the reverse would
necessarily be true. But I would hesitate to make even that much of a
weighted distinction. The trouble with theatre critics when they write about
films is that they don't know the important values in the cinema, and some
people who are good film critics are very weak in their judgment of acting.
They simply don't know what they're talking about, even when they write
about acting in films, and they know much less when they write about it in
theatre. They're just talking out of caprice.

Q: The technical aspects of film certainly take a lot of the viewer's attention.

A: Yes, and they are worth a lot of the attention. It's very possible, as I say, to be illuminating on the subject of films without really knowing much about acting. The parallel is not really possible in the theatre. Admittedly there are plenty of people writing drama criticism who don't know beans about acting, but we're speaking ideally.

Q: How important is it for a critic to have also been a practitioner of the craft? That is, you are an artist, as well as a critic of art.

A: Well, I've certainly stubbed my toes trying to be an artist all through my life. Again, that's a highly personal answer; there are those who believe that to have tried and not succeeded notably in art is very bad for a critic, because it puts a film of jealousy before his eyes when he looks at a work of art. I think that's utter nonsense. My own view is that if you have, yourself, at least bungled your way through some of the processes of the art you're talking about, you have much more insight into what's going on. When I was working as an editor in publishing houses, I know that I was able to help writers from the inside out because I'd done some writing myself. I had some concept of what it is to start with blank paper—a concept which most critics and editors don't really have.

Q: Some playwrights who started as actors feel that they have a better understanding of what the actor has to do on the stage because of their own experience.

A: I think that's absolutely true. It used to be a truism in the theatre that the best directors were failed actors. I have never myself made a film. I've written screen treatments and been involved in talking about films, but I've never actually made one. I would love to make one; I think I'd be a better film critic if I had an actual day-by-day part in the making of a film. I would not lay down any law that one should or one must, because the moment one does lay down laws like that then up comes the example of a fine critic who never did anything of the kind. All I can say is that I'm glad that I had some experience in the making of at least two of these arts before I began to criticize them.

Q: As a theatre critic, you chose to attend the final preview performance rather than the opening night. Do you believe the rush and pressure of having to write a life-or-death review in the space of about an hour is detrimental to theatrical criticism?

A: Almost always. There are occasional plays where one could write the criticism in fifteen minutes; it doesn't matter. I also note that in the eight months I was on the *New York Times,* I didn't always attend final previews. I had to, for one reason or another, write first-night reviews, I suppose, at least fifteen times while I was on the *Times.* Hated it!

Q: How much time did you actually have while you were at the *New York Times,* from the time you left the theatre, until you had to have the copy in?

A: An hour is a fair approximation. I'll give you an example of one particular play. This was a play that needed thought and analysis. In my opinion, it was an unsatisfactory play, but it was one deserving of criticism, which not all are. It was deserving of a full day's thought and writing. I left the theatre, which was some blocks away from the *New York Times* office, at a quarter after ten. I had to get myself to the *Times* building, go up the elevator, and get seated. Every thirty seconds weighs on you. . . . There wasn't time to look for a taxi, so I had to hustle through the streets. And I'm talking about what's common practice; I wasn't in any unusual position. The last sheet of my copy had to be passed in by 11:30. That means I had an hour and a quarter to get there, write it, look at it, revise it, have second thoughts, and so on.

Q: I can imagine trying to write a review of something as provocative as Pinter's *The Homecoming.*

A: It's dreadful! The whole idea is dreadful! It is inimical to art. There is no argument for it that I have heard that makes any kind of sense. One newspaper reviewer, whose name I won't mention, told me that he understood my point of view, but he added, "A review to me is like urine. I must get rid of it all at once." Well, I didn't answer him, but I quite agree that most of his reviews are like urine.

Q: This encourages the kind of instant reaction that's so often encouraged in school: that is, the glib, fast, superficial response.

A: Phrase-making and hot reaction, not reviewing. The pat justification is that you know what you think of a play when you walk out of the theatre. Well, sometimes I *don't* know what I think when I walk out of the theatre. The better a play is, the less sure I am immediately of what I think. I want to think *about* it.

Q: It has to be on a simple, obvious level if you know immediately.

A: Yes, many times, you can say I like it or I don't like it. But of what use is that? That isn't criticism; it is a Consumers' Union shopping service.

Q: I suppose that the role of the critics has become so firmly established that producers won't accept any other.

A: Well, it's become established in this country and in Great Britain. It's not universal practice. In most countries critics are invited to what is called the *répétition generale,* and in some European countries if a play opens on a Wednesday night, there's a performance at 10 o'clock on Tuesday morning for the press: to allow time for the reviews to be well done. But my argument was never to see a preview as such; it was only to have twenty-four hours to write the review. If the *New York Times* had gone along with the idea of printing the review the day after, that would've suited me even better. It would have obviated all this silly fuss and controversy, this irrelevant sniping. . . .

Q: I should think it would even be difficult to watch a play, knowing that within an hour you've got to regurgitate something about the work.

A: Any reviewer who says he can watch a play equanimously, when he knows he has to review it, is lying.

Q: You have to be looking and writing at the same time.

A: I'd have to expand that by saying that anyone who sees a play, knowing he has to review it, and says he's not conscious of the fact while watching it, is lying. But this is true of any book critic who's reading a book. You read a book differently if you know you're going to review it. Those things must operate on you. It's nonsense to deny them. You're being two people while you're reading instead of one, but, of course, the pressure is much stronger if you know that within fifteen minutes after the curtain comes down, if you're unlucky it's as long as fifteen minutes, you'll have to be committing yourself to paper in front of some millions of people—and influencing the fate of that particular production very heavily. I've never understood why in self-interest, in *self*-interest, producers don't want the critics to have more time.

Q: Are the professional New York critics as influential as it would appear, and is the *New York Times* the most influential paper?

A: I can't see any solid argument against the producer's claim that the *New York Times* review, in the vast majority of cases, makes or breaks a play. There are occasional exceptions. There's a musical on at the present moment with two great stars in it that had a huge advance sale. If you read the *Times* review very carefully, you find out that the critic really didn't think terribly well of it, but it will have a run, because of its stars. I can't think of many shows like that. The *Times* review certainly does make or break most, I wouldn't say all, of the productions in this city. To that must be added the fact that this situation has come about through the producers' own doing. They have made the critics gods, and now they're complaining about it. They never complain when they get good reviews. They're happy for the good reviews; they exploit the good reviews, but, of course, when they don't get them, they complain, not just about the bad review, but about the power of the critics. It's absolutely irrational; they want it both ways.

Q: I wonder how much this influences professional theatre in your country—the playwriting, the producing of plays?

A: Well, one cannot talk about negatives and unknowns. In other words, we can't say what doesn't get on because of reviewers, but certainly it would be hard to understand a producer who didn't take into consideration what the newspapers might think, because the economic situation on Broadway is just dreadful and getting worse! These are well-known facts. They're so well known now that it's not even depressing to talk about them.

Q: We could start a repertory with what *Kelly* lost.

A: Yes, or with what something called *A Joyful Noise* lost. It's a fact of life; we know that Broadway is a roulette wheel, and that the chances for a winning number are getting fewer and fewer, while the bets are getting higher and higher.

Q: To get back to criticism for a moment, we talk about objectivity as if it were some noble, necessary quality: how objective can or should a critic be?

A: Very, very slightly, I should think—I should hope.

Q: We're sort of paying you for your prejudices actually. . . .

A: Shaw said that he wouldn't give tuppence for an unprejudiced critic, if there could conceivably be such a thing. I want a critic who goes to the theatre full of hope and full of taste, full of hates and full of loves, not a reporter. That's the kind of man who can do something for me when I read him, if I find him. Objectivity is for judges in law courts, and even they don't have it.

Q: For a long time we've heard about the need for repertory theatre in America. Now in a brief period of time we have Lincoln Center, the A.P.A., the Guthrie, and others. What is your view of repertory theatre in America?

A: First of all, if we're going to use the language accurately, the only one of the theatres you just mentioned that is a repertory theatre is the A.P.A. Repertory means *repeat*. These other theatres don't keep plays in repertory from season to season, repeating them. They are what used to be called stock companies. They do a play for a period of time, then drop it, then do another play, and so on and so forth. The A.P.A., whatever its faults, is at least a true repertory company. It's still doing plays that it did when it started and is adding to its repertory. It's been called the best repertory company in America, but it's really, I think, the *only* repertory company in America in any true sense.

The other idea that's operating in places like Lincoln Center and the Guthrie, and there it's not operating with whole success—and I'm just talking about theatre practice in general, not their productions in particular—is the idea of a permanent acting company with one or two or three permanent directors. That, of course, is optimum practice from the point of view of actors. Well, repertory is actually the optimum practice, but this is the next best thing. It keeps actors fresh, flexible, wide-ranging, yet unified in style. That's why actors have liked it, but actors are historically deluded if they think that that's why it started; it isn't. Repertory started for economic and social reasons, because there wasn't enough audience for long runs in the days when theatres began to grow up, and one had to vary the bill to keep audiences coming. Actors in a certain ideal sense got spoiled by repertory, by the idea of being able to play eighteen or twenty parts in a season.

Henry Irving started his career in a stock company in Scotland, in Edinburgh I believe, and in the first three years played something like two parts a week; he said that that was his school. Well, of course, many bad actors came out of that school. What they learned was a lot of tricks that got them over humps very quickly, and they never went any deeper than the tricks. But if one were as serious and gifted as Irving, it was possible really to use it as a school. Actors looking back at the history of the theatre retrospectively remember that aspect, and not that it started for economic reasons. Whether that kind of operation is still relevant in our society is very much an open question. Ideally, I think it's very nice to have a true repertory company that presents a variety of plays in which you can see actors playing different roles within a week or two or three weeks' time. You can get some idea of their skills and range and imagination, but whether it's relevant to current threatre-going, even at its most tasteful level, I'm not sure. Whether it can survive against the current economics in the theatre in New York or elsewhere is an open question. There are now about forty resident theatres around the country. The ones that I know anything about are operating on a very high level of play selection. The plays they do are generally very good. They're trying to be permanent companies but, I think I'm right in saying this, they're all operating at a loss. Their phrase for it is "deficit oriented." They need to be subsidized by foundations, by the community, and so on to survive. I don't see anything wrong with that. I'm very much in favor of a little help to get the kind of theatre that's interesting to attend. But, if you're taking a step forward, this calls for a whole process of re-education in this country to accept the subsidized theatre, instead of allowing it to be a freak thing that can be dropped at the whim of some millionaire or some foundation. What I'm saying is that naturally, intrinsically, spontaneously, repertory doesn't seem to be connected with the present day; it has to be fostered and nurtured. I think it's worth fostering and nurturing, but there's no reason at the present moment to think that the conditions of repertory and the economic-cum-cultural appetites of our country are ever really going to mesh as they once did. The basic disparity between the two may persist for a long time to come.

Q: Robert Brustein, in the *New Republic,* was critical of Elia Kazan and Robert Whitehead for producing primarily trivial American plays such as S. N. Behrman's *But for Whom Charlie.* Herbert Blau and Jules Irving were criticized for producing primarily difficult period pieces, or so-called classics. What kinds of plays should an American repertory company be doing?

A: Well, an American repertory company—if I may stretch your word "should" to its utmost—should be doing a repertory of great American plays. Now such a repertory does not exist. There is no repertory of great American plays, if we're going to use the word "great" seriously. I think that repertory theatre, working with what it can at the present moment, should fulfil two functions. It should serve as a really living museum. You should be able to go and see a good performance of *Hamlet* or *The Misanthrope* or *Phaedra* or *The School for Scandal.* Everyone, some time in his life, should have the chance to see those plays well done, and perhaps a company should be consecrated just to that task, as is the Comédie Française in France. But for the general health of a theatre, it should have those things, plus some plays of particular relevance, some pertinence, to the lives of the people in its audience. They should feel some direct response in particular, as well as the classical response in general. A play should speak to them about timeless matters in timeless terms, and there should also be plays that speak to them about timeless matters in particular terms, *timely* terms. That's a function our resident theatres are not yet fulfilling, and it's one that some of the more intelligent resident directors around the country are very keenly aware of, because they have the devil's own time getting audiences to come to new plays, and they're very chary about putting them on. Audiences will flock to see a really quite difficult play by Beckett, for example, pack the house for that, and perhaps stay away from a new, much more accessible play by an unknown writer. Robert Brustein's criticism is leveled against a couple of new American plays, and, by and large, I agree with his criticism of those plays. I'm sure that Brustein does not mean to criticize the effort to keep a good theatre in close touch with the lives of its audience. Basically, I suppose his criticism was that those plays were not doing the job well enough.

Q: Last April in a *New York Times* article, you were pessimistic about the Lincoln Center Company. What are your feelings now, one season later? Any change?

A: No, I'm afraid there's no reason for any. . . . We're talking now while *Yerma* is on; there is no reason to feel any cheerier about it. I thought the production of *The Alchemist* was quite poor. I think *Yerma* is a poor choice; I'm not fond of that play. What depressed me even more about *Yerma* was that it's done by another director, named John Hirach, whose work I saw last summer at Stratford in Canada. He did a production of *Henry VI* which was very good indeed, brilliant; I don't know whether it's the geography or the atmosphere of the Beaumont Theatre or that inflexible play, but I was terribly distressed by his work in the *Yerma* production.

Q: *Galileo* is a good choice.

A: *The Life of Galileo* is a beautiful play, I think. What will happen with it, we do not know as yet. *Galileo* is a drama that ought to mean a great deal to an audience, can mean a great deal to an audience. But as you've probably read, they're having trouble with that now. The leading actor they engaged for it has left.

Q: How can an actor develop himself for the stage today? Is there enough work available for the struggling actor?

A: There isn't enough in New York. To answer that question completely involves many other things. There's possibly enough work for some of them, not all the aspirants, in resident theatres around the country. There they do get the chance, if they're lucky, to play a lot of good parts, seven or eight parts in the course of a season. The money is not much, not nearly sufficient. For a married man it just doesn't work out, unless his wife is also in the company, or unless she gets some kind of job.

Q: Sounds like college teaching.

A: There are certain similarities, I suppose, but then other problems, such as ego satisfaction, come into it. I mean if you do seven plays very well in Chillicothe, Ohio, or wherever Chillicothe is, the time is going to come when doing those seven parts well for one hundred and fifty dollars a week, with no one knowing about it, except the Chillicothe *Bugle* and the Ladies' Auxiliary of the Theatre, is not going to seem like enough in life. And you're going to feel an "itch" in one way or another. New York audiences and New York critics, horrible as this may sound to us, are the best in the country, and every actor, sooner or later, wants to measure himself against the best possible standards. Decentralization is the only factor that's going to give him that chance outside New York, the only factor that's going to fundamentally increase the number of working opportunities for actors in this country. In Germany, if you're an actor, you can spend your life in Munich and feel very happy if you never set foot on a Berlin stage. In this country, you can't spend your whole life in Tulsa and be completely satisfied. When that situation changes, then the whole outlook for work for actors in this country will be much brighter. As far as building careers in New York is concerned, it's farcical, just farcical. The more serious you are, the worse it is for you here.

Q: Even with television?

A: There's no television in New York. Figuratively speaking, there's no television. There used to be, but not now. There's no work in New York; all the actors have moved to California.

Q: What's been happening in the past few years to Off-Broadway?

A: Well, it has subdivided, of course, into Off-Broadway and Off-Off-Broadway. Off-Broadway itself has become so expensive relative to its early days that cautions are in effect there. I still think that there are interesting things being done from time to time on Off-Broadway, but it lacks the freedom and adventurousness that it once had.

Q: Is that primarily because of finances?

A: To a great degree. I'd made up a little list in my eight months at the *New York Times* of what I'd seen Off-Broadway, and there were an overwhelming number of two- and three-character plays and one-act bills. The large production has almost left Off-Broadway, and I don't take largeness as an index of anything except range and scope. I don't exactly know why this should be the case, because there are good plays that have not yet been done here, interesting plays from abroad, and others. I know this from first-hand knowledge in a few cases, and I hear about many other scripts that are worth production, scripts that would make an interesting if not a completely satisfactory evening, but still one you'd be glad you went to. These plays just don't get done Off-Broadway as they once were. I can't see much reason, other than economic, for the slow-down there. Then, of course, if you proceed from that to Off-Off-Broadway, you get into the matter of adventurousness without competence in most cases. You get into a theatre where, out of necessity, amateurism is elevated to an aesthetic.

Q: That's well put!

A: I've talked to some of, in my opinion, the best people who are operating theatres down there, and they really put forth as a serious principle that one must not be too skillful and polished in order to preserve freedom and imagination. Well, I think that is a happy way of looking at a necessity. I have seen many, many refreshing and stimulating things Off-Off-Broadway; however, I've never seen one that I did not think could be vastly improved by being really well done. I saw much more than I wrote about while I was at the *New York Times,* because many of the things I didn't think were worth reviewing.

Q: At least this is a place where young playwrights can see something done with actors on the stage.

A: Of course, it's better than not being produced, but what one gets a little impatient at sometimes is overpraise and a kind of compulsion to encourage. I think that encouragement is something that should be just as stringent in the theatre as any place else, and speaking out of my publishing background, I think that the fiction equivalent of some of these works would never see the light of day. It is just that the theatre is so bankrupt, so desperate.

Q: I was thinking about how many old comedies are now being turned into musicals because there's such scarcity of material for musicals; there are plenty of songwriters, however.

A: Well, even the songwriters are not doing so proudly by themselves these days. But the guiding rule is usually the guaranteed property. If you make a musical from *Auntie Mame,* you're starting several miles ahead of someone who's starting from scratch.

Q: Are the "happenings" of any value?

A: To some people they're the apex of value. To talk about them seriously—and I think if one is going to put them down, one has to at least put them down seriously, not simply dismiss them—they represent one outgrowth of a fundamental aesthetic view of today. That is, that traditional forms are played out, exhausted, in all the arts. This is the theatrical manifestation of that belief, the belief that not only new forms but new aesthetics must develop, and that all the "old" anthropomorphic views of art are outmoded and irrelevant. Any interest in characterization, theme, structure, design is called antediluvian and irrelevant to a rapidly changing society. Now painting, relevant painting, has been defined by its chief critical spokesmen as not design but the encounter between the painter and the canvas. And all new painting, according to such men, is action painting, whether it's abstract or op or pop. There are, of course, very intricate designs in op and pop in execution. But the essence of new art is what happens when the artist puts the brush on the canvas, not the planning in advance, not the distillation of experience.

Q: They're anti-humanistic.

A: They believe that the humanistic tradition in art is becoming a sentimentality. My own view of this matter is that artists have always operated to some degree in the subconscious. Finally, ultimately, fundamentally, no artist can tell you how he works. He can tell you what he thinks about after he has started working, but he cannot tell you exactly from the moment "go" why he picked that word or that color or that note. He can tell you what he consciously did with it after he picked it, but the absolute inception, he cannot describe; there's always been that element of the subconscious in art. But after that point, the element of design and plan has played a very strong part. To resign all that, as we are now asked to do, is to put your faith in one of two things—the subconscious by itself, or divine guidance—if you happen to believe in divinity. For myself, I'm at least as interested in my conscious as I am in my subconscious, and I don't think that God is a particularly good artist. If he were, we wouldn't need art, you know. So, I, no doubt an antediluvian, a sentimental anthropomorphist, can see "happenings" for the sake of some initial visceral response, but I quickly get bored; I don't see in them the artistic value or resonance that many of their apostles do see, although I recognize intellectually what they're talking about when they theorize about these "happenings."

Q: That's a point; as an intellectual protest, it has some kind of validity.

A: I'm not being facetious, but like a lot of contemporary art of all kinds in the theatre, in drama, in film, in painting, and in music, its principal purpose or *raison d'être* seems to be to provide occasion for criticism that's much more interesting than the art work itself.

Q: Many of the emerging artists of the theatre whom we've interviewed have been Negroes. Is Negro talent coming into its own in the American theatre, films, and television?

A: I think that it would be a large statement to say that it's coming into its own, but I did write an article in the *New York Times* in which I said that I thought the theatre was probably the institution in this country in which integration is most genuinely advanced, proportionately speaking, I mean. The aircraft industry employs a lot more people than all the theatres combined, but in terms of proportion, I think the theatre is the place in which integration is more genuinely advanced than anywhere else, and I think that is one of the most salutary things about the contemporary theatre. For myself, it's probably irrelevant that I have no faith in the *Negro* theatre that Douglas Turner Ward has spoken about at length. I don't see why it should not exist; I'm not against it; I'm not going to boycott it, or mililtate against it, but I think it's about as relevant to the future of the American theatre in any large sense as the Yiddish theatre was to Jewish actors in this country. It's possibly a parallel line on a lower level, but there's no future in it. There's only one future for the American theatre that I can see, and that is absolute color blindness. It's simply a matter of education, isn't it, beginning with children? The only qualification should be aptness for a role and acceptability in a part. I've seen Negro actors in roles that the playwright never dreamed would be played by a Negro. In Strindberg, for example, or Shakespeare. Where I was conscious all through the play that the man was a Negro, it was simply because he was not very good in the part. I've also seen Negroes in parts—parts *written* for Negroes—where I almost completely forgot about skin color.

Q: You simply suspended disbelief as you normally would during an aesthetic experience. . . .

A: And it's just a question of extending the disbelief a little further, that's all. You never really forget that an actor's a Negro any more than you forgot that you're watching a play, but . . .

Q: A great deal of "forgetting" does go on.

A: Yes. This whole psychological analysis of what actually happens when you're on the stage or in an audience has been debated for years, and it will never be settled. It's obviously extremely complex, but we're talking in large generalities. Here one can forget to a great degree that a man is Negro if he's good in the part. Also obviously, it's easier for a Negro to play a white part in a non-realistic, non-contemporary play, like one by Shakespeare or the Greek dramas. I've seen Negro actors and actresses in mixed casts in Greek plays and in Shakespeare. For reasons that don't need to be belabored, that's easier to accept right from the start than more contemporary casting. I was asked by one of my most intelligent and unprejudiced friends, a well-known drama critic, if my beliefs in this matter derived more from a social imperative than an aesthetic one. My answer was a hearty yes, and I don't see why this should not be so, if one adds to this, and never forgets it, that the sole criterion should be acting ability and aptness for the part. Then color blindness is an imperative.

Q: Of course, Douglas Turner Ward was talking more from the standpoint of the playwright. And Godfrey Cambridge made the point, too, that the Negro playwright writing for a white audience has to do some translating.

A: I think that's true, although I can't think offhand of many Negro playwrights who have written for white audiences—at least, produced ones.

Q: James Baldwin's *Blues for Mr. Charlie.* . . .

A: But *Blues for Mr. Charlie,* first of all, is such a terrible play. Second of all, it was written, perhaps not deliberately—yet certainly as it works out—to fulfill the function of a masochistic device for guilt-laden white people who came very aptly and patly for that reason. It wouldn't have today the amount of success it had a few years ago.

Q: I think we're more sophisticated. Douglas Turner Ward's *Happy Ending* and *Day of Absence* didn't need translating, I think.

A: No, those were Negro plays about Negroes.

Q: Certainly professional theatre and television are not using Negro actors to the fullest; is this possibly because of a lack of Negro talent, or, as Godfrey Cambridge put it, because of a lack of guts on the part of producers?

A: I simply can't give you any answer to that, because it implies a statistical knowledge that I don't have. I would assume, by analogy, that there are many talented Negroes who are out of work, simply because there are many talented people of all kinds who are out of work. Since most casting—in spite of what I just said about the theatre—since most casting is certainly done of white people, not just *by* white people, but *of* white people, for television, for films, and for the theatre, it just stands to cruel reason that there must be much Negro talent that is not being used. In any unemployment situation, Negroes suffer more than whites do, and I don't see why this should not be true in the theatre. I would certainly assume that there is much good Negro talent that is not being employed, and from that it follows that there is much Negro talent that is not developing. It follows too, that by the time you get around to tapping those people who have been jobless, they're not nearly as good as they would have been if they had had a chance to be working in the interim. So it's a vicious circle.

Q: Part of the problem is that Broadway theatre is middle-class, bourgeois, and often has no relevance to the Negro.

A: Unless he's out to be bourgeois himself, as, of course, a good many Negroes are. A very large number of them want to have debutante parties for their daughters, and so on and so forth. I don't mock that; it's too human to be mocked. I don't see why you should mock it any more in a Negro than in a white man. But another reason is, just to follow up on that matter of the audience, that the economic and educational background of Negroes hasn't been such as to make a theatre audience out of them. The theatre is not within their price range, geographical range, or their caste range.

Q: A theatre as an adjunct to Harlem might help these problems.

A: It might make Negroes more aware of theatre. The idea of a Negro young man taking his date on Saturday night to the theatre in New York is relatively new.

Q: You don't actually see many Negro couples in any Broadway audience now. It was, therefore, interesting to go to Ward's plays and see that half the audience there was Negro.

A: When I saw *The Blacks,* which I think is the best play on this subject—written by a different kind of outcast—a lot of the members of that audience were Negro. That was one of the few times, not in a literal sense but in a metaphysical sense, that I was thoroughly frightened in the theatre.

Q: It was an assault! We asked Godfrey Cambridge what he would say if somebody asked him to join a Negro repertory company, not to do just Negro plays, but Willy in *Death of a Salesman,* for example. He said a producer had approached him to do Willy. The cast would be a mixed one, with Willy's family being Negro.

A: What would be most interesting would be to have Willy black and, for the rest of the cast, use the best actors available. I think that to make Willy black and his family black, together with his boss and all the others, is to distort the play, is to put a value in it that Miller didn't intend. To cast it color-blind by talent is not to distort the play.

Q: How far can the theatre go? Are we ready to have an inter-racial love scene?

A: I dare say that if the scene itself were convincing it would be accepted. I've seen it happen in classics and contemporary plays.

Q: We hear much more about censorship of films, rather than the stage: yet we seem to be seeing films that are more frankly explicit with regard to sex, for example, than are plays on the stage: *Night Games, Dear John, The Silence.* Why do you think this is so?

A: Well, I don't think that it *is* so. I think that on Off-Broadway, particularly on Off-Off-Broadway, one sees things that haven't yet been in films. If you limit yourself to Broadway, the reverse may be the case, but it's a false comparison to match films and Broadway. As for American films, they are not really explicit. Many foreign films, however, are not only artistically ahead of most Broadway plays and American films, but are also ahead in terms of moral scope.

Q: Both the New York stage and films shown in New York have been dominated in the past few years by foreign artists. What's happened to the American product?

A: Well, the potential American playwright has been discouraged by the conditions of writing for the theatre. The playwrights we have had, predominantly Miller and Williams, have simply been betrayed by their ages and by the passing of time. Miller is a full-grown product of the thirties and of that decade's thinking. He's been having a very hard time trying to update himself, although he's a talented man, no question about it. Despite the justified criticism, *Death of a Salesman* is still a very moving experience. Tennessee Williams is very gifted, but his "message" has been delivered, and hasn't grown at all. He has a vein in him that he's given us glimpses of from time to time, and it came out in the second of his two one-act plays last year . . . a possibility of really wildly raffish, slashing slapstick humor. Wild stuff—I don't mean cute little verbalisms and ploys. If he really let go, he'd probably write some very funny plays; there have been hints of it, not necessarily of black humor, but certainly blackish humor. At any rate, since most good plays in the last few years have been British, we've been seeing a lot of British actors.

Q: What are our new playwrights concerned about? Are themes emerging out of their work?

A: Very hard to perceive anything crystallized enough to be described. Much is made of the theatre of rebellion, or revolt, or satire, but there are really only a few isolated instances of it. I can't agree with my friend, Robert Brustein, that at the present moment there is anything like a cohesive, organic "third theatre." There is *MacBird;* there was *Viet Rock.* But there doesn't seem to be any fountain flowing in that vein. Satire as a cabaret item is sometimes good, sometimes not. New playwrights in any substantial sense don't seem to have any focus, as the playwrights of the thirties did, as the playwrights of the forties did, or even of the fifties. One sees young writers coming along like, for example, Jean-Claude van Itallie, whose principal interest is in a mode of theatre practice rather than in theme. It's true that *American Hurrah* and his other plays are satirical of contemporary mores, but that hardly seems to be their primary impulse. Their primary impulse is to be works of the Open Theatre, to be material for the Open Theatre, and it wouldn't surprise me in the least if his future works were quite different in tenor and tone, in terms of their content, from the things he's done already. But he plans to keep on working with the Open Theatre, and I think there are other writers of his age and conditioning who are more theatre-oriented than writer-oriented. I'm not saying that's good or bad, but it's very different from the writer who is influenced, for example, by Chekhov, by Pirandello, or by Shaw.

Q: You've written about homosexual drama and its disguises. Does the homosexual playwright avoid dramatizing homosexual relationships directly because it would be bad box-office, bad personally, or for other reasons?

A: The first point is that a play by a homosexual that dealt with his homosexual life straightforwardly would be very difficult to get produced on Broadway. It has often happened Off-Broadway, and Off-Off-Broadway; on Broadway it's very difficult.

Q: Still a taboo subject?

A: Yes. It is not good box-office. I wouldn't say that it could never be done; it has been done. There have been homosexuals in plays. *A Taste of*

Honey comes to mind at once. But homosexuality is not really an open subject on Broadway. Fiction now is freer than it used to be . . . of course, we can look at *Of Human Bondage,* which, it's common knowledge, was really about Maugham and a little cockney waiter that he converted into a waitress.

Q: Film seems to be freer in its portrayal of homosexual themes—*Leather Boys* and *A Taste of Honey,* for example—although the latter was a play first. . . .

A: I think what I said before on that comparison is fairly true in terms of homosexuality also. If you take our theatre as a whole, not just Broadway, along with the theatres of London and Paris, it's probably at least as free as the film is. I just want to add one point: the things I wrote on the subject of homosexuality were wildly misinterpreted by a lot of people, and I had to write a second article, answering letters. One of the wildest misinterpretations was the inference that I had said homosexuals can't write about anything else but homosexual relations, which, of course, is utter nonsense, and has been nonsense for generations. All I was talking about was this one specific point: when we hear that the American drama of post-war years has been dominated by homosexuals, and that therefore the portraits of American women and wives in those plays are distorted, we must remember that we have a share in that disguising and masquerading, because we have insisted on it; that was my sole point really.

Q: It does rather limit the homosexual who is writing to have to do all that disguising. . . .

A: We've had this kind of masquerading before in the theatre. Between wars, we had a very successful Jewish writer of high comedy in the American theatre. He went through all kinds of agonies of readjustment of values, re-casting of stories, and distortions of characters, so that he could write plays that would not have a Jew or a Jewish phrase in them, because he felt that plays about Jews would not fly. He probably was right at the time, unless it was a sentimental Jewish play, like *The Jazz Singer.* So this matter of having to disguise is an old problem in the theatre, and possibly it's a sign of progress that it's gone past disguising political principles in allegorical terms, gone past disguising Jews as gentiles: now it's reached the border of the question of whether homosexuals need to disguise their lives.

Q: For a long time, film was a theatrical second-class citizen, but now, more and more, it's becoming a separate, accepted art form. It seems to me that the newest things, the most interesting and exciting things, are in film rather than in the theatre.

A: Well, I don't know about the future, but I certainly would say that this has been true of the last ten years. A few years ago I wrote an article called "End of an Inferiority Complex," which simply articulated its title. I'd been trained for the theatre, and even though I loved films, I'd automatically, unthinkingly, assigned them to be in Number Two position. After I'd been writing film criticism for about five or six years, I had occasion to look back and compare what I'd been seeing in the theatre as against what I'd been seeing in the film, using as international a view in one as in the other. What I'd seen in the theatre came from all over the world, so I looked thus at the film too, and in that comparison it was quite clear that the most interesting things in that period had been in films. This is still the case, I believe. This is not to say that the film is a better form than the theatre; there's no point in debating which is the better form. I think it's incontestable that better art works have been made in the film in the last ten years than in the theatre. And I could, if I had the kind of mind that remembered titles, give you examples of this phenomenon, but I'll give you one name. In my view, the best theatrical artist whose work I've encountered in the last ten years, using theatre in the widest sense, is Michelangelo Antonioni. As far as art appetite is concerned in this country and in many other countries, especially among young people, the appetite for film is much keener than it is for the theatre. Not to say that there's no appetite for the theatre; we're not talking about blacks and whites but about shades. I went into my guesses as to why this is so in a long essay, which is the concluding essay in my book *A World on Film*. In fact, the essay is called "The Film Generation," and I tried to explore why I think that's the case.

Q: Is there anything happening in so-called underground film that's of interest?

A: Much is happening, but not much that's interesting. This is due to several reasons—some of them are too large to take hold of here and now, even for a garrulous person like me. Part of it is because the underground movement covers a wide range of different kinds of filmmakers. Underground is really meaningless as a term, except to describe the kinds of places where they're shown. There are very straight documentary-makers in the underground; there are wild abstractionists whose work you can't recognize, not only as anything human but as anything. And there are all kinds of things

in between. Part of the reason that there's not much that's interesting to me
is because of what we just talked about before in relation to happenings.
Much of the underground film is an attempt to reflect or to implement the
impulses towards a new aesthetic, and I've actually seen films *of* happenings.
As you know, films have been used *in* happenings—in other words both
ways. There are occasionally films in the underground that show humor, films
that show a kind of artistic daring, films that do things that are at least briefly
worth doing, that aren't done anywhere else. But the net effect of seeing
program after program of underground film as I have done is an experience
of people in an art saying, "Don't look now, wait twenty years until we find
out what it is we're doing."

Q: Television drama seemed to have reached its peak ten years ago or so.
Has television, with the commercial limitations, gone as far as it's going to
go or can go in dramatic offerings?

A: I don't know. Educational television in this country, which is by now
unfortunately the fixed term for non-commercial television, is not literally
educational at all, although I hope it educates. . . . Educational television is
trying to do serious things well. The commercial networks have largely given
up on this for very simple reasons—it didn't sell cigarettes and automobiles.
There's no proof that commercial television did at first, really. There was the
so-called Golden Age of Television, simply because they didn't know what
television was, and the first thing they could think of was plays, and they did
them with a certain amount of freedom. Then other things came along, and
they found out that other things attracted wider audiences than heavy-handed
symbolic plays about race relations or whatever it is they were doing so
breathlessly back then. There's a great deal of nonsense talked about the
Golden Age of Television. It's just not true. There were more plays done than
are being done now; there were greater scope and freedom than there is now
in terms of sheer numerical opportunity for television playwrights, but the
level was not all that high. And some of us said so then, when people were
telling us that it was the new Elizabethan age because there were oh-so-many
hours in the week, and they all had to be filled up, and that this inevitability
would produce a generation of great television dramatists. So I don't think of
the fate of commercial television as indicating anything about American art.
It can only indicate something about American cigarettes, soap, and automobiles.

Q: Well, it indicates something about American tastes, unfortunately. . . .

A: Yes, if one wants to use the word taste as applicable to a television audience. A television audience of thirty-five or fifty million people can't possibly represent anything in taste. It's too much; it's unfair to say that that's America, because there's plenty of America that isn't like that, or is looking at it just to laugh at it, or is *not* looking at it—in the bedroom or something. There are millions and millions of people who take television the way some people take drugs; there are people to whom it's a sort of iron lung. They can't breathe without the television being on.

I was out of town last week to lecture. In the motel where I was, I had breakfast, and a television set was on. This little restaurant had truck drivers, businessmen; it was out in the country and had various assorted types, eating those huge breakfasts that you never see anyone eating in New York, piles of stuff with potatoes on the side. And the television set was behind us with a children's program on, and nobody was paying the slightest attention to it. But you felt that if anyone had turned it off, they'd all have felt that the air supply had been cut off. So I have nothing but uninterest in most television; I don't think it reflects anything. I don't think it is interesting, except during actualities: news, political events, those few sports events that I care about. Once in a while, there's a documentary that's worth something, and that's about it. I'm very active in television myself; I spend a great deal of my time working for Channel 13, but I'm sort of egocentric about that. I don't think of it primarily as television; I think of it as work about films and about the theatre, and I just happen to be doing it on television. When I write for the *New Republic,* I don't think of myself as being in magazines; I'm just doing more about books, or some other subject, and it happens to be in a magazine. When I was on the *New York Times,* I didn't think of myself as a newspaper man; I was simply doing more about the theatre, only it was in a newspaper.

Q: Is the government doing as much as it should to aid the arts?

A: I can't answer as to what it "should"; I must say that there's a tremendous revolution going on in this country, or a change at least. I'm talking about a revolution connected with culture. For all the talk and publicity, I don't think it's even yet fully appreciated what it means that the government is spending money on the arts in a programmatic way. It's staggering! To be spending six million dollars a year regularly on painters, on the theatre, and so on . . . who would have dreamed ten years ago there would be such a thing? There were plans then that were laughed out of Congress, and this doesn't mean that Congress has become enlightened; it means that politicians have a sense of what the public is interested in and are pleasing the public.

But so long as they do it, that's all for the good. Of course, when we get into the question of "as much as it should," then we have to compare the six and a half million dollars that the National Endowment for the Arts is given in this country, as against the approximately twelve million dollars that the Canadian Arts Council has received in a country of about eighteen or twenty million people. In that light, six and a half million dollars is ludicrous. Of course it's very easy to waste six and a half million dollars. But I have to say that I'm not consistently unhappy about the way the money's been distributed so far. I think that there have been more good grants than I would have expected.

Q: We have one question for you that we normally ask all actors: Do neurotic people go into the theatre, or does the theatre make them neurotic? I posed this very elaborately to Robert Symonds, and he said, "Do you mean are actors as nutty as they seem?"

A: Well, of course, any reply to that question has to start with a truism: Freud said that all artists of every kind are neurotic and that any artistic work of any kind is the product of neurosis.

Q: Do you buy that?

A: Yes.

Q: I think I do, too . . . I think it's more true than not.

A: And acting, since acting involves the person, calls for certain qualities of exhibitionism and extrovertism that a writer doesn't have to have, possibly shouldn't have. Moreover, the circumstances of theatrical life are such that they would have to heighten any neurotic drives, partially in the direction of sex. Then you have to remember, too, that the theatre lives, it absolutely lives, in an amniotic fluid of sex. One of the purposes of the theatre is sex stimulation, deliberately and tangentially. No leading actress can really succeed unless subconsciously the men in the audience want to sleep with her, and this is also true of actors and women. How could that be a prime condition in the theatre without its having some effect on the people who work in the theatre? When this subject comes up actors are always saying that they're hard-working and they're no more immoral than stockbrokers. I don't know about morality or immorality; they're not choice words of mine. But it's simply nonsense to pretend that there are not a lot of fancy goings-on in the theatre all the time. It does go on; it's inevitable in that hot-house atmosphere, where sex is the prime currency; I don't see how it could not be the case.

Q: The neuroses, to some extent, would have to follow from that, too.

A: They would certainly be intensified by it. But just on the subject of actors' behavior, I don't know that anyone could make up any batting averages as to whether or not there's more playing around in the theatre than in advertising circles in Westport, or whether there's more homosexuality among musical comedy people than there is in the Navy. I wouldn't be prepared to say; all I can say is that for theatre people to deny that the atmosphere of the theatre is conducive to free sexual life is nonsensical. Why deny it? Why bother to deny it? What the hell difference does it make?

Q: Do you see any emerging trends in films or theatre that may develop into something larger?

A: I think that there's one trend certainly that is bound to develop, because it's part of a general social trend, something that should be viewed with some caution, and that is what I call the worshipping of youth. I think there's absolute, abject worship of youth today. All you have to do to be interesting is be under twenty-five.

Q: That's right. A girl of seventeen is over the hill now.

A: Yes. Look at *Time* magazine recently, their issue on Youth. The examples are innumerable. . . . To be young is to be true, pure. . . .

Q: And at the same time sexy. . . .

A: Yes . . . sexy, unshackled, and full of promise. The young would say that I have my own reasons for disagreeing. I certainly do have; just as they have their reasons. And I'm a person who goes out on lectures around the country twenty or twenty-fives times a year, at considerable physical wear-and-tear, to make money, of course, but also and importantly because I want to keep in touch with young people. I have no children, and the only real way I can get to talk to interesting young people is to go and speak at colleges and universities, and get bugged by them afterwards, and I love it. So I'm not speaking from any tower of snobbishness about age, or out of necessary wisdom because of age. I just think that this thing has gone too far!

Q: There's such a catering to this market in literature, for example.

A: Let me give you one more instance of why this is so. My wife's nephew, a very intelligent, very nice young man whom I like very much, just married someone his age; they're both twenty-one. She's English; he spent a year at the London School of Economics, and he met her there. She's a farmer's daughter, which is quite a nice union, because he's from a wealthy upper-middle-class Jewish-American family, and here he is married to the daughter of a Lincolnshire farming family that goes back for hundreds of years; they make a very nice combination. They came to the house for dinner a few weeks ago. I tried to tell them—without being unbearable about it— that all their radical plans, all their distrust of elders, sounded familiar to me, because I'd once said the same thing myself, and they looked at each other with a shrug of disgust and the feeling of, "Oh, it's that old put-down." "We can't do it," they said, "because it hasn't been done. We can't change the world, because the world hasn't ever been changed." Well, first of all I don't agree that the world hasn't been changed. I think it has been changed; I think that everything in our world tends to get better, and I quite seriously believe that. I'm not talking about the arts now necessarily; I'm talking about social conditions, education, health, working conditions. The fact that we're sitting here now is one index of it. But it certainly is true that the progress is slow. And it's also true that the young people themselves change, as marriage and children come along, and one doesn't want to belabor young people with such an observation because one doesn't want to dampen their spirits in the slightest.

Q: Besides, nobody believes you.

A: No, they don't believe you; what's worse, both sides kid themselves. They don't believe that what you're saying is true, and you kid yourself that you really can remember what it's like to be their age. You can't . . . and even if you could, it wouldn't be relevant because being young in 1967 is not the same thing as being young in 1937. I don't really remember; I only think I do. I know that. But I am tired of this overemphasis on the quality of youth as the prime good in everything.

Q: It's very unhealthy.

A: Unhealthy . . . And one sees it in the film world particularly. In the comment about a very gifted director like Godard, whose chief virtue, if you analyze all the criticism about him, is that he is young, understands his youth, and can use it.

Q: Mr. Kauffmann, thank you so much. Perhaps ten years from now we can look back and talk to you again.

A: It has been, and would be, my pleasure.

Film to Me Is Another Art

F. Anthony Macklin / 1972

From *Film Heritage* 8, no. 1 (Fall 1972): 16–36.

Macklin: How did you begin writing for the *New Republic?*

Kauffmann: Well, it started with an amusing accident. I had been writing film reviews for a very short time for a now defunct magazine called the *Reporter,* and things had not progressed so well between them and me. It ended with my having a review that I wanted to place somewhere because I wasn't going to put it in the *Reporter.* This was in early 1958. I put it in an envelope and sent it to the *New Republic.* I didn't at that time actually know whether they had a film critic or what was happening with them. I hadn't read the magazine for a time. I sent the review to them in Washington, and a couple of weeks later, let us say on a Wednesday, I hadn't heard from them and I sent them a card saying, "Don't be embarrassed or hesitant—if you don't want it, just return it, but it will be of no use if I don't place it some-where soon." And the following day, Thursday, I got a copy of the magazine with my piece in it and their check. And the *following* day, Friday, I got a lovely letter from the review editor saying that they had read my piece care-fully and unfortunately they could not use it [laughs]. So I said to my wife, "This place is for me." And the man who wrote me that letter, Robert Evett, and I became excellent friends, not only because of that, but certainly partly because of that little incident. They asked for more and I sent more, and after about five or six weeks, Gilbert Harrison, the editor-in-chief, wrote me and asked me please to consider myself their regular film critic. And I said I would with pleasure.

Macklin: What's your relationship with them now? I've noticed that sometimes it appears that you're not doing many reviews.

Kauffmann: There have only been a very few issues that I've not been in. In 1969, I believe it was, they asked me to be their theater critic also, because Robert Brustein who is, in fact, still their official drama critic on very ex-tended leave, was unable to write for them because of his duties as Dean of Yale Drama School and running the Yale theater up there. In this year to come he's going to be the critic of the *London Observer* during his sabbatical from Yale. I said I would do theater reviews, too, with pleasure and would apportion the space as I thought the occasions dictated.

Macklin: You find the *New Republic* a very compatible forum for you?
Kauffmann: Absolutely, the most congenial place I've ever written.

Macklin: Why?
Kauffmann: First of all, the attitude of the editor and literary editor, who is now Reed Whittemore, toward me—very inviting and congenial. Everything about what I do is left entirely to my discretion. I choose my own material. There is no interference in what or how I say it. And there is also an element that I've noted in both my books, which are mostly collections of *New Republic* pieces—that sense of congeniality between me and the readership, the letters I get, the responses I get, the lectures that have arisen—many of them out of this *New Republic* tenure—make me feel that I'm writing in the right place for me.

Macklin: I think that Stanley Kauffmann probably is the major critic who is least quoted.
Kauffmann: You mean in ads?

Macklin: Yes. Do you ever feel that you would like to be more "powerful"?
Kauffmann: I had a good dose of power in the *New York Times,* and I wasn't entirely happy about it. No one becomes a critic out of modesty. One would like to be quoted. On the other hand, the distinction (if there is one) of *not* being quoted has nothing to do with me personally. It has to do with the circulation of the *New Republic,* the commercial clout of the magazine. I don't have to name a lot of other magazines and journals that have five, six, ten times the ciruclation of the *New Republic,* which has a very healthy circulation for the kind of magazine it is. Its minimum these days is about 150,000 which means that anywhere from 300,000 to 400,000 people read it every week. And that makes me very happy—to be read by that many people who have some discrimination and apparently to be interesting them to some degree. But that's not the same thing as a magazine with six million circulation and twelve million readership. The people who write for magazines like that, of course, have much more widely known names. And even if their names are not known, the name of the magazine they write for is known. I just have no strong feelings about being left out of ads.

Macklin: When one looks at the various major critics, he can identify them. Maybe labeling is not a good idea. But one can label critics—John Simon's love of art; Pauline Kael's hatred of sham; Sarris's *auteur* criticism. I think you may be the most difficult to do this for. How do you identify yourself as a critic?

Kauffmann: It's awfully difficult to answer because I flatter myself that I can't be subsumed under a simple label. But there is a direction I could indicate, in that I refuse to think of the film as lesser or more circumscribed than any other art and I insist on judging it by the same standards, generally speaking, as I would—as I *do*—judge literature and the theater. In other words, to put it as briefly as possible, the film to me is *another* art, not a place where one slums.

Macklin: How would you react to people who say, "He's a specialist in acting in terms of films, that that's the thing about Stanley Kauffmann that stands out most importantly"?

Kauffmann: If people recognize that I have a strong interest in acting—I was an actor for a brief time in an obscure way and have had something to do with it off and on in various periods of my life, also did a little directing—I would be pleased that they see that I had some, at least, interest, if not particular expertness.

Macklin: Do you think there is any critic writing today who has a greater interest?

Kauffmann: I can't think of any. But I would hate equally to think that that's all I have to bring to the discussion or that's the only good judgment (if it is good) that I have about film. My strong feeling on the subject of acting in film criticism is not that it ought to be italicized at the expense of everything else, but that it has been completely *ignored* in most film criticism or written about in such a superficial, sweeping way that all it did was betray the writer's ignorance—I'm not going to give you examples—and it still *is* handled that way in the vast majority of cases.

Macklin: Do you find that people are aware in their letters to you about the acting—do you get much response to your discussions of the acting?

Kauffmann: Often. It's not the only thing people write about, but certainly it's picked up.

Macklin: Anything specific?

Kauffmann: The latest thing . . . I did a review on the Soviet film of *Uncle*

Vanya a few weeks ago, and I got several letters commenting on my discussion of *Uncle Vanya,* first as a play in relation to the film which was made of it, and then to what I said about the acting of it.

Macklin: What should one look for in film acting? What makes film acting effective?

Kauffmann: I can answer you in a way that sounds evasive, but really isn't—a quotation from St. Augustine that I've used before. He said, "I know what God is if you don't ask me." I know what good acting is, but I know it empirically, not by any set of rules.

Macklin: Let's get specific then. I disagree strongly with you on your view of Jane Fonda in *Klute.* You thought she was fairly mechanical and just doing what she does well without any real creativeness in her acting. I wonder why.

Kauffmann: If we're going to talk about Jane Fonda, I'll have to take that particular subject back to its beginning and toot my own horn a little bit. When Jane Fonda first appeared in films, I was the first, if not the *only* one, who took her talent seriously and was roundly derided in person and in print by people for talking seriously about this girl's talent.

Macklin: What films?

Kauffmann: The one in Louisiana where she played a sort of girl of the streets—*Walk on the Wild Side.* Then, *Period of Adjustment,* from a Tennessee Williams play. A bad film that she made in Greece with Peter Finch—*In the Cool of the Day.*

Macklin: What was it that you saw in her?

Kauffmann: I *heard,* first of all, a voice that's really a first-class actor's instrument. I heard the way she used it with acuteness, with sensitivity, with a musical ear that wasn't musical for its own sake; it was musical for the sake of not merely reproducing life, but of commenting on the life she was reproducing. The quickness of her ability to mime graphically what it was she was feeling. A punk picture like *The Chapman Report*—she was absolutely first class in it. She went to the core of what she thought she had in hand and found a fresh symbology, an actor's symbology with which to express it.

Macklin: How so?

Kauffmann: I can't remember the details of the part, but she played (as I remember) a repressed wife who was thinking about having an affair. And all the usual things you might have expected in a film actress's performance of repression and wakening desire she discarded, and she went to root sources of observation of life and a fresh system of actor's signals to convey them to her audience in a characterization. There was freshness, there was creation in what she was doing, not merely reaching on the shelf for a lot of things that a lot of other people had used before in cognate places. And so on through the things she has done through the years. Until we got to *Klute,* where I felt—well, she's still enormously gifted and I think *Klute* doesn't mean the end of the road or the fall of Jane Fonda—I simply felt that she was doing a little bit of exactly what I said she was *not* doing in these earlier pictures— coasting a bit, settling for the easy gesture, the easy reading, still very effective because *she's* effective.

Macklin: Most critics began to become aware of her talent in *They Shoot Horses, Don't They?*

Kauffmann: Well, you see by that time she was, in my mind, long established as a good actress. *They Shoot Horses* is rather late in the Jane Fonda story for me. Although I did say these slightly negative things about her in both *They Shoot Horses* and in *Klute,* for me those remarks are in a perspective of long standing admiration for her and a slight feeling that in those two pictures, where other people are, in a sense, just discovering her as a valid, genuine actress, there's just a touch for me in both of those pictures of her taking it a little bit easy and *riding* on what she is, instead of working as hard as she can.

Have you seen *Period of Adjustment?* That's a first-class comic performance, imagined freshly. It couldn't be more different from these two later films we're talking about. We're talking about the impulses behind the work she does. There's a quality of energizing behind that performance that is not quite—not *quite*—present in those last two films that she did. I have a feeling that her mind is not as centered on her work as it has been, and I *don't* think it's because I'm aware of her extra-cinematic activities, which to me are sometimes quite admirable.

Macklin: I thought there were so many surprises to her performance in *Klute.* The things that you had recognized in her performances earlier I thought she still generated in the film.

Kauffmann: She doesn't *not* generate them. I'm talking relatively. I'm not talking of a complete debacle. I'm talking of, simply, a level. Acting— genuine acting—is a very very difficult art and it calls not only for gifts; it

calls for a kind of absolute, almost—and I'm quite serious—religious concentration on what one is about, to make the most of those gifts. Fever-
pitched, white-hot moments—even if they happen to be technically quiet
moments in the film. (Quiet moments are very difficult to do. It's easy to
shout.) And I don't feel in those last two films quite that utter summoning of
every molecule of power in herself to make the most of everything. Anything
she does she's going to be somewhat good in. She couldn't be bad.

Macklin: I got a different feeling from reading your review. I got more of
a feeling of negative . . .

Kauffmann: I set up in a proprietary way about actors—or any kind of
artist whom I have been terribly fond of, uninvited and quite presumptuous,
but I can't help it—a token of concern. And I feel that someone has to say,
if he feels it, "Careful, here, dear Jane. We all know you're good, but don't
you know it!"

Macklin: It strikes me that there are two other mechanical actresses that
do this more than you seem to feel Jane Fonda does. What about Glenda
Jackson and Maggie Smith—in movies more than on the stage?

Kauffmann: I don't think of them as mechanical actresses.

Macklin: Well, does Glenda Jackson get this "white heat"?

Kauffmann: Why, yes. I think Glenda Jackson has done some very vapid
roles, which made her look ridiculous because she was expending on them
an enormous amount of energy in a situation which was like pouring water
into a sieve. That dreadful Tchaikovsky picture where she was writhing and
rolling around—it was just silly. It was like emotional outpourings with no
container. But in a film like *Sunday Bloody Sunday,* that was a very beautifully modulated performance—felt, understood, communicated, sympathized
with, and commented upon while she was making it. I thought she was beautiful. In that D. H. Lawrence picture, *Women in Love,* the same thing. I can't
remember any film of Glenda Jackson's of which I would have said that she
was merely coasting. I have felt at times, as in that Tchaikovsky picture and
a ghastly picture called *Negatives* about three or four years ago, that she was
overexpending energy, that she was conscious that she was working in a Jello
situation, trying to solidify it a bit. Quite the opposite of mechanical, however.

Macklin: You don't get the feeling, then, that this is an actress and she is
always making the audience aware that she is an actress?

Kauffmann: If I answer yes to that, it's going to be misleading. You see, I like that feeling, but I have to be very guarded about saying that because it seems to be saying that I like actors to be phoney or to be hammy. I don't mean that at all. I mean that acting, like every other art, is a tremendously complex matter. And *one* of the components in this complexity—granted that the artist has all the other things we've been discussing—is a certain pleasure in the execution of the work. I can't believe—I know for a fact the reverse— that artists don't get pleasure out of doing their work well. And I can sense that in Glenda Jackson's work. But it doesn't obtrude between me and the work; it simply certifies that she is as good as I feel she is.

Macklin: In reviewing *The Prime of Miss Jean Brodie,* you said that Maggie Smith played the affectations instead of a woman with affectations. And I thought that was a very astute point. What about Maggie Smith?

Kauffmann: At times she has been excellent. I've seen her in the theater a few times—not as often as I'd like because she does most of her theater work in London. But she has a wider spread of effectiveness, I would say, than Glenda Jackson has. In *The Prime of Miss Jean Brodie* she was to a certain extent at the mercy of a rather mechanized role as written. I don't think the role as prepared for the screen or the stage was on a level with the character created by Muriel Spark. The adapter went for the tips of the iceberg, with nothing of what's beneath. I saw Maggie Smith once in the British National Theatre in Chekhov's *The Three Sisters,* and I was terribly disappointed with her. She came over as a shrewish rather than a strong woman. On the other hand, in various kinds of roles, she's been captivating. In a trifle—really a trifle, powder-puff picture—called *Hot Millions* with Peter Ustinov, she was enchanting. She's a woman of gifts, distinction, and beauty. But I don't have quite the confidence in her that I have in some other people. For example, in that ghastly picture of Richard Attenborough's where she came out to do a song in a revue, *Oh! What a Lovely War,* she acted like the great artist coming on to prove that she was regular and all-around, and she simply didn't know how to use her hands and arms in a musical number.

We're leaving out of this discussion, by the way, another actress, also English, whom I think at least as highly of, if not more so—and that's Vanessa Redgrave, who has been extremely fine, often in bad pictures, like *Isadora.* Again, I think it was in *Oh! What a Lovely War* she had one small scene as a suffragette. It was enchanting. In this regard she's like Jane Fonda; she steps on—figuratively—and you know you're dealing with an actress, with a being who *belongs* there, that her *vocation* is to be there, her chromosomes are attuned to her appearing before people, making them look at her so that something will happen as a result of it. She just *is* the goods, besides being beautiful.

Macklin: Who else would you say are the best that we have—actors and actresses?

Kauffmann: Well, here are some names. Olivier is probably in the English-speaking theater the most distinguished that we have, the closest to a *great* actor that we have living today.

Macklin: Does he adapt well to film, do you think?

Kauffmann: He has done some beautiful work in films and sometimes, again, in negligible pictures. I remember his quiet, gentle, very good performance in an Otto Preminger thriller set in London—*Bunny Lake Is Missing.* A very taking, small performance that he gave. I've seen him in a large number of things in the theater. In fact, one of the three or four best things that I've ever seen in my life was his *Oedipus* which he did here in the Old Vic in 1946, and I saw that three times. But there are people who are more generally known to film audiences . . . Mastroianni, Max von Sydow, several of the people called the Bergman company. There's a wonderful Swedish actor named Per Oscarsson, who appeared in *Hunger.* Marvelous actor. Jeanne Moreau at times has been very fine.

Macklin: When?

Kauffmann: She was very fine in *La Notte,* I think.

Macklin: Well, that's interesting. Antonioni is a director who supposedly doesn't work with actresses very much.

Kauffmann: And she hates Antonioni. The one time I met Jeanne Moreau she told me she disliked Antonioni so much that she never saw the film. Still, she's very fine in it. Actors and actresses are not always the best judges of their own work.

And then you have a couple of Japanese gents named Toshiro Mifune in his Kurosawa pictures. And Takashi Shimura in pictures like *Ikiru.* Very, very fine.

Macklin: That brings up another point. What about something like *Rashomon* which I was somewhat surprised to see on your top ten of all time. What about Mifune's performance?

Kauffmann: Oh, I think it was a wonderful performance. But I ought to say I put *Rashomon* in that list simply because I wanted to put a Kurosawa in. I could have put in *Ikiru* and certainly I could have put in *Seven Samurai,* which is one of the best films I've ever seen. But I chose *Rashomon* because it seemed to me to have a little more resonance.

Macklin: You, I thought, underrated *High and Low.* You said there wasn't much going on in the film. Have you seen it again?

Kauffmann: No, and I'd like to. There are things in that film that I'll never forget, that stick in my mind—things like the camera movement in the opening scene in Mifune's house, where the camera has a choreography of its own as it moves around with the detectives and with Mifune. There's the confrontation between Mifune and the man in prison, the way the picture ends. Marvelous, marvelous. I really would like to see that film again. But, on the other hand, anyone who writes criticism—you must know this for yourself—would like to see or read everything over again and rewrite his reviews every ten years. My own feeling is that anyone who says precisely the same thing ten years later about a work that he criticized ten years before is petrified. He may like it more; he may like it less; he may like it *more so* in a way he did, but he can't like it exactly the same, with the same degree, with the same caloric content—it's impossible, if he's alive. So I'm perfectly willing to concede that I might think better of *High and Low,* just as there are some pictures I've praised that I would probably think less of.

Macklin: You did select *Rashomon* as your choice of a Kurosawa film. Why *Rashomon?*

Kauffmann: I suppose a simple reason: at the moment it was the Kurosawa film that was absolutely clearest in my mind. The letter that we got, all of us who contributed to that poll in *Sight and Sound,* said, "Please, make sure you've seen the picture lately." I teach at Yale; I have a theater seminar and a film course, and I had seen *Rashomon* very recently. It was the clearest in my mind; I was surest of my ground about that one so I chose it. But I was choosing among gems, Kurosawa gems.

Macklin: Does Mifune's performance or Mifune as an actor make extra demands upon the viewer? Can one go to that performance the same way that he would go to Olivier?

Kauffmann: Different cultures make different demands upon you. Japanese actors often use different sets of symbols and different sets of references than Anglo-Saxon actors. We saw that when the dramatization of *Rashomon* was done here on the stage, and it was pathetic. Or when the faulty transmogrification of *Rashomon* was done in Mexico with Paul Newman, *The Outrage*. An excellent actor, Newman, one who certainly belongs in the category of first-class actors of our day. But nothing jelled in the way that part was conceived or realized because the ethnic roots were waving in the air. Mifune has a kind of animal assault in *Rashomon*, making demands—maybe the word isn't "demands"—on you. It's like being locked in an elevator with a madman. You may be uncomfortable, but you pay attention [laughs]. There's a familiar story about Kurosawa and Mifune in making that picture. They were preparing it, rehearsing it, and Kurosawa got a print of a travelogue about Africa in which there were some roaring lions and said to Mifune, "That's the bandit!"

Macklin: Did you see "roaring lions"?

Kauffmann: Well, I certainly saw as sheer an animalistic performance—I don't mean in sexual bestiality, I mean just in feral quality—as I can remember in pictures.

Macklin: You mentioned Newman; has he ever delivered a performance that is anywhere within his potential? He would be my Jane Fonda. I would think Paul Newman would be an actor that simply has coasted through horrendous roles and really glided through performances.

Kauffmann: Would you give me an example of where you think he's glided?

Macklin: I think *WUSA,* for instance. When he played a drunk, I thought he was just awful. . . .

Kauffmann: Oh, that's such a ghastly picture. I'd hate to judge from that, but let's take some examples. I've just been writing a piece about Stacy Keach and I compared him with Newman, apropos principally of Keach's performance in *Fat City,* a very disappointing film, I think, in which Keach *could* have been very good, but is coasting. And in my own mind, I compared it with Newman's performance—small performance, a vignette part—in the Hemingway thing, *Adventures of a Young Man,* a wonderful small piece of acting. Or in the Rocky Graziano picture, *Somebody Up There Likes Me*—which wasn't much of a picture, it was a characterization.

Newman is a very subtle actor. He's much more subtle than he's given credit for. I wrote about two of his recent films: a mixed-up picture that he

directed himself called *Sometimes a Great Notion;* followed immediately by
one called *Pocket Money* that he made with Lee Marvin. Now if I could take
clips from those two pictures and show them to you side by side, figuratively
(I used to do this on television), I think I could demonstrate to you what I
mean about subtlety of imagination working its way out through vocal inflec-
tion, physical attitudes, personality aura, and all the other factors that go
towards subtle delineation. He *thinks* differently in his pictures. He has a
strong personality that doesn't change. It's not a question of a stock company
actor putting on hook nose and beard and becoming "somebody else," a man
of a thousand faces or anything like that—that's easy. He works from a core
outward, differently. And you would find, I believe, that his whole system of
timing was different in *Pocket Money* from what it was in the logging picture.

Do you remember his performance in *Hombre?* . . . a doughy western in
which he played, do you remember, an Indian who had come to live among
white people, and how easily he signified to you that this was a man of two
worlds—not in any heavy-handed way that a more obvious actor would have
done—that this man had physical characteristics, habits, conditioning that
contradicted those of the people around him. He *lived* in a different way.
Very nicely done, I thought.

Macklin: I get the feeling when I see Newman that he has to be loved,
that he's afraid not to give the audience what it's prepared for.

Kauffmann: Well, he didn't do that in *WUSA.* Oh, I don't see how you
can say that. You didn't see *Sometimes a Great Notion?*

Macklin: No. I didn't see that. That may be a change. I'm talking about
up to that picture.

Kauffmann: I don't think there are many actors who will risk playing
unsympathetic roles like that, genuinely unsympathetic roles.

Macklin: Take Robert Redford in *Downhill Racer*—I don't think Newman
at that point in his career would ever have allowed himself to play that kind
of hollow character. Compare Redford and Newman in *Butch Cassidy and
the Sundance Kid.* Redford creates; Newman coasts.

Kauffmann: We're talking here about really two different things. We're
talking about choice of role and method of execution. If I may say so, I've
heard this before about Newman—as probably a valid criticism—that he's
interested in being liked too much. I recognize that, I think. I mean I understand what people are saying when they say it, and I also think that he hasn't

extended himself in obvious range as much as, let us say, Marlon Brando has. No American screen star has tried as many different things as Brando has.

Macklin: Let me give you another example. Jon Voight in *Midnight Cowboy,* a film which I think, if I remember, you didn't like. . . .
Kauffmann: Oh, I liked it pretty well—principally because of the acting.

Macklin: Well, Voight seemed to me to do so much—no hard sell at all—that people really didn't relate to him in terms of this is a great actor because he was so quiet and he was *so* understood.
Kauffmann: And he certainly was very good in it. He's a very good actor. I saw him in the theater before I saw him on the screen. By the way, Dustin Hoffman was his understudy in an off-Broadway production not far from where we're sitting now. But Voight had one big advantage in that picture—he was an unknown. Also, Newman couldn't play that part now because he's too old for it, but I can't see why the Newman of ten years ago wouldn't have been at least as good as Voight in it and why he wouldn't have approached it with the same reticence.

Macklin: You think he understates? You think Newman is an actor who understates?
Kauffmann: He can. I think he can understate when he chooses to. That pug, for example in the Hemingway film is an understated piece of acting. I think people who don't respond to Paul Newman are reacting on a matter of personality, rather than art. They just don't like *him.*

Macklin: Well, I find he sells his personality. The personality is always there and to me it overwhelms the art.
Kauffmann: This doesn't happen to me very often. He has a strong personality, but it's not like Kirk Douglas.

Macklin: How about actors or actresses that you think have turned out to be disappointments?
Kauffmann: The one I've been writing about lately is Stacy Keach, who, as he climbs higher and higher up the golden ladder, seems to me to get dimmer and dimmer. His last two films, *The New Centurions* and *Fat City,* both of which are not very interesting pictures anyway, show him sort of imagining himself as something he is not, as some kind of powerhouse personality who can just be on screen and overwhelm audiences. And I don't

think that's true of him. I think Keach is effective only when he is someone *else*. You know Olivier says he never appears on stage or on screen in his own nose. He has to do something to himself; he has to act. It helps him to come on in some kind of disguise.

Macklin: Keach should come on in somebody else's eyes, shouldn't he? Don't the eyes kill him?

Kauffmann: He looks dopey some of the time. But he *doesn't* when he's playing a part that is further removed from himself, when he did Buffalo Bill in a play called *Indians.* He had to reach to get there at all and to stay there; he couldn't sink back into himself.

Macklin: Could you see his eyes from where you were?

Kauffmann: You can see actors' eyes in the theater. That's another fiction about comparisons between theater and film.

Macklin: Not from my seat you can't.

Kauffmann: [laughs] You can get the effect of what they're doing with their eyes certainly, which is the important thing. He did *Coriolanus* with the professional theater at Yale—not a good production—but he had an idea, an image of something he was doing and went to it the moment he leaped onto the stage. I can remember *one* picture in which I thought he was really very good—a relatively small part—made from a Carson McCullers novel with Alan Arkin, *The Heart Is a Lonely Hunter.* Keach had a scene in which he got furious and punched a wall. He was very very good in it because he *went* to someone.

Macklin: What about Katharine Hepburn?

Kauffmann: She's gotten very much worse as she's gotten older. I understand she has physical problems, which wouldn't be my concern if she weren't an actress. But she is an actress appearing before the public. These things get thrust at us. She's become tremulous in a way she never was before. God, I must be old—I saw her on stage before she ever went to film. I was quite young at the time, and the few people who saw her in those plays saw something that was later revealed to the world at large—a fresh, vital, *extremely* winning, intelligent personality. Her personality breathed intelligence. One of the things that Hepburn isn't given sufficient credit for as an actress is that—in addition to her beauty, which she certainly has, and her crispness as an actress and her delicious sense of social comedy—she made intelligence an *emotion*. She made intelligence a viable theatrical element.

Macklin: How so?

Kauffmann: Because you got the sense from her that this was a woman with some brains, and that the factor of her brains was an added attraction to her. You wanted to know her, to go to bed with her *because* she was so intelligent. I can't think of another film actress before her who used that sort of intellectual flair in quite such a sexual manner.

Macklin: I shouldn't talk about actresses without letting you have at least a short comment about the divine *Barbra*.

Kauffmann: Harris, you mean [laughs].

Macklin: No. Maybe, we should leave it at that.

Kauffmann: You mean Bar-bra?

Macklin: Yes.

Kauffmann: Well, I thought she was very amusing in *Funny Girl* on the stage and again in the picture. I simply don't think she is divine or a goddess or endlessly interesting. And I think she's sometimes absolutely dreadful, as she was in the visionary musical—*On a Clear Day You Can See Forever*. As she also was, I think anyone would admit, in *Hello Dolly*. I have no animus against her; I just have an animus against the inflation that surrounds her. She's a singer of ability—that's quite clear. But, there's a cheapness to her that bothers me a great deal. Merchandized vulgarity that isn't vulgar in the way that Marie Dressler was lovably vulgar. There's a tremendous conceit that comes across in Barbra Streisand, which is not the same thing as personality.

Macklin: You've done some interesting work on the entertainer, not as actor, but as having a kind of presence. I wonder if you've seen either James Taylor in *Two-Lane Blacktop* or Kris Kristofferson in *Cisco Pike*?

Kauffmann: I missed *Two-Lane Blacktop,* but I saw *Cisco Pike*. I hate to dredge up this dreadful cliché, but there's probably some kind of generation gap operating here. He was simply to me a dead-end fellow with a husky voice.

Macklin: With no presence?

Kauffmann: No, I had no interest in him, and the picture itself was such a contrived piece of hokum to capitalize on what it thought were certain chic things about young people that it put me off very badly. I had no response to him.

Macklin: You wrote a review about *Pocket Money* saying it was a pleasant film. I think that you made a decision somewhere as a critic to accept imperfect films because they had something that in your eyes was worthwhile, but I know for a fact that a lot of your fellow critics are disappointed when you will find something in a film like *Pocket Money* or *The Hired Hand* and say that this is a film that has some quality to it.

Kauffmann: They're two different categories, they're two different kettles of fish there—*Pocket Money* and *The Hired Hand.* I'm not referring to anyone personally—you haven't told me who and please don't—but I think there's a certain amount of lack of self-confidence in some critics, a fear of liking things that are "popular" because they'll look a little less highbrow. In my supremely confident whatever-it-is, ignorance, I don't have that kind of fear at all. If Rona Jaffe wrote a novel tomorrow that I liked, I would say so, although I don't think that's likely. *Pocket Money* to me—it wasn't a question of liking it despite its faults—I would have liked it better if it had been a *better* "pleasant picture." What I wanted to draw attention to there was simply that it's possible to make a film of no particular significance that is pleasant to watch. And that it takes a certain kind of courage to set out deliberately to make that kind of film. That's a species, a genus of art—not at the same level as *Rashomon*—but it has a right to exist, an artistic, an aesthetic right to exist.

The Hired Hand is a more complicated subject because there was an attempt at a very serious picture, very severely flawed. But I think it's the critic's busines, is it not, to *discriminate* within a work and to find out what in the picture he thinks, he feels, is good and is bad. Now there are critics I know, and again I'm not naming names, who feel that if critic A disagrees with them about a particular work he has breached the faith. In other words, they take their opinions as legislation. It seems to me to be at least a two-way street. If it's thought that if I like a film directed by Peter Fonda, and Peter Fonda is on nobody's gilt-edged list at the moment, that by liking parts of a film or the intent of a film that Peter Fonda made, I've let down certain secret codes, it seems to me utter nonsense. Take *The Hired Hand* as a case in point. I recognized, I thought, in *The Hired Hand* an attempt at a very large American theme: the role of the male on the frontier and the friction between that role and, let us call it, the civilizing process. There were certain circumscriptions which had to be accepted by the free male if society was to progress. That, to me, was an impressive choice of theme to begin with. I saw, I thought, a good deal of the ingenious cinematic exposition of that, mixed in with a great deal of pictorial sentimentality, a not very impressive performance by Peter Fonda himself, and some other things which seemed to me forced and strained. It would have been to me a kind of dereliction of duty to empty the baby out with the bath and say that this picture was bad. For me, it had things in it that made it worth seeing or worth knowing about or worth recognizing, at least. What I object to, to return to something I just said before in this matter of critical back chat in which I don't indulge much, is that critics take their opinions as law.

Macklin: Did you go through some process to arrive at that . . . you see, I'm still troubled by this question of discrimination.

Kauffmann: Well, what you're troubled by, if I may presume, is what all of us are troubled by—we're looking for some kind of absolute. I don't suppose that we should dampen our ambition for absolutes in art—we just have to be very careful not to arrive at any. It would be very nice if we could say that X was faulty in liking that element in that picture because we *know* that element is capital B Bad. But nobody knows—*nobody* knows whether that element is capital B Bad. One can only say that in the light of his own experience, his own psyche, his own pair of eyes, his own experience from his moment of birth until that moment when he saw that film, it struck him as bad and he can explain with internal consistency, at least, why he thought so. That's the *most* that anyone can say. Of course, if we pursue that to a ridiculous extreme, it would mean that everyone is a good critic. But the way you tell good from lesser critics—for yourself again, only for yourself—is through an experience with them, an experience either that shows them corroborating what you feel or establishing differences which you can respect, but *never* absolute die-stamped standards, which is one of the reasons, of course, that I object so strongly to the old *auteur* theory—it promulgates pantheons with lists.

Macklin: If critics and readers are saying we are trusting in Stanley Kauffmann to stand up at the gates of art and to defend art and to look out for art, and here he comes along and he is being cordial to works like *Pocket Money* and *The Hired Hand* which are minor art at best and perhaps inartistic in many ways. . . .

Kauffmann: If—let me take that sentence as given—if they believe the first part, why can't they believe the second? If they believe that I have any credibility as a critic, why can't they believe that I knew the risk I was taking and deliberately took it because I refused to be cowed by the fact that this particular film or these particular films had no greatness about them? I would just as much refuse to be cowed by the *lack* of pretense of those films as I would refuse to be cowed by the arrant pretense of many films that are taken seriously as great art or given to us as impressive spectacles—*Nicholas and Alexandra* is the first example that comes to mind.

Macklin: [laughs] Oh, so you *are* like Rex Reed.

Kauffmann: [laughs] You know what Winston Churchill said about a rival who once agreed with him on a particular point. He said, "Even a stopped clock is right twice a day."

Macklin: Do you think you've mellowed?

Kauffmann: Oh, I'm afraid I have [laughs].

Macklin: Why are you "afraid"?

Kauffmann: I would like to have some of the arrogance that I had when I was younger—still. I'm afraid that I sometimes see the *rationale* behind things I dislike. I'm even beginning to understand a little about Hitler, for example. If that's "mellowing," it's happened to me. But let's stick more to our muttons here. If "mellowing" implies anything akin to a lowering of standards, I think that that's simply untrue. Changing, alteration, reconsideration of standards because I'm now fourteen years older than when I began writing film criticism regularly, yes. I should hope things have happened to me in that time. If I could see again say, the first six pictures I reviewed in the *New Republic,* I would hope I would write differently about them. But I strongly resist any imputation—for example, these two pictures you just mentioned, *The Hired Hand* and *Pocket Money*—that there's any sliding off in my standards. On the contrary, I think it's prosecution of my beliefs that leads me to look for the glimpse of gold in the dross. The easiest thing to do to get yourself a reputation for being demanding and knowledgeable is to be consistently negative. That's easy. To me that's just as cheap as the people on the popular press who are always consistently positive as a way of keeping their jobs. I have no patience with either as a blanket policy.

Macklin: Well, are you a critic for whom art is the priority?

Kauffmann: Absolutely. Absolutely and irrevocably. And that's just what I've been trying to make clear about these two pictures—that it's a poor critic, I think, who can't see what's good in an imperfect work and who is afraid to say so because he thinks he'll lose face with his highbrow pals.

Macklin: When you affirm something worthy in an imperfect work, do you always mention the imperfections? Do you always put it in that kind of setting?

Kauffmann: I certainly hope I do. I'm *not* going to get into critical back chat, but it would be easy for me to pick examples of films or plays that were praised by some people in "highbrow" criticism that I thought were utter garbage, utter *garbage*. I mean these are two-way streets.

Macklin: You hit upon arrogance. Is that a critical necessity?

Kauffmann: If you use the term and the idea lightly, *lightly*—yes, it's a critical necessity. Arrogance in the sense that one cares about nothing but one's probity and one's devotion to the art and to one's completeness of response to it. That strikes some people as arrogant. But the worse aspect of arrogance, particularly in our time, is the whole business of critical elevation that is going on—critical exaltation, focus on the critic, "the critic as super-star" as someone just said—I'm very much against that. I think that critics have a necessity to be—vis-à-vis the art in which they're engaged—relatively humble. They are mediators, teachers, but they're not creators of the art. There are various reasons adduced as to why critics are getting so much attention these days, particularly in the film world. Whatever those reasons are, in that respect, I'd like to be humble and reticent and just write my pieces and let people read them if they're interested. I hope they are.

Macklin: Is it *possible* to be modest as a critic?

Kauffmann: It's not possible to be intellectually modest or you wouldn't be a critic. But it's possible to be *socially* modest and that's something else again, and the distinction is not always clear with every person.

Macklin: You are one of the critics who is pretty nicely hard on comedy like *Putney Swope* and *Fritz the Cat* and these faddish, trendy things. What would you say is good comedy?

Kauffmann: Well, for example, I think the best films of Richard Lester are marvelous film comedy. I think, and maybe this is my King Charles's head, but I'm willing to stake a good deal on the opinion that Lester's *How I Won the War* is one of the most important films of the last decade. It's beginning to come into its own. I have had personal experience with that film over the years. I show it every year in my film course, and I can sense differences of response to it in the people who see the film. I think, for another example, that *Some Like It Hot* is one of the best film comedies and farces ever made. We're not bringing into this discussion any of the star comics—we're not talking about Chaplin or Keaton or the Marx brothers.

Macklin: No.

Kauffmann: We're talking about acted comedies with actors playing parts. *Some Like It Hot,* to me, is a superb piece of work. I've just written a long article for *Horizon*—I'm doing a series for *Horizon,* one essay a quarter each on a different film. I'm mild on some of the things that are thought a lot of these days, like Woody Allen. I think Allen is a very, *very* funny writer, but a very, very limited performer and an absolutely dreadful director. He's better when he doesn't direct, and he's best when the thing he does lies *exactly* within his small range of the put-upon Jules Feiffer, damp little creature. *Bananas* was a very funny script, but a terrible picture. And another example of that in a different way is *The Producers* by Mel Brooks, another very, very funny writer and stand-up comic, but a very bad director.

Macklin: Maybe the piece of criticism by Stanley Kauffmann that is best known is the two-parter on *The Graduate.* From today's vantage point, what are your thoughts on it?

Kauffmann: From one factual point of view I've been proven right. I said the film was a landmark.

Macklin: A milestone.

Kauffmann: Milestone, is that what I said? [laughs] And milestone doesn't mean "great work"—it means "marker." And it certainly was a very clear marker in what was happening. That's proved, retrospectively. It breached and opened up new dimensions in American feature fiction films. I think that's incontrovertible. You may like or not like what followed it, but it certainly is a milestone. Anyone who writes the history of the sixties in American films cannot disregard *The Graduate* as a milestone. I haven't seen the film again within the last three or four years so I can't second-guess myself about it. I have a suspicion, however—I'm not going to use the term "overpraise"—that *one* of the reasons I praised the film was because I thought Nichols did such a very good job with the actors in the picture. Whatever one thinks of him as a director *en tout,* he certainly is a first-class director of actors. And the performances he got from Dustin Hoffman and Anne Bancroft, who hadn't been very good previously, and that girl, Katharine Ross, who was never any good before *or* since, gave the picture a quality for me that made it stick.

Macklin: What about in the church when Anne Bancroft becomes like a banshee. It's just caricature, which I think Nichols does far too much of.

Kauffmann: I don't agree, but, since you mention the church, the exchanges between the girl and Benjamin in the balcony in that scene—I saw the picture three times—just pulverized me each time I saw them.

Macklin: Why was that?

Kauffmann: Because I felt that there was a sense of *anti*-romance in it, there was sense of "my God, I *know* that our getting together won't make the world right, but what can we do *except* this? This is the *only* log we have to cling to, it's not going to turn it all into technicolor roses down the path forever, but we'll *drown* without this. We've *got* to have this." I got that very clearly from the exchange between them, the looks between them in the church and from that last moment on the bus which was very distinctly *not* a happy ending. It was an iron lung ending. "At least we can breathe now." There are cartoon elements in the film—I've mentioned some of them. My readers, people who pay me the compliment of talking about those pieces, usually overlook the fact that there are some very strong criticisms of the picture in them, although I certainly come out in its favor.

Macklin: You say you didn't overpraise it, but you . . . what would a word be?

Kauffmann: I would say that I weighted the effect of the acting on the theme more heavily than many people did. I think that many of the people who judged that film more or less restricted themselves to it as a script and as a piece of cinematic work. And in both of those regards it has faults, some of which I certainly detailed. But most of them omitted the quality of creation that Nichols brought about with the people who were playing it.

Macklin: A hundred actresses couldn't have done what Katharine Ross did?

Kauffmann: But they couldn't have done it without Nichols—that's my point. Katharine Ross never did it before or since.

Macklin: What did she do?

Kauffmann: She made it true.

Macklin: What about the new book you're working on?

Kauffmann: Oh, it's to be published in the late fall of '72 probably, perhaps early 1973, by Liveright. It's an anthology of American film criticism from the very beginning—the date of the first review is April 24, 1896, the first public showing of the Edison Vitascope in New York—up to *Citizen Kane.* I had the very considerable help of a research associate named Bruce Henstell. It ends in 1941 with *Citizen Kane* simply because the book is very long as is and secondly, because I wanted to throw the heavy emphasis on the pre-Agee period. There's a common fallacy that serious film criticism began in this country about the time of James Agee. That's simply untrue. And one of the things this anthology is trying to do is to explode that fallacy. I hope also that it's intrinsically interesting. I can speak this way about it because I didn't *write* the pieces; I know that there are very many rewarding things in the book.

Macklin: Finally, I presume you get the kind of opposition anybody who has a literary background gets. What do you answer to people who say that you can't deal with film the way it should be dealt with because you have a literary background?

Kauffmann: If I want to answer them in their own terms, which I think is a mistake, but if I wanted to, I could say that their objection isn't really precise. I have a theater background, I was trained as an actor; I worked with a theater company, a repertory company.

Macklin: But you read books. . . .

Kauffmann: I can't help that. I'm sorry. And I also review books quite a lot. My aesthetic objection is to the *idiot-savant* approach to film—the idea that one can and should know only one thing and that the arts don't enrich one another. I simply disagree. My own conditioning, training, and inter-ests—strong interests, I presume to think—are to write about three fields: theater, film, and literature. And I can't see any more logic in my being debarred from film criticism because I review books than vice versa. I know a good many distinguished literary critics and not one of them has ever said to me, "Oh, you're a film man, you shouldn't review books." There's a certain nervousness in the film world which doesn't obtain in other fields. There's a certain eagerness to preempt territory and sometimes the person's sole claim to preemption is that he doesn't know anything except film. That's pretty slim qualification for film criticism, I think, as nothing but theater knowledge would be slim for theater criticism.

Literary Criticism: Stanley Kauffmann

Stanley Rosner and Lawrence Edwin Abt / 1976

From *The Creative Expression,* edited by Stanley Rosner and Lawrence Edwin Abt (Croton-on-Hudson, NY: North River Press, 1976): 203–20.

Q: Perhaps a good point of departure would be for you to tell us something about what you do.

A: I occupy myself principally these days with two functions, teaching and writing criticism. The teaching is not relevant here, of course, although it's connected to and derives from the criticism. And my criticism is concentrated in three areas. Right at this moment, two areas take precedence over the third—those two being film and theatre, the third being literature. I'm the film and theatre critic of the *New Republic,* and I write literary criticism occasionally for them and occasionally for a lot of other journals too. I used to do a great deal more literary criticism than I have time for now.

Q: Can you direct yourself to what you see as the function of a critic? We know that's a difficult question.

A: Yes, it's a question that has to be answered either with a snap phrase or really with a book, but let me try to strike a medium. I think of criticism as a form of literature. Not paraliterature, not a substitute for literature, but a kind of art concurrent with art. To me it's not a substitute vocation. It's not a haven for foundered artists, although many such have ended up that way. It's a profession, and the point of the profession is to act in several ways. First, as a mediator between art work and audience. Second, as a very necessary sounding board for the artist. And always I'm talking about criticism at its optimum, without at the moment making distinctions among critics. I'm talking about the function of criticism. I know that there are innumerable instances through Western history, in the last three hundred years particularly, of great artists animadverting against critics. I've just been writing a piece on Giuseppe Verdi, a man I love, and he hated critics. But in the careers of any one of these men or women, you can find instances where they relied on critics to a degree sometimes they weren't aware of, for some kind of resonance in regard to their work. I don't mean fame, success, celebrity. That's the publicity aspect of criticism which, of course, is inseparable from it. I mean in terms of enabling the artist to ask: "Have I done exactly what I meant to do? Maybe I've done better than I knew I was doing." Which is often the case. Those are two primary functions, one would say, or obvious functions.

There's a third function that derives from the proper execution of the first two—again speaking optimally—the critic himself is creating a literature. If you look through the index of the collected drama criticism of Bernard Shaw, who was, as far as I know, the best theatre critic who ever wrote, look through the index of his three volumes of collected criticism, you'll find that you would not know the names of, at a guess, 95 percent of plays that he reviewed, excepting classics. And you have no desire to know. But in reading what he wrote about them, you encounter a form of experiential examination which is hard to divorce from the experiential examination of art itself. Just as a novelist can write about a man walking down the street and buying an ice cream cone in such a way that it illuminates the human condition through that commonplace and trivial action, so a good critic can write about the most ephemeral nonsense that has happened in the theatre or the films in such a way that it illuminates his life and, therefore, yours.

Q: You're suggesting, then, that Shaw, for example, would have had a place in history as a critic independent of any plays that he had written himself.

A: I think it's absolutely indisputable that if he—it just happens that he is the best playwright in the English language since Shakespeare, but that's almost incidental here—if he had written only his theatre criticism and his music criticism, one or the other, he would be immortal. With both together, he's got a base of immortality before he writes Play One—absolutely. In every sense his criticism is beautifully written, ideological, analytical, and philosophical, and it's a fine kind of contemporary history.

Q: Would you say that a function of the critic is to set standards for the arts? Do you think that that would be a significant function?

A: Yes, so long as one treads gently with any didactic overtones of that phrase, I do agree with it. As T. S. Eliot said, with his usual courage in criticism, the function of the critic is the elucidation of masterpieces and the improvement of taste. Setting standards sounds a little as if you had a rule book from the U.S. Bureau of Standards and you could measure anything

against it. It has the hint of absolutes about it, which simply don't exist
because, at the last, any opinion—Shaw's, or Joe Blow's—is only his opinion.
But, still, one of the measures of a critic's validity and worth is the passion
with which he subscribes to his opinion. In other words, if it's important to
him, really important to him, that such and such be adhered to or pursued,
then what he's saying is, in effect, (a) that the art will be better if so-and-so
is pursued, and (b) if art is really important and not embroidery on life, life
will be better if so-and-so is improved. I've just been reading a very remark-
able book, first translation into English, by an Austrian named Karl Kraus.

Q: Karl Kraus—oh, sure.
A: Exactly—exactly.

Q: Right after the turn of the century.
A: He was a kind of mordant, bitter genius. His principal function was
really that, rather than editing a biweekly magazine in Vienna for many years.
He had a great influence on Wittgenstein, Schönberg, on Adolph Loos, and
God knows who else in Vienna at the time. He wrote a play in five acts and
259 scenes called, *The Last Days of Mankind,* which is a cataclysmic horror
play about the end of civilization through World War I, an immensely pro-
phetic play. But what's interesting about Kraus is, and something that's lost
to somebody who doesn't really understand German, and I really don't, is
that everything he believed in philosophy, in politics, in art, in ethics was
rooted for him in language. The ethical, esthetic use of language. Part of the
political horror of this play is based on the way language is manipulated to
make people react in certain ways, and his opinions of the language are only
his opinions, but to him they were fiery convictions, that if you maltreat
language, you automatically maltreat everything else in life. It's inescapable.
And so there is a clear example of a man who believed that standards, in his
case linguistic standards, were the absolute fundament of ethical, esthetical,
philosophical necessity. Yes, that's criticism at its highest.

Q: There was a piece in the *Sunday Times*—we don't know whether you
saw it—an interview with Menotti, in which the author makes some of these
points, we think. Menotti is very much upset with Harold Schonberg and the
attitudes he shows towards his compositions, and we think there is the same
implicit notion of standards.
A: Well, without getting into specifics about personalities, which I'd rather
not do, but since you mentioned music, and we are talking about optimums

in criticism as a ground for our discussion, whenever I'm feeling depressed about theatre criticism and film criticism, which I often do feel, even literary criticism, which is much better than either of those two, I think of music criticism and I cheer up considerably.

Q: We would like to ask you, in line with your earlier comment which suggested that, as you see it, criticism is every bit as creative and an independently creative profession, as any of the arts, what you would have to say about the notion of making something from nothing.

A: I have to make just one reservation about your statement, which is that I don't believe it's every bit as creative as "the arts." I think the *process* is every bit as creative as the arts. If you ask me whether I would rather have written T. S. Eliot's "Tradition and the Individual Talent" or T. S. Eliot's *The Waste Land* I would certainly prefer to have written *The Waste Land.* I think it's a greater achievement, but what I'm saying is that the process of his criticism is itself a creative process, not a lesser process. I think art comes first. My insistence is that the means by which one makes the best criticism is not in itself a different, parasitic process. But to pursue what you said, a simplistic rendering is this: that the artist works from the material of life and that the critic works from the material of art plus life. Oscar Wilde, of course, who is only coming into his serious own these days, who is really a much deeper man than anyone gave him credit for in his lifetime, said that, therefore, criticism was superior to art because the critic has to deal with two bodies of phenomena and the artist with only one—only with life—whereas the critic has to deal with life and art. And in fact, Oscar Wilde is very much to be admired. Richard Ellman, himself a first-class critic, edited an anthology of Wilde's critical writings a couple of years ago called *The Critic as Artist* a lot of which was surprising, although a lot of it was printed before the turn of the century. One could almost call it a modern view of the importance of criticism. And in Wilde's case it's particularly welcome because it doesn't come from a man who was artistically bankrupt. We know he is talking as a man who himself created art. In fact, one of the most astonishing things about criticism in English, which is the only language I really know, from the Renaissance on, you would find that if you applied as rigorous standards as you could to the selection of the authors in your anthology, probably 50 percent of them would also have been first-class poets or novelists as well. So there's a symbiosis going on there between the critical process and creative process. My own hunch about it is that it's simply not an emphasis in genes, in the psyche, in whatever. It's not a distinction. It's like being male or female. It's just an emphasis, not a distinction.

Q: Let us try to play the devil's advocate. One question that comes up again and again in our work is the issue of where do ideas come from; and one answer to this is that the artist, again, is able to create something from nothing. The playwright can sit down, put a blank page in a typewriter, and begin to get ideas or an artist who puts a blank canvas in front of him. Can we make such a distinction here, where, when the critic goes to work, he's taking off on something that already exists?

A: Well, there are two parts to the answer. The first is, as Harold Bloom, who teaches English at Yale, has been writing, poems don't start from nothing. They start from other poems. The history of the creation of poetry is the history of a philology. It's an open guessing game as to whether a man brought up on a desert island would ever write a poem without a book of poetry ever to read. Poems write a poem, one could say figuratively. There's a degree of emulation, of "I want to do what he did or she did" in the writing of poetry. It has nothing to do with sincerity; I'm not questioning the poet's sincerity. I'm talking about the process by which the poem comes into being out of the most convinced things. I fall in love—my heart is broken—I want to do something about it. Oh, Robert Burns wrote a poem about it. It's my own heartbreak, but if Burns hadn't shown me something about how to do something about it, I might knock my head against the wall or just keep it stuffed up inside myself or have to dance a jig, but I wouldn't have a poem. Poems come from poems. I think that's fairly well—I won't say established, that sounds like scientific fact—it's widely believed and there's a reason to believe it. Second part of the answer to that point is that a blank sheet of paper is a blank sheet of paper. And it's just a question of whether the phenomenon that's going to operate through you to reach the paper was a love affair or a musical comedy you saw the night before.

Q: Then in terms of the birth of ideas for you, what would you say about that?

A: Well, "what kind of ideas" is a little loose, but let me try to draw this rough distinction. I've written a lot of novels, as it happens, and I've written a number of plays too, but nothing much happened with the plays. The novels have been published here and in Britain and have been translated and so on. Published seven of them, as a matter of fact. Anything one says in this vein is a little ludicrous because it's being reduced to words and you're dealing really with things that are not verbal—they're impulse, and, you try to catch them in words. A series of things happen to you, as experiences—phenomenological experiences—and they resonate against whatever your frame of mind and emotional composition happen to be, and for a complex of reasons including ego—I want attention, including money, including desire to mediate between yourself and the experience, including a desire to ingest the experience—the experience resonates against your being and if you have the gift, out comes a novel. There are other reasons for writing novels. There are sociological reasons, there are programmatic reasons, there are reasons which emphasize much more heavily one or the other of the factors I mentioned.

But maybe that's a satisfactory rough-hand sketch of everyone from Tolstoy to Harold Robbins. The critic who's serious and who takes the function seriously begins with the immediate phenomenon of having been affected or influenced by the work, the novel, the play, the film, whatever it is. And if he keeps on working and there's a series of such stimuli of plays, novels or films, he begins to have to arrange his experiences in some kind of order. That is, he sees that all the plays he saw in the last year have left-handed heroes, or all the films he saw were photographed on mountains and from his sequential experience comes, what you might call, inferential philosophy. There may be, broadly speaking, two methods of criticism. One is prescriptive as one starts with some esthetic theory—some great critics like John Dryden have written that way—the other, which happens to be my own bent, is inferential. A series of things happen to you and then you examine what they were and what the relationship among them is. People are always asking critics, "How do you know what a good play, film, book is? What standards do you use to judge a good play or novel or film?" And the only true answer always sounds like an evasion. The only standard I have to apply is myself, my experience of everything—plays and life and the hot dog I had last night. It sounds terribly evasive, but if you have lived your life as a—let's say, a kind of mobile litmus paper—that's all you have to apply to the experience. It isn't a conscious set of things—I'm going to see whether a plot develops within the first three minutes after the curtain comes up, or whether I'm into the story by page thirteen. Obviously such tales do exist—I caricature them, but they do exist and are taken seriously by some people—but they're irrelevant to me. To me it's experiential and the idea, to my sense, is inferential from the experience.

Q: So this places a very heavy emphasis upon your own bent in the sense that a critic who very rarely has something nasty to say about a piece of work, compared with a critic who seems always to have something nasty to say about a piece of work, can then offer a reflection of his own feelings about himself, about the way he views life.

A: It could be that a lot of other factors enter into it. I've written a little on that, as a matter of fact—again not naming any names. There are other factors that enter into the practice, the profession of criticism. One of them is popularity. The desire to succeed, and there are certain ways of succeeding with certain audiences. One way of succeeding with one kind of audience, the larger, is to like a lot of things. To be pleased by a lot of things. Another way of succeeding with the so-called intellectual, high-brow audience is to dislike a lot of things. The people who think of themselves as superior are always glad to read that most of the stuff that they haven't bothered to see is no good. This puts them in not just a negligent company, a superior company. Ever since the days of people like James Gibbons Huneker and H. L. Mencken, there's been a kind of popularity through negativism in this country, and in a way it's a kind of playing to the gallery—a smaller gallery than if you were writing for the *Daily News* or broadcasting on NBC, but still gallery playing. One could almost make a rule of thumb that the yea-saying critic is bound to be a defective critic, because most things are not good. The nay-saying critic can be either really a person of thorough discrimination or a person of modest discrimination who is leaning on that modest taste to succeed in his particular niche.

Q: What do you feel, Mr. Kauffmann, are the things in your own background that are most relevant, we would even say pertinent, in connection with your work?

A: Well, as it happens, I'm unusual, I think, in one respect in that I'm actually trained in some of the things I'm writing about. I didn't happen into them. I have been trained and I am experienced.

Q: Would you tell us about that please?

A: I'm a graduate of a drama school. I went to New York University and I took a major in dramatic art and spent a total of ten years in a repertory company. In fact, I thought I was going to spend my life in it. It was primarily a Shakespearean repertory company. I was a very minor actor, which was fine with me, and a stage manager. The hope was that some day I might be the director for that company. The company was split by a number of factors.

We're talking about sort of ancient history, but the company came apart in 1941, and the war was one of the reasons it came apart. So there's a background of some specific education and practicality, which I don't think every theatre critic has, to put it very very calmly. And that wasn't the end of my theatre experience. I wrote a number of plays, whether they are good or bad is not really the point. The point is I stubbed my toes on them.

As far as literary criticism is concerned, as I say, I've written seven novels published here and abroad, short stories and so on, and worked for a total of eleven years as a book publisher's editor and worked with some quite well known authors, so I have some nuts-and-bolts experience of the process.

Film I've never had any first-hand experience with, although I spent an enormous amount of time around film people at work. And for five years on Channel 13, New York, I conducted a weekly program called "The Art of Film," most of which was devoted to interviews with professionals of one kind or another in films. I don't mean just film stars. There were very few of them. Directors, cameramen, script writers, composers, editors, and everything else.

Q: We remember this series.

A: I'm glad you do. Well, that was educative, I'm told. I keep meeting people in their twenties now who tell me how they grew up on it ten years ago. And, of course, it was very educative for me, too. But for me it had the temporal position of coming after my experience in theatre and in literature and summoning them up.

When I was in drama school, I was taught—I think truly—that in order to do anything in the theatre, to direct or write, certainly to criticize in the theatre, you had to know all the arts. Because every one of them, from architecture to dance, has its place in theatre function. I would go further now for film and say that you have to know everything that feeds into theatre plus one step more, to become involved in film work. Graphic arts become more pertinent, even more pertinent than they are in the theatre. So I see what I'm doing as a cumulation.

It happens to be my own shape, internal shape, that led me along this road, along with a specific competence, something that I suppose I have and that, whether I have it or not, I believe in very strongly—critical talent. I think there is such a thing as critical talent. Just as there is singing talent, there is critical talent. I taught for five years at Yale in the drama school there. I was in a doctoral program that concentrated on people—a small group of vigor-

ously selected, wonderful young people interested in criticism. They are
weeded out on the basis of things they send in. They select a maximum of
five a year for admission at Yale. And what is looked for, quite properly, is,
in addition to the intellect, which is of course, a requisite, is that less defin-
able element of talent. There is such a thing as critical talent. And once you
recognize that and believe in it, as I most certainly do, then the whole practice
and profession of criticism becomes something else.

As far as the profession itself is concerned, now there's a growing recognition that criticism involves ability and training. When I was in drama school,
if I had said—which I wouldn't have said because I had no idea at the time—
that I wanted to be a critic, that's why I was going to drama school, I would
have been thought to be some kind of loon. Criticism was something you
maybe do a little of en route, but to train to be a critic would have been, to
put it mildly, eccentric. There was no place in the United States, certainly,
where you could train to be a drama critic.

Q: Is there a place now?
A: Yale is one.

Q: Yale where one can actually be trained in criticism?
A: Yes, exactly, and you can do this in film too, in several places.

Q: We would like to go back to our previous discussion and ask whether
you think that your own transitory moods from day to day would affect the
way in which you would view something that you are going to write a critical
account of. If you get up on Monday feeling lousy and you go to see a play
that night, is that going to affect the way in which you evaluate that play?
A: I can't absolutely state that it would not. I would try not to ever have
that be the case, but who can say? The psyche and the soma are pretty closely
connected. But I have known specific instances where I've felt rotten, just
physically—bellyache or headache or something—and deep within myself,
within my headache I felt myself laughing at a comedy. I didn't have the
energy actually to laugh, but inside I knew I was amused. I could take the
experience away with me and the next day, when I was feeling better, write
something about it. Only some kind of superman or saint could say that he's
not affected by mood when he sees things. But for a man or a woman who
takes the work seriously, it's not nearly as capricious as it could be made to
sound. You know the critic had a quarrel with his wife that night before he
went to the theatre? It doesn't really operate that directly. What does operate,

which is much more serious, I think, is the passage of time, and therefore the heightening or lessening of various enthusiasms, the increase of various experiences, and so on. Which is why I maintain that all criticism should be dated. It obviously is dated when it appears in a periodical, but it also ought to be done if the criticism is reprinted in a book, as mine is from time to time.

If everything I said before is true, that criticism is what you are able to say at any given moment is a result of everything you've done up to that moment; then when there are more moments, they can change your view of the thing you saw back there. It's a commonplace experience for anyone to go back to work that he has thought well or ill of earlier and find that he thinks differently of it. He likes it more or less than he did then, or his feeling gets intensified. And also sequence affects the way you react. When you see your first—let me pick an example out of the air—when we saw our first social-realist film from England around 1960, it had a certain effect on us. When we saw our eighteenth social-realist film from England which may have theoretically been as good as the first, it must have a different effect on us. A friend of mine says that if a man from Mars who had never read a novel came down to earth and by some device could read *The Godfather,* he would be absolutely stunned by its magnificence. But if you come to *The Godfather* after you've read *Crime and Punishment,* it means a little less to you. I'm not discounting the immediate effect of things or their importance. All I'm saying is that to anyone who takes this work seriously, such matters as quarrels, headaches, constipation, sexual problems don't apply any more than they do to every other moment of that person's life.

Q: Do you feel that time for reflection, for example, on something that you're writing a critical piece is important?

A: Very strongly.

Q: If you're trying to make a deadline, as you've had to in the past on some occasions, that's rather different from the opportunity to reflect, isn't it?

A: You may remember that I was theatre critic of the *New York Times* for eight months in 1966. This subject was a chief bone of contention before I started work and while I was there I told them that I thought—I've written an article about this that you might want to look up, it's in the first issue of the *New American Review*—the idea of rushing back to an office and putting into fixed immutable words within an hour your opinion of a work that might represent the conglomerate efforts of seventy-five or a hundred people over a period of five years was ludicrous and was worse than ludicrous when you were doing it for the *New York Times,* which is central. It would be ludicrous for the *Blatsville Blade,* but when you're doing it for the *New York Times,* which is—I don't have to expatiate on what its power is—it's criminal. In theory, the management of the *Times* agreed with me absolutely—in fact, their then managing editor, Clifton Daniel, did everything he could to implement it, and he ran into all kinds of opposition. Most of it came from the sources that felt one of two things, (a) other critics had trained themselves to do this practice and should I be an exception, (b) they want the hot reaction. They don't want you to be able to reflect.

There was another source of opposition, too, which was that in order to do this I had to go to the last preview. Of course, this was partly the *Times*'s fault. I wanted to go to the opening night and then hold my review forty-eight hours. They didn't want to be beaten journalistically by other newspapers. I thought that was a little silly at the time and still do. So, in order to get that extra twenty-four hours, instead of moving it that way, we had to move it back to the last preview. And there was opposition from the people who believe in this terrible mystique, this stupid mystique, of the opening night as the high point. I did go to a number of final previews when I was on the *Times* and I went to a number of opening nights. Sometimes I went to both because the condition on which the producer would let me go to the last preview was that I also go to the opening night. I could write my review in the intervening day but go to the opening night to check out any differences. I did that maybe fifteen or eighteen times, the double thing, and in every single instance, except one, the preview was a better performance. You know, and this is just a parenthetical note, the United States and Great Britain are the only two countries in the world where this opening night review thing is practiced. A child of eight could tell you that it's a stupid way to handle the matters of import in such time and other countries simply refuse to subscribe to it.

Q: Well, of course. We just wanted to say that you're drawing probably a very necessary and important distinction between reportage and criticism.

A: Well, it was exactly my point. When I spoke about this to a man named Friedrich Luft, who is, I suppose, the dean of German drama critics and I asked—I've been in Berlin a couple of times since I was on the *Times* and we talked about this point—he said that after the performance he sends in a paragraph, two paragraphs, describing the occasion, and his readers know that they'll get a critique of it the day after that, which seems so sensible that you know it will never be followed here. It's just too logical. In fact, this business of deadline applies only in two fields. It applies only in theatre and in music. Even in music sometimes it's delayed if there's a new work, a big new production; the critic will stay. The Metropolitan, we'll say, begins at seven-thirty, eight o'clock, and he doesn't have time to get back to write that night. The review appears two days later, instead of the next day. Films, not one film out of 500 that gets reviewed in the *New York Times,* is reviewed that night between the premiere and the first edition. It's seen at a screening two days or two months ahead of time. Why this particular idiotic hobble should be placed on the theatre is beyond sense. It has nothing to do with sense. It has to do with publicity and razzmatazz and glamour and all the rest of it.

Q: You're very consistent with what you said before, in terms of your view of criticism as an art form in its own right and the great respect you pay to language.

A: That, I hope, plus responsibility to the work. I could give you an example. I won't mention the play's name. It was said by my opponents, who were not few, that one of the reasons I was opposed to the opening night review was that I couldn't do it. Now, I knew that one of the reasons I was opposed to it was because I could do it too easily. I didn't want to get good at it. I didn't want to become adept at something that I thought was shoddy practice, but I had to do it sometimes. On one occasion, there was a production of a play that had been hailed ahead of time as an important piece of writing, a long play. The curtain went down at about 9:40 opening night. The theatre was about six blocks from the *New York Times*—this is all important. Too far to be close, too near to take a taxi, therefore I had to run, virtually run through the streets, certainly hurry through the streets. Had to wait for an elevator—I had to go to the bathroom, had to come back. I mean all these stupid details matter in order to get a review done by 11:00 which is the last moment, 11:15 possibly. And then there's the practice of writing reviews on a newspaper—a paragraph or two at a time on a separate piece of paper which you hand to a copy boy. So by the time you've finished your last paragraph, the first paragraph is already in type. What has this to do with critical process?

One of the rebuttals was, how interested are the readers the next day in any kind of critical analysis? Do they want just sort of a fleshed-out description? Well, I know from experience many people did want some kind of critical analysis as point one, and point two, that was all that I was interested in. So it got to be an impasse and they were quite right to replace me. In fact, it's just a matter of fact, my wife could confirm, although they did fire me, I was talking very seriously with her about not continuing after my contract was up. That's not sour grapes, that's just a fact. I'm not saying I would have, but I certainly was not sure that I wanted to spend the rest of my life doing work in that fashion. All this is a circuitous way of getting back to your point in the original question, what is criticism if it's just reaction? Your Uncle Willy could do it. He can walk out and say I liked it or I didn't like it. The whole point of criticism is not only to have a good human, normal reaction as a member of the human race. That's important, that's essential, fundamental. But the difference of a critic from the other 999 people in the theatre is that he then can examine his reactions. And if it didn't affect him satisfactorily, how could it have been done in such a way that it would have?

Q: We would raise a question about pushing the forty-eight hours to forty-eight days. What we're getting at is, have you found that you've seen something and two days, three days later you wrote something about it, but then a month later or two months later you started to have some other ideas about what you had seen, and is there still room for . . . ?

A: Well, once we leave the relatively small parish of newspaper criticism, which in terms of the profession is a small parish, of course that happens. And it happened with me; I can think of a specific instance with Harold Pinter's play *Old Times,* which I saw in London two years ago. I'm a great admirer of Pinter and I was quite disappointed in this play, but it kept nagging at me. Then I saw it in New York with a different cast, a much superior cast in New York, I thought, which opened up the play to me even further, and I saw what it was that had been nagging at me. Then over the next six months to a year, I read the play again two or three times and I discussed it in a seminar of mine at Yale and just recently have completed an article about it which is going to be in the *American Poetry Review.* There's a concrete instance of a work growing for a critic. There has to be some amount of sympathy or active antipathy to a work to get that kind of continuing reaction to it. I'm not ashamed of the article I wrote when I reviewed it in New York, but it is, for me, a transitional review as against the *APR* article. Possibly I might write another one ten years from now, should I happen to be alive ten years from now.

Q: Putting the shoe on the other foot. Do your think, for example, that artists, whether they are playwrights or painters or filmmakers, should pay a lot of attention to the criticism that they get of their work?

A: I have to speak again in the large and in the optimum, because the immediate answer to your question is, in cold fact, that they shouldn't and nobody else should pay attention to most of the criticism that's published in any field. That's a cold turkey answer to what you're saying, but you're speaking in principle. About the word "should." I don't think an artist "should" do that. I do know that some have, and I have to center it on myself. I know it has happened with others. I don't say it's only happened with me, that a novelist, a filmmaker, a playwright, a director, more than one of each, has said to me, "That was interesting." I won't mention his name—a man I admire very much who is an actor, playwright, and a director—said to me, "I read your review of X. It was all a lot of gas except for that one phrase in there, I'll never forget it. And I'll remember it when I sit down to write my next play."

What it amounts to for the artist vis-à-vis the critic is an extension, an amplification, heightening if you like, of what happens with the ordinary reader and the critic. You read, you yourself read a film critic, let's say, and nothing happens to you as a result of reading him two or three times, so you don't bother. You find another critic, and whether you agree with him or not is not the immediate matter, and some kind of confidence you can place in this man or woman has a vigor for you to the degree that you don't even have to see the film sometimes to know that you're getting something from the review. That happens with an artist. He can find a critic, or several, and the artist says, "This man seems to understand what I was trying to do. He's getting it from my works, so there's some kind of sympathy between him and me, and if things didn't happen to him exactly as I wanted them to, maybe he's telling me something." I've heard that—I know I'm not the only one. I've heard it from one of the greatest artists alive today. It's one of the proudest moments of my life that he said it, that two of the best artists alive today have said it to me about reviews of mine. I don't say that they respond like a schoolboy's obeying a teacher. I'm not talking about obeying, I'm talking about stimulation.

Q: And in a way learning—

A: Yes, in the biggest sense. Because what I wrote about their work became part of their experience of their work. Now it doesn't happen often because (a) most criticism is not worth the paper it's printed on, and (b) many good artists of every kind have a mind set against critics as ignoramuses, publicists, free loaders, and one has to sympathize with that view, to a considerable extent. A work of art of any kind is a tremendous investment of ego, of self, of nakedness. Even if it's the worst play or film ever made, you still exposed yourself in it. If someone tells you you're deformed after you've exposed yourself, the more truthful he is, the more you hate him.

Q: It's a narcissistic blow of the worst type.

A: Yes, I know critics who disagree with me about this and say, "I'm just criticizing his work." But if a man or a woman hates me for negative things I've written about him, I never resent it in the slightest. Why shouldn't he? Why shouldn't she? How could I in reason expect him or her to like me or to say, "Well, that's reasonable." I don't expect them to be reasonable about it.

Q: What is there in your family background that predisposed you to what you speak of as talent, which we think we can understand from our experience, and is there anybody else in your field in the family?

A: There's nobody in my family who is in anything like my profession, but my father, who is a dentist, was always interested in music. He is an amateur pianist. In fact, when he was a high school boy, he used to be a program boy at the Metropolitan Opera House, and, when he became a dentist, the man he worked for became a patient of his. When I became a high school boy, I got a job—I didn't become a program boy—but I used to write little fillers for the old Metropolitan House program and be paid in tickets, and I was going to the opera house in the most wonderful days, the end of the twenties, when it was empty—figuratively empty. They had these great casts that people now pay fortunes for on records. I just wrote an article about Verdi, and I mention this point. A high school boy, fourteen, fifteen, sitting in a box at the Metropolitan with my feet on a chair listening to Gigli, Ponselle, and so on. I had that interest inculcated in me by my father, who was always very bookish as well, but no specific antecedent, no artist forebear that I know of.

Q: Was there any opposition to your studying drama when you went to college?

A: None. I had family difficulties, as a lot of people have, but one difficulty never appeared, and it's astonishing when I think of it. There was no objection to my decision to become an actor, to go to a university to study to be an actor. When I entered high school, there was a kind of an assumption, to which I subscribed in just a sort of romantic way, that I was going to be a doctor. My father is a dentist, I'd be a doctor. That was just sort of said. When it came to the crunch, when I graduated from high school, I knew I didn't want it. I'd done a lot of amateur theatricals. I'd begun to write. I'd published poetry in magazines, not school magazines, when I was in high school. And all these amateur theatricals I'd been in interested me very much in acting. And I announced this, and I still don't know why it was, in the depths of the Depression when everything was as shadowy as could be, there wasn't the slightest bit of opposition to it. My parents said, "All right, if that's what you want to do." They warned me about the difficulties, but they certainly put no kind of block in my way. There was never the slightest opposition, and there wasn't very much money. In fact, I couldn't have made it through the university without help from my grandmother. Also, while I was still an undergraduate, I got financial assistance from the university—I was tutoring by the time I was a sophomore—I was a tutor in drama school—things like history of the theatre.

Q: Was there anyone there who was a prime influence?

A: Yes, there were two. Both dead now, inevitably. One lesser one was a man named Roy Mitchell, who was a Canadian, who wrote a book called *Creative Theater*—hailed at the time and lost for a time, now having a resurgence, a revival. An idealistic dreamy kind of book about what theatre might be. He and his views put forth in this book had a great influence on me, but the prime influence was a man named Randolph Somerville, who was much more of a traditionalist than Mitchell, who had had his own training under a very fine English actor who had been an associate of Bernard Shaw's. That actor's family had had a Shakespearean theatre in England for many years—a famous theatre. Their name was Calvert, and Louis Calvert had been a teacher of Somerville's and I was, one might say, a disciple of Somerville's. He had a great influence on me—most of it, though by no means all, beneficial. He was the director of this company that I was a member of, which worked tangentially with New York University. It was not a university function, so for the better part of four years while I was a student and for six years after I graduated, I was still a member of this company directed by Somerville, until 1941. From '31 to '41 he was the single biggest influence. I had to learn to throw off some of the things he taught me. He had, I discovered, narrower limitations than I had thought, but I wouldn't want to have missed the bulk of the experience I had with him.

Theatre in America: A Dialogue with Stanley Kauffmann

Bonnie Marranca and Gautam Dasgupta / 1978

From *Performing Arts Journal* 3, no. 1 (Spring/Summer 1978), 19–34.

PAJ: Let's start with the current state of the theatre—in terms of the American past, that is.

Kauffmann: It happens that it's just fifty years or so that I've been going to the theatre. And I don't think there is any question that Broadway was an infinitely more interesting place fifty years ago. The 1927–28 season was the high point numerically, as there were 234 productions. Long ago the number sank below 100, and has never got anywhere near it since. O'Neill got the Pulitzer Prize in that 1927–28 season for *Strange Interlude*; *Showboat* had its premiere. The Broadway range was much greater in those days than now—not just the quantity but the qualitative range. For a very simple reason: Broadway was the whole New York theatre, more or less. Therefore, if a play was to have any kind of production in New York, which meant in effect in America, it had to be done on Broadway. The situation has changed in the fifty intervening years, and changed most rapidly fairly recently—beginning about fifteen years ago. Nowadays it's perfectly obvious that Broadway is only one locus in New York. This city doesn't own the whole American theatre the way it used to, figuratively, but we can still say that New York is, in terms of theatrical energy, easily as active, in sum, as it was fifty years ago.

There are 160 theatres that are numbered in the Off-Off Broadway Alliance—we're talking about energy now, dedication and commitment. And this leads to a kind of cultural paradox. We are in a city that teems with various kinds of theatrical vitality. Yet we ask each other, as you just asked me, "What do you think of the American theatre?" in really a kind of almost despairing tone, or at least an unexcited one, which I share. So we have at the moment a city—one of the world capitals of theatre—in which activity is immense and in which quality is nonetheless a recurringly desperate issue. It may be that we're in for a long period in the theatre where we are going to have—not as the equivalent of but as the replacement for genius—committed activity, committed pursuit of ideals rather than actual accomplishment.

What happens in most of the theatres throughout the country, and I don't say this with any glee, is more or less imitative of New York still. There are very few theatres around this country that are generative in themselves, either in terms of new plays or of new approaches to the theatre. Some of them are what's called experimental. But the majority of the first-line residential theatres take their guiding genius from what happens in other theatre capitals, primarily New York, in terms of plays and styles. No New Orleans writer of consequence, for example, thinks now of writing for a New Orleans theatre.

What has to be accomplished underneath the structural change—which, thank heaven, has occurred in this country in the last thirty years with the establishment of regional theatres around the country—is a return culturally to a condition that existed 100 to 150 years ago: a local audience with pride and taste and ambition. That means, too, a local criticism of consequence. If you are an actor or a director or a playwright working at a resident theatre, you starve after a while for recognition that you can respect. I certainly don't mean that the New York critical corps is a body of Lessings and Hazlitts. But in the sheer vulgar currency of fame and energy, New York critics and the audiences they guide are still the most vital.

PAJ: The American theatre underwent enormous changes in the sixties. Attitudes toward drama, acting and directing techniques, the audience, the performance environment, and critical theory were revised and expanded to suit the spirit of the times. Now, in the seventies, we are again witnessing sweeping changes in the experimental theatre, most notably in its relationship with the press, the university, foundations, theatrical institutions, the audience, and the other arts. As a person who has been active in the theatre during both decades, how do you view the changes which have taken place?

Kauffmann: A chief difference between the experimental theatre of the sixties and of the seventies is that the latter is less political. There is still some politics and there is considerable social subject matter (drugs and prisons, for instance), but the politically revolutionary content of experimental work seems to have dwindled sharply. The most-discussed new groups to appear in New York in recent years—the Byrd Hoffman Foundation, the Ontological-Hysteric Theater, and the Mabou Mines company—have no discernible political concern whatsoever.

The reason for the change, obviously, is the end of the Viet Nam war. But this fact throws some retroactive doubt on the legitimacy of sixties politics because it means—and I've caught some hell from students for saying this but not enough to dissuade me—that most anti–Viet Nam action by young people in this country was not political. It was self-preservative. I surely don't think this is a trifling reason, but neither is it a political reason. If all the groups who were doing anti-war pieces had been motivated by political conviction rather than by immediate political disgust or the wish to preserve self and/or friends, political theatre would not have dwindled.

PAJ: What about the end of the so-called anti-literary theatre of the 1960s?

Kauffmann: The end of the "anti-literary" theatre has not happened. Some commentators feel that, when the calendar changes decades, predictions of change are obligatory. We had much "anti-literary" work through the sixties, therefore (yes, almost *therefore*) the seventies would be different. But there seem to be just as many groups working in a non-literary manner as before; also, there are just as many non-commercial playwrights writing non-commercial plays.

Still, a relation exists, I think, between the written and the non-written theatre. If there were more good new plays, there might well be less non-literary theatre. Speaking in generalization and allowing for exceptions, I think that when a group becomes discouraged about new plays, the idea of "performance" theatre becomes close to obligatory if those people want to work at all. (Who wants to do still another "version" of *Hamlet* or *The Doctor in Spite of Himself*?) To put it the other way round, if such a group found new scripts that absorbed them, particularly in their early days before exigency dictated principles, their philosophy might be different.

In the traditional theatre it is now considered a prime sin to give an actor a line reading. I think this became a sin because, unlike in the past, there aren't many directors who *can* give an actor a line reading. In the experimental theatre, the mining of the members of the group for materials, instead of relying on scripts, may have followed something of the same pattern. There have certainly been some positive results, some beautiful results. But I don't imagine that many of those "performance" groups bravely turned their backs on new scripts that absolutely thrilled them.

PAJ: But monist doctrine continues to be a burden, doesn't it? The theatre "is" This; or "is" That.

Kauffmann: Not for me. Six months after Grotowski enlarged my imaginative life, *Boesman and Lena,* a linear naturalist play, had precisely the same kind of effect on me.

PAJ: Let's talk now about the problem of funding for the arts. Who should be funded? Should the financial support be private or public? The country seems right now to be at an impasse on this subject.

Kauffmann: I think that the whole idea of funding theatres from established governmental sources is based on a European idea—on European *thought*—where countries are much smaller. In Germany every town with over 25,000 people has its own professional theatre and its own independent productions. We can't do that here; the possibilities for really big money on a national level are not present. If anything is to be done, it must be done through cities and through states. Yet while this idea of governmental funding comes from Europe, it hasn't come forcefully enough.

There's a paradox in this. Our country is, always has been, a democracy, whereas the idea of subsidy that prevails in Europe and elsewhere was originally an aristocratic notion. It's been taken over by many socialist and many democratic countries that have an aristocratic tradition long behind them. It doesn't shock anyone in Germany that huge subsidies go to theatres and opera houses. This doesn't strike Germans as out of the ordinary because the grand duke so-and-so was doing it 300 years ago and now they're proud to have taken over the tradition with republican hands. The once-aristocratic system now belongs to the people.

This country was founded on self-reliance, but as applied to the arts that's a blind principle. It assumes that if you open a grocery store on the corner, work hard, and deal fairly, you will succeed. And if you open a theatre and behave in the same way, the same thing will happen. In point of fact, however, the better your theatre is, the less likely it is to make money. The fact that business and art are not analogous has taken about 250 years in this country—from before America was founded—to sink in. There is a further analogy that is harmful. If you work in TV or film, your salary corresponds to the market for television and cinema, but if you work in theatre, especially a non-profit theatre, your salary has no such huge commercial impetus to reflect. Yet you must buy your food in the same supermarket as the TV or movie employee, pay equivalent rent, etc. In the theatre, the ballet, all but popular music, the situation is ghastly. And it's the kind of situation that, if allowed to harrow down to the roots of art institutions, may destroy things past recovery.

PAJ: Let's go back to a point you suggested earlier: we can't have a national theatre in the United States, but we can and do have city theatres, even "state" theatres. And yet they cannot be compared to the national theatres of Europe in terms of accomplishment.

Kauffmann: Here's my definition of a true national theatre, derived from European models: a permanent company playing in a repertory that consists to a considerable degree of the great dramatic literature of *that* country. Now the prime handicap here is that there is only a handful of truly great American plays. So that sooner or later, any American artistic director who runs such a theatre—if he deals honestly and doesn't want to blow up out of all relativity items that really don't belong on the scale of European names you and I could cite by the dozen—has to make the bulk of his repertory foreign.

Even that would be fine and necessary from another point of view. If we're not going to have any theatres comparable to, let's say, the Comédie Française, then we ought to have in New York—in many cities—what one might call a museum theatre, a theatre that is absolutely essential and sadly lacking anywhere in this country. This would be a theatre that does for great dramatic literature what, for example, the Metropolitan Opera tries to do for great operatic literature and what the Philharmonic does for great symphonic literature. In other words, give everyone in his lifetime at least some chance to see and hear the great works. Such a museum theatre is generally derided nowadays, particularly by young theatre people. Derided, I think, because it's outside their competence rather than because of any conviction on their part. I think that a theatre like this is culturally imperative as one part of the theatrical spectrum. The reasons that mitigate against it are obviously expense and obviously, too, the difficulty of retaining anything like a permanent company.

PAJ: It's astounding that, with all the money being poured into theatres and the great number of people studying theatre, there is such a lack of genuinely creative talent. There aren't many artistic directors who are very creative, and there aren't many good directors anymore, or playwrights for that matter. Why do we have diminishing returns when so much is going into the building process?

Kauffmann: There's not necessarily a connection between the first part of your statement and the second. That is, education doesn't create talent. Maybe we put false expectations on education for the theatre. This is by no means an argument against it, because the more people know, the more likely they will be able to make things happen. But things haven't been happening in a period of a mere twenty or thirty years, which is really what we're talking about.

One important aspect must not be overlooked, however, when we say glibly that we have no great dramatists. Fifty years ago, almost all the playwriting energy went into Broadway, and we had a lot of prolific writers who usually had one play a year there. There is, I think, even more playwriting energy nowadays; you know the names, both of you, better than I do. And very few of them dream—as O'Neill dreamed—of going to Broadway. They dream of getting their plays done as they want them done. Here is one thing that, I think, must be said loud and clear about contemporary American playwriting: on the whole, it is much more serious, liberated, and personal than it was fifty years ago. I'm talking about the general level; the peaks don't exist yet. I can think of one or two exceptions. I always want to make an exception of Sam Shepard.

PAJ: It seems that theatre criticism is what we should discuss now.

Kauffmann: I have a clipping at home of a movie ad—for a terrible picture. They found one sentence to quote: "One of the better movies of the week." The only thing that cheers me up about the state of theatre criticism—which is a large part of the American theatre's problem—is that it's *never* been any good. We think reverently of the great critics of the past, but if you read their contemporaries . . . In terms of power, there is only one critic in this country, and he works for the *New York Times.* It's the most powerful critic's job in the world in any art form.

And playwrights suffer—I mean suffer terribly—from the mindless overpraise dished out by most reviewers. One thing happens as a result of this, which did not happen in the Broadway of old. You find a playwright writing his sixth, eighth, even twelfth play for Off Broadway or Off-Off Broadway, with the same faults—curable faults—that he had in his first play. You find wasted talent because of critical pampering and because of the very reaction against the Broadway regimen. There's hope that this situation may be changing now because the profession of dramaturg—another European institution—is coming into some prominence in the United States.

Now, nothing is a solution, but the idea that there should be someone on the staff of a theatre, one of whose chief functions it is to be interested not just in finding good plays, but in fostering the art of playwriting, in finding and developing dramatic talent—this is a great step forward. Yet there's been this conduit atmosphere—mostly on Off-Off Broadway—in the last twelve to twenty years that implicitly argues: if it exists on paper and has some promise of talent or poetry, let's put it on. And the twelfth play by that author, which is in the same state, is produced as well. I will name one theatre—La Mama, run by Ellen Stewart—which has operated on the assumption that it's better to do something that merely shows talent than not to do it at all. And in the long run—and we're getting to be in the long run now after about twenty years—we come to a situation where people ask, "Where are the new playwrights?" What has happened as a result of all this? Part of what has happened is the disappearance of artistic discipline—lack of discipline proceeding from lack of craft if not dearth of knowledge.

PAJ: We've covered a lot of ground concerning artists, critics, and institutions. Let's move on, if you don't mind, to the changing tastes of audiences.

Kauffmann: Fine, let's talk about New York audiences. The audience of fifty years ago was by and large a middle-class audience—with a certain view of itself as the apex of Western history. Middle-class values were considered to be the *summum bonum* and, although there were radicals who disagreed, no one took them very seriously. The bulk of the audience today—on Broadway and much of Off Broadway (at the Public Theatre, for example)—is still middle-class. I don't think there is any discernible difference between the audience that goes to see *A Chorus Line* uptown and the one which goes to it downtown. But these audiences have different attitudes nowadays towards themselves and towards their own middle-classness. There is more of a sense of guilt about being middle-class because of events that have occurred in the intervening fifty years, because of the ferociousness of attacks on the bourgeoisie, and because, as against their forbears, these members of the middle class are in the majority college graduates and therefore have at least different kinds of pretenses, if not different basic ideals.

So there's a kind of openness to artistic innovation that the previous middle-class audience didn't have. There's also an openness to kinds of sexual behavior, to sexual language, that would have been unthinkable, not fifty but fifteen years ago. Still another change in the middle-class audience is that it now contains a good number of black people, which it certainly did not contain before. And that's been reflected in Broadway productions of plays by and for blacks. Another chief component of the present-day audience in New York, which itself did not exist before, is the audience that goes to Off-Off Broadway—an audience that I believe is centrally different from the uptown one, even from the Off Broadway audience. The people who go to see Richard Foreman's theatre do not conceivably go to see *Annie*.

PAJ: Or Foreman's *Threepenny Opera* when it played uptown at Lincoln Center or *Stages* on Broadway.

Kauffmann: Right, and they don't go in any great numbers to see John Guare's plays, either. To use an old-fashioned word, these people are "bohemians" and they represent a special theatre audience in New York City—the most cogent and recognizable one, as a matter of fact. There's a defect in this audience, as there is in almost every virtue, in that it has become a coterie group which almost conspires to keep its theatre sort of amateurish. But I must also note that there are many Off-Off Broadway theatres which, thankfully, at least have an organizing principle—based on certain kinds of plays, on a particular type of directorial approach, on an ethnic or social slant. The feminist theatre, for one, has emerged in the last five or six years, as have several avowedly homosexual theatres. All these theatres represent elements in the New York social fabric that, to put it mildly, wouldn't have been represented fifty years ago. The curious thing about the theatre and its relation to society is that obviously it's the product of the society in which it exists. But the best theatre is always prodding the society at the same time. It's always trying to make it a little more disturbed, at least, if not better, than it was. And I'm not talking, by any means, of political theatre. Very little political theatre has been successful, artistically, in terms of vision. But theatre people finally can't do more than what they can do within their professions.

Just one last note about change that is not entirely tangential. When I was going to Broadway, certainly up until the time of the Second World War, the place itself, the physical place, had great attraction and glamour. It glittered. What Broadway meant to the world, it meant to me. There was real excitement. Even if you said to yourself, "Oh, I'm above all this," you loved it. You *loved* it. You loved going to a smart, glittering musical. You were thrilled to see the latest George S. Kaufman play. I once asked students in a critical seminar to write on what they thought of Broadway *today,* and a very young playwright said Broadway is a place where, if you're lucky, you get a job in a play and you go there eight times a week and you do the same part for three years. This, he said, is called the Theatre of Cruelty.

PAJ: Was it true during the twenties, thirties, and forties that musicals had one audience and straight plays another?

Kauffmann: Not in any really distinctive sense. There were people who didn't like the plays that the Theatre Guild did because they thought these works were too heavy, and other people who would only go to musicals and comedies, but this was more a matter of taste than of severe class distinction. The point I want to make, however, is that now there are three theatres in

New York: Broadway, Off Broadway, and Off-Off Broadway. And you know when you're seeing an Off-Off Broadway production.

It's silly to have to be fooling around with these acronyms, but the Off Broadway playwright who existed before the Off-Off Broadway playwright became firmly centered Off Broadway, then moved uptown if he could and if he was invited to do so. I think what I'm getting at is that the Off Broadway play is now more transferable; it may be written with the same Off Broadway intent but it's more transferable.

PAJ: David Mamet and Albert Innaurato fall into this category, but they couldn't really be called Off Broadway playwrights, in the experimental sense.

Kauffmann: That's what I mean.

PAJ: There is another problematic point regarding playwrights. Today we have dramatists who come out of some of the best universities in the country, where they are exposed to great dramatic literature, yet they are for the most part incapable of writing anything more than television-level work. Indeed, some would *rather* be writing for TV or—even better—the movies.

Kauffmann: I understand your point but, once again, what you're really doing is criticizing an educational system for not creating talent. And that shortage of talent may come down to the fact that the United States is an inheritor country, a scion country of culture that's made its own distinctive contributions but did not originate much in art.

PAJ: Except in musical comedy.

Kauffmann: But that specialized fact, which is an historical and not a judgmental one, is part of an attitude towards the theatre in American writers that's very different from the one in Europe. Point one: most European plays are written by men and women who are more than playwrights. Very, very few of the greatest plays have been written by people who wrote only plays. Theatre was part, *part,* of the instrumentality of their culture. It's a lie that novelists can't write plays; that's only true of English-language novelists. The theatre has always seemed for the elite European writer—and I mean the term with respect, not pejoratively—as an avenue open to him for one kind of poem, a dramatic poem rather than a lyrical or narrative one.

Point two: Europeans operate out of a more homogeneous culture and see themselves as immersed in the tensions, the polarities, of an organism more than Americans do. Why, for example, have there been so many good Southern writers in this century? Because they are the most homogeneously "culture-conscious" of Americans. The English, for their part, believe—despite all the talk of "diversity" on American university campuses—that they're more diverse than Americans within their own particular organism. And because they are, in a sense, more compact or contained, they're more acutely aware of their differences. The class-conscious early plays of Edward Bond—in my opinion his best—are very keenly aware of what's it's like to suffer in the English countryside, à la Thomas Hardy. That's something for which we have no exact equivalent in the contemporary American theatre. I think two or three of the German-Austrian playwrights are among the best now writing: Peter Handke, Wolfgang Bauer, Franz Xaver Kroetz.

American plays are trying to sense or satisfy this—let's call it community hunger—by the transmogrification of pop culture. Sam Shepard has done such, particularly in his rock plays. But it is not quite the same thing. I don't know if there's anything to be done about this except for the country simply to live a little longer. I'm just trying to understand in my own mind why more interesting writing is coming from England, Ireland, and elsewhere than we're getting today in the U.S. . . . This is not a general American phenomenon; it's an American *theatrical* phenomenon. There is very fine American poetry being written now. There are some fine American novels being produced. And there are good painters and architects at work. I think the problem of playwriting has deep roots in American attitudes towards the theatre. In terms of theatre *seriousness,* this is a very young nation.

PAJ: The topic of playwriting has taken up a good deal of our time. Acting is a subject that we haven't covered yet in this discussion.

Kauffmann: I think one of the problems of acting today is that there is so much of it—in theatre, films, television, commercials. And what has become the obsessive criterion of all this activity? *How much it does not look like acting.* . . . This criterion has to do with photography, with American film, with the kind of fiction we like: with embarrassment at large gestures. It has to do with art as a buffer against deep emotion and large experience. This factor is militating against much serious theatrical activity in this country. When you see a man come along like Stacy Keach, whom I saw in very early appearances at Yale Repertory Theatre, you see a genuine talent. But it's chewed up, not only because of commercialism or on account of the fact that there is no vital theatre to step into, but also because all he can sell is *not appearing to be an actor.*

PAJ: You have had the opportunity through the years to watch several actors fulfill their careers in a number of great roles. And you have also had the opportunity to write about performance of diverse kinds. I, for one, feel cheated out of the chance to watch good actors grow over the course of time.

Kauffmann: It's true that there have not been many auspicious careers opening in the last fifteen years. When I think of actors who have grown in the last ten or fifteen years, I think of two principally: James Earl Jones and Geraldine Fitzgerald. A kind of inertia has settled in on people who could have grown. Think of Marlon Brando, who has settled into a life of rich self-loathing out in Hollywood because he's not doing what he could have done. Or consider magnificently talented actors like Paul Newman and George C. Scott. They are men who have achieved the kind of power in our commercial theatre that would enable them to do whatever they wanted, yet they choose to do nothing except the occasional film that appeals to them or a revival. Scott is a wonderful actor but he has no sense of career in the sense we are using the term. The last actor I can think of in that position in the English-speaking theatre, who insisted on having a career, what he considered to be an aesthetically honorable career, was Olivier.

PAJ: We know there have been great actors in the past. Were the directors quantitatively better?

Kauffmann: Meyerhold represents something that's happened with the directing in this century, which is that the director has taken over from the actor. Now the best *production* I've seen in my lifetime since O'Neill was a play by Athol Fugard that I mentioned earlier—*Boesman and Lena.* And that did present opportunities for excellent representational performers. Ruby Dee was in it, and she's one of the fine, unacknowledged actresses of our time. But in her case that's not only an acting or critical problem, but also a race problem. We have in the representational mode a very fine director of actors with almost no artistic ambition—Mike Nichols. He knows how to direct actors, but in what does he direct them for the most part? I don't have to answer that question.

By contrast, Foreman—who is, I think, within strict limitations an interesting artist—isn't remotely interested in representational acting. And it would be a mistake to say that it's a fault in Foreman not to be producing theatre in the Stanislavsky vein. If he is going to have any benefit for us at all, he has to be what he is and not what someone thinks he should be. I think that directors make their theatre. And the only directors I can think of in New

York or in the entire country, over the last fifteen years, who have generated enough enthusiasm to have people follow them, are non-representational directors.

PAJ: You've painted a despairing picture of contemporary theatre in America. What can we hope for in the coming years?

Kauffmann: Trouble. Money trouble. Social trouble, too, which automatically means trouble in the theatre. But one good thing that theatre education has been doing, the education that you're impatient with for not producing masters, is to produce—let's call it—a certain disgust. At least some of the people who are coming out of good educational programs are disgusted with trick-dog theatre that sits up when a bored audience snaps its fingers. These people want to do something more with their lives than serve such a theatre. We can't look forward to geniuses—that's like pinning your hopes on miracles. But we can reasonably look forward to honor an commitment in the exercise of talent—in the face, moreover, of a cloudy situation getting cloudier. It's even not impossible that audiences throughout the United States will get again that sense of possessiveness towards their theatres that once made the theatre truly decentralized in this country. And there's one other thing— part of all this and, in my mind, not one whit less important. There's good reason to hope for some improvement in the level of theatre criticism. I don't mean the production of scholarship by professors, but the exercise of critical talent by writers who understand the art of theatre because they've mastered the other arts as well.

Stanley Kauffmann on the Dick Cavett Show

Dick Cavett / 1979

From the *Dick Cavett Show* no. 1361, New York, New York, 1 October 1979.

Dick Cavett: (*Applause.*) Thank you. If you're anything like a regular viewer of this show, you might have heard me on occasion mention a critic's name here and there. And certainly one that I have mentioned more than once is Stanley Kauffmann, who reviews films and theatre for the magazine the *New Republic.* There are even times when I have quoted him and not mentioned his name but have used his ideas anyway. That's excusable when you're a talk-show host. Finally, I thought, why be content with Stanley Kauffmann at second hand when I could have him first-hand right here on the show?

He has an interesting background for a critic, you might say. He's been an actor, a playwright, a novelist, an editor, and still is a teacher. So, obviously, he's well informed on the subjects he writes about. I think what I especially like about his criticism is that he never seems to be stampeded. That is, he doesn't seem to fall in with publicity hype, hot trends, or what all the other critics are saying. And he doesn't give in to the temptation to write a contradictory review just for the sake of being contrary or making an effect. It's so noticeable when that happens to critics. He has quite an amazing equilibrium; he's always himself. He's pithy, intelligent, unpredictable, often witty, and has that irritating quality of making me think that he's right even when I don't agree with him. I think you will find him all of those things in person. So if you'll welcome, please—Stanley Kauffmann. (*Applause.*)

Well, here we have that dreaded creature, a real live critic right in our clutches. I would love to define what that is, if there's any way of doing it.

Stanley Kauffmann: "Live" or "critic"?

DC: Critic. (*Laughs.*) No one has ever defined what it is to be alive, but one way of maybe getting into the definition of a critic would be to talk about the poll taken some time ago, God knows how, by *Variety,* in which you were voted "the critic hardest to please." Did that bother you?

SK: Well, that's like being voted tallest in a line of pygmies. It's not really terribly much of a distinction. The only way it would bother me is if people thought I were "hardest to please" in an effort to create some kind of trade-mark for myself, or worse, as an act. It just happens that, in summary, in retrospect, it seems that I like fewer films—the poll was about films—than most people seem to like. But that, of course, doesn't define anything.

DC: I don't know why that should bother anybody because what one should worry about is a critic who is easy to please.

SK: That's not a pressing worry!

DC: Not in the commercial side of the business, but I don't see why it shouldn't be a worry on the artistic side. Would you go along with this figure, although it isn't scientific: that, by definition, 95 percent of what's produced in any field of the arts is junk by comparison with the masterpieces?

SK: Yes. The only exceptions to that that I can think of offhand are poetry, which is relatively good in this country at the moment, and literature in general. Not specifically the novel or nonfiction, but literature in general seems to be more interesting. That leads to some questions about why one would bother to be a film or a theatre critic, but I've answered them for myself, at any rate.

DC: I don't suppose there's a child anywhere who says to his little friends, "I want to be a critic when I grow up."

SK: I have to contradict you. Child, maybe not, but the whole attitude towards criticism and the training for it has changed drastically since I was a college student. I majored in drama in college, and the idea of becoming a critic then would have been a premature admission of complete failure. It would have been like admitting that you couldn't be an actor, a playwright, et cetera.

DC: "Those who can't do, criticize."

SK: Well, that's another statement that needs a little revision. But now there are, not many, but some young people, men and women, throughout the country who are actively, deliberately, choosing to become critics of film and/or theatre. And there are now programs set up at both the undergraduate and graduate level to accommodate and perhaps help them. I teach in two of them.

DC: You don't mean that you can major in criticism?

SK: Well, major isn't quite the right word, because most of the serious work in this field goes on at the post-graduate level when you choose it as a profession—you hope—and work at it as if you were preparing to be a historian or musicologist or lawyer or whatever. Criticism is perceived as an accessible profession now, intrinsically, if not in actual occupational terms.

DC: Suppose you do a luncheon somewhere and ask for questions from the audience and somebody gets up and says, "Why do we need critics, anyway? Why don't you just let the arts be and let us enjoy our plays and our movies, and stop telling us what's good or bad and killing off shows, Mr. Kauffmann and others of your kind?"

SK: Well, first of all, the others of my kind may, but I don't kill anything. Second, to a person like that there is no reply to make. If he doesn't want to read criticism, why in the world should he? And if he wants to blunder around and make his own choices, why in the world should he not? But there *are* some who read criticism with something more than utilitarian interest, more than a consumer-service interest.

DC: Real criticism is not a shopping guide.

SK: Right. You see, here's a curious fact. Big circulation magazines like *Time* and *Newsweek* always insist on carrying criticism of the theatre. I wouldn't want to hazard a guess on what percentage of *Time* and *Newsweek* readers actually see one professional show a year, but their reader surveys—of which they surely conduct many, constantly—must tell them that the theatre is a subject. That's *one* of my contentions about criticism: that it is a way of choosing subjects to write about as well as being, in sheer review-form, a consumer guide.

DC: That's right. *Time* and *Newsweek* are covering theatre in one city in America, yet these magazines are read all over the world.

SK: They travel a bit: they try to cover other cities, but that's an impossible dream.

DC: Have you covered up the evidence of your own acting career?

SK: It didn't need much covering. (*Laughs.*)

DC: What exactly was it?

SK: Well, when I was still in drama school, I became a member of a theatre company that I thought was going to be my life's work. I never dreamed that I'd be doing anything else. It was a repertory company and was founded by a man who happened to be the head of the school in which I was enrolled at New York University. It was not a school company, but there was this affiliation. And I was in this company for ten years from, believe it or not, 1931—when I was fifteen—until 1941. It was mostly a Shakespeare company, and I was a very minor actor in it. I did a lot of stage management, some lighting, and music, which meant picking selections from records. It broke up, as much as anything else, because of America's getting into the war, when things got rocky. But I thought that was going to be my life. And, in a certain sense, I've measured everything else I've done against that ten-year experience—in which I, along with others, created a theatre.

DC: Was there a particular role that the critics said Stanley Kauffmann played brilliantly? Did you give the definitive performance as Mercutio or another comparable character?

SK: Mercutio! I never played anything that grand. I found out very quickly what young people—fifteen-year-old boys—do in a Shakespeare company. They play ancient men. You put a wig and a cowl on a kid and that will cover up his youth. But he can't be, let us say, a forty-year-old man with a naked face because he *looks* like a fifteen-year-old boy.

DC: So you did the Bishop of Ely, Cardinal Pandulph and—

SK: Adam was my star role, Adam in *As You Like It.* And before I played it, at least five different people took me into a corner and said, "You know, that's the part that Shakespeare himself used to play." Whenever anyone came near me, I used to say, "I *know.* I *know.*" (*Laughs.*)

DC: Is there any secret to your success at doing what your admirers feel is the best aspect of your work as a critic, which is that you have remained unswayed—what I was talking about in my introduction—and steady and intelligent, and have not taken up fads, or have not been caught praising works that are then seen as junk a couple of years later?

SK: Well, I wouldn't want to claim that my escutcheon is spotless—

DC: No, of course not. I wouldn't want a "spotless-escutcheoned" person on the show. (*Laughs.*)

SK: I saw the sign outside. (*Both laugh.*) Well, T. S. Eliot said, "It's the critic's first duty to be intelligent." And he might have said—this is going to sound terribly immodest, but I'm trying to answer your question—that rule number two is, the critic must have talent. There is, I feel distinctly, such a thing as critical talent, and one discerns it—now as a teacher I try to discern it in students and help them nurture it. With those two qualities, intelligence and talent, all other matters just fade away. Going with this or that tie or flavor just doesn't seem to matter. There is important work to be done, which is wonderful in a sense because the work is important even when the material you're treating is terrible. Criticism is important even when the film or play is bad. I mean, there's a kind of analogy with a novelist or a playwright or a filmmaker, isn't there? Such an artist has to be equally good about good and bad people, and a critic ought to be equally good about good and bad plays, films, or whatever.

DC: Interesting parallel. I have this fantasy, by the way, in which all the critics, for a benefit perhaps, do a play and each takes a part—
SK: You have to say whose benefit. (*Laughs.*)

DC: Well, I mean the old-fashioned kind of benefit. And the audience is made up of prominent actors who then have a day or so to write their reviews of you, John Simon, Pauline Kael, Clive Barnes, Vincent Canby, and all those people. I don't know whether you critics would have the guts to face such an audience, but it's just a weird fantasy of mine. All we need to do now is find the right property with which to fulfill it. (*Pause.*) The word "great" is thrown around all the time in the press, in every blurb about almost every show—
SK: It's where criticism begins. That's the ground floor of most criticism—"great"—then it goes *up* from there.

DC: It's either "great" or "better than great." But in those people that we know are great, like Brando, Chaplin, and others, have you ever come up with whatever the "X" factor is or the common thread that runs all through their work? The quality that tells us, when we see them, that they're great.
SK: You want a serious answer?

DC: Yeah, I'd love it.
SK: They transform your life. They *transform your life.*

DC: That's it?
SK: That's how you know they're great. You think differently, you feel differently, you *see* differently after a great experience in art. I'm doing a film course now at one of the places where I teach, Yale. And just the other day, I showed two Chaplin films: *The Rink* and *City Lights.* I know them quite well, those two films. And when I sat to watch them with this lovely group of young people, I thought I could predict exactly what was going to happen to me during those pictures. But they're fathomless! They have no

bottom. You keep digging deeper and deeper each time. This sounds a little ridiculous, but it's not: I'm a different person now, having seen those films for the umpteenth time, than I was before.

DC: That's fascinating. Do you understand what that "difference" is, or do you just know that it's there? Can you tell how you're better now, or different—?

SK: I didn't say better—different. (*Laughs.*)

DC: It could be different *worse,* though. Are you worse after seeing a Nazi film, for example?

SK: You're disturbed. You changed the subject, but I'll follow your line for a moment. When you see a film like Leni Riefenstahl's *Triumph of the Will,* you come out shaking with fear because half of you is revolted by what you've seen, and some portion, maybe not half, is terribly *excited.* That's really vicious, isn't it—when art can use you to make you doubt your reason? So there is such a thing as being hurt by an effective work of art.

DC: But do you have to fall back on phrases like "X-factor," "genius," or other mysterious, indefinable terms to say what makes a Chaplin, on the one hand, and just another good comedian, on the other? One of them is just a comedian, but Chaplin is far beyond that.

SK: Well, to say that I myself don't sometimes have to use words like "genius" as a last resort is to claim that I can always define exactly what it is that a great performance is, and I wouldn't claim that. Sometimes you have to use such upholstery words to cover up your own lack of precision. But if you live with great artists like Chaplin long enough, you get to feel that what he is doing, in a sense, is giving you models or exempla. His physical grace, for instance, is not just an example of how I'd like to be able to move. Everyone would like to be able to move like Chaplin or Keaton. But the being he is on the screen, with that physical grace, is what I'd like to be *inside.* I'd like my morality, my moral sense, to be as graceful as his physical grace.

DC: I remember something you wrote about Chaplin, in *The Rink,* I think. Wouldn't it be that film, or does he skate in another film?

SK: Well, he skates in several of them—

DC: In any event, he does a preposterous sort of maintaining his balance while his feet are going so fast you can barely see them. And you pointed out that he is just incidentally able to accomplish those physical feats better than most people who have devoted their lives to doing only that, plus he has everything else.

SK: That's what's fantastic about seeing these two films together, *The Rink* and *City Lights*: Chaplin does things physically in these short films that you cannot *believe* while you watch them. You can't believe them at the moment of actually seeing them. And then he goes on at several points in *City Lights,* most notably the last few minutes, to do acting that can only be called "great." And to put this acting and that physical prowess next to each other, well, it takes your breath away. You just don't know what to say. It's a kind of boon, but it also does something for you. It's not just a matter of gaping and awing in response or, as that French filmmaker said, of getting out your handkerchief. Chaplin manages, by his genius—this is true of any artist, especially a great one—not only to comment on one's own experience, but to have an impact on your life. He subtly clarifies issues concerning your perception of the world and your reaction to the people in it. That's why art, for me, is not a question of culture with a capital "C"—something you do when you have the spare time to go do it. It's that towards which everything else seems to go and seems to need.

DC: I had Jane Fonda on the show once and I said, "You must be upset by what Stanley Kauffmann just said about you." It was my coy way of reading to her something she hadn't seen, in which you said she has become, or was becoming—I forget which, though I suppose it's important—"the preeminent American screen actress."

SK: I think so, anyway.

DC: I remember looking back at old reviews of yours in which you wrote about Jane Fonda and other performers. They're fun to read because, through them, you can follow the development of an actor like her or Brando over the years.

SK: That's just *my* longevity. (*Laughs.*)

DC: You've been on the beat for a long time. (*Laughs.*) Way back when, you predicted wonderful things for Fonda. Have she, and Brando, borne out your expectations?

SK: Well, Brando has become a pain in the neck, I think.

DC: Pain in the neck?

SK: I'm tired of hearing big, successful actors talk about how they hate acting. This is not to say one word about the cause of the Indians, which is a grave and serious cause. But when Brando's asked questions in public about his acting, he responds, "To hell with that, let's talk about the Indians." I'm not going to try to equate the two subjects, but I want to hear Brando talk about acting. That's what he's gifted at. And I think this false or genuine despising of acting shows in the work he's done lately. He's just ludicrous, I think, in *Apocalypse Now.* And in *The Missouri Breaks,* you felt he was just bullying—bullying the director, bullying the cast—and saying, "I'm going to do what I want to do, and that's that." It's been a long time since he's taken acting seriously. If he had done so, and if he'd taken film as seriously as other actors have—I don't derogate film as some theater people still do—he could have stunned the world with his accomplishments instead of being the sort of hyped-up presence he's become by now. You know, he made his Broadway début in a play of mine.

DC: So I learned.

SK: A little children's play, two acts in rhymed verse. It was done at the Piscator School on 12th Street—the New School now—in 1944, and then they moved it uptown. And Brando was a guard, a walk-on, in it, and he got hit on the head and fell down. He was wonderful.

DC: Every night he fell—

SK: Every afternoon—it was a children's play.

DC: Did he have a way of falling that set him apart from other actors?

SK: He had a way of falling that made you know that he'd thought about how to do it a different way from the way every other actor had ever done it, and yet his fall fit into what was going on. It wasn't merely freakish. He's a man of *enormous* talent. When I say he's become a pain in the neck, which I mean euphemistically, what I'm talking about is his betrayal of himself.

DC: I thought he was awfully entertaining in *The Missouri Breaks.* I had the feeling that he just decided this was a movie not to be serious about.

SK: But no one else thought that, no one else decided that. His was a sort of solo decision, and it was a little egregious.

DC: You made a staggering assertion in an interview you once did. I wrote it down, in fact. And this is the quote: "Everything in our theatre and film world militates against the development of talent." That's an incredible in- dictment, and I'd love to hear you expand on that.

SK: Let's take Jane Fonda, for example. When she first became figuratively visible, it was clear that she had extraordinary talent. She was just *made* to act. Everything about her screams "actress." The first worrisome question you ask yourself after your pleasure at her presence is, "What's going to happen to her in our world?" Because there are—in the theatre as well as film—all kinds of people who have not the slightest interest in her development as an artist, only an interest in her as a vehicle for exploitation.

DC: I remember you once pointed out in a review, early in her career, that "This woman has now done three roles of extreme variety, and no one seems to have noticed."

SK: Yes, so did Brando, by the way. He's been the most versatile screen star we've ever had in this country, yet no one's paid that versatility any attention.

DC: And yet everyone imitates him by mumbling.

SK: Or imagines him in his torn undershirt. That's what it is to have an icon made of yourself, despite the variety of roles you've done. Fonda, for her part, has worked moderately hard at progressing artistically. But most of her energy of choice these days seems to go into subjects of social relevance. Who wants to quarrel with that? Somewhat less attention is paid by Fonda now to her fulfillment as an artist.

DC: But to say that everything in our theatre and film world militates against the development of talent?

SK: That's extreme. That's hyperbolic. But Bernard Shaw says, "Never apologize. Repeat your assertion." (*Laughs.*) It's close enough to the truth to be chilling. There isn't much in the commercial processes or systems of theater and film in this country to help a serious artist develop. In the theatre world in general—as you certainly know because you have appeared in some theatres away from New York—an enormous and varied amount of work is going on to give actors and other kinds of theatre practitioners a chance to develop seriously. What the result is, is another question. But in so-called mainstream theater, within a few blocks of where we're now sitting, there isn't any interest in such development or growth. I don't blame the producers or the money-men. If it were my million dollars, I would worry about my return on it, too. I'm being a bit blithe with regard to money, but I'm *not* being blithe about artists and their art.

DC: It must be astonishing to some people to see a production outside New York—at the Williamstown, to name one of those theatres, where audiences perhaps take for granted the brilliance of what they see—and then come to the city and see a piece of junk that is not worth mentioning in the same breath with this production at Williamstown or Long Wharf or wherever. Maybe the problem is that those out-of-town actors have as their goal a New York career, and yet they are destined to have to go back to the "province" to really work again.

SK: For a while—this is beginning in the early or middle 1960s—I thought that a new breed of theatre person was coming out. What you might call "the educated theatre person." I don't mean conventionally educated, I mean educated in or for the theatre. When I was a drama student, the worst thing you could say if you went for a job anywhere was that you had been to drama school. Such a place was then a subject of ridicule. That situation changed drastically. There seemed to be a new generation coming in the mid-'60s that was going to stay away from the mainstream theatre supermarkets in New York—some of which, occasionally, do very entertaining material, even good material. Let's not paint with too wide a brush. But that generation is not as staunch as it once was, or the ones who are coming along now are not as staunch as they once were. It may be a double fault or double defect: theirs and a certain disappointment in what's called the regional theater around the country. I'm not sure, but I don't have the conviction that new people entering the theatre are as dedicated to fulfilling themselves as they are to getting on. I regret this and do all I can to sway them the other way, but I find it a little hard to argue with an actor who's offered a job at several hundred dollars a week and takes it in lieu of something at seventy-five dollars a week elsewhere. Sooner or later—it's what I've been saying about Brando—that actor has to make his choices, but I try not to be too moralistic about the matter.

DC: In the minute we have left, I'd like to throw one more question at you. You worked as the drama critic for the *New York Times* for a while. Whoever holds it, that's the most influential position in the American theater world.

SK: That influence, of course, is a function of the paper's own wide influence.

DC: Does your having been unhappy there tell us something damning about the *Times,* about us, about the theatre, or what? In forty-five seconds.
SK: Me, mostly.

DC: You?

SK: Me. It's a dreadful position in some ways, I can tell you, and I think it has become considerably worse. But I'll say just one more thing. When the job was offered to me—and it *was* offered to me—what I thought about by myself, in my study, what I examined myself very carefully about, was whether I could take this job with hope, with true hope. I was able to answer that question satisfactorily, so I took the job—and found out I was wrong. (*Laughs.*)

DC: You answered that within the time limit. Stanley Kauffmann, the time has flown by. Thank you for being here.

SK: Thank you for inviting me.

DC: Good night, everyone.

Interview with Stanley Kauffmann

Contemporary Authors / 1981

From *Contemporary Authors* (Gale Publishing), 17 February 1981.

CA: In your memoirs *Albums of Early Life* (1980) you write about the "series of alternative lives" your life has encompassed. As your careers as actor, director, editor, writer, and critic have overlapped, have you ever felt torn between jobs?

Kauffmann: Constantly. I'm never satisfied with what I'm doing. I feel that about every four or five years I ought to be changing my life, but I'm running out of chunks of five years. I love what I'm doing just now, teaching and writing criticism, but I keep thinking of other things I *might* be doing and that makes me a little discontented. Maybe that's good for the thing I'm doing.

CA: You wrote also in that book, "I graduated in 1935 with a good warped education. I had learned a lot about what interested me, much less about most other subjects." In view of how that education has served you, would you do it differently in retrospect?

Kauffmann: Very differently. I would, first of all, ground myself in at least one, preferably two foreign languages. If there's one single, salient, depressing gap in my education, it's in languages. I'm not really competent in any foreign language. I can struggle along with a couple, but I've missed very much the fluency that I wish I had in at least two other languages. And I wish I had some formal training in philosophy, in which I read a lot as an amateur. I have no real grip in any serious sense on science, and I wish I had at least some grip on the philosophy of science. This could go on endlessly; who isn't dissatisfied with himself? I do know something about music, and if I had my life to live over again, really from scratch, I think I would be a musician. I think I'd like to have been a pianist and a conductor.

CA: Do you use music to relax from your writing?

Kauffmann: No, I use music to tauten my writing. Music infiltrates my whole life, and I flatter myself—I hope not too foolishly—that things I hear in music affect my writing beneficially, in a rhythmic sense—even, one might say, in a melic sense.

CA: You were writing successfully as a very young man. Where did the ambition come from?

Kauffmann: That's difficult to say. Probably these things begin with emulation. My father wasn't a writer, he was a dentist, but he did a lot of writing for professional journals, so I was around a sort of writing all the time. I began to read very early, thanks to my mother, who taught me some reading before I went to school. I was in an atmosphere of words very early on.

CA: Was the writing encouraged at home?

Kauffmann: Very much so. Not professionally, of course, because no one thought of that in the beginning, but certainly to do it, to write, yes.

CA: What does being a film critic mean to you? More specifically, why do you write film criticism? Whom do you hope to reach and what do you hope to communicate to them?

Kauffmann: For me, because I've been with the *New Republic* almost continuously since 1958, being a film critic is like having another residence. I go to that residence once a week to think about the films I've seen in that week, to investigate what, one way or another, they have done to me. This is what I try to convey to the magazine's readers who, I can now gratefully believe, are interested.

CA: Back in the 1960s you wrote, "The Film Generation can help make the foreseeable future of film interesting and important. Let us see." Do you think that's happening?

Kauffmann: No, I think at the present moment the film situation in this country, and to a relative degree throughout the world, is quite shadowy. One of the strong reasons is that the economics of film is always closely tied to large sums of money, and the costs are increasing. *Profits* are increasing, but the very fact that profits are increasing on the successes makes the chances more difficult for films that may not have huge success. Money is a strangulating factor for the present film situation in this country, because of both the great losses and the great successes.

There's also the fact that, in my view, film education in this country has been misguided, has been partial instead of holistic. I'm making broad statements here, speaking in generalities, but American film education has tended to turn out technological experts with nothing much in themselves to make films *about*. The difference between this country and Europe is not black and white, not by any means, but the film schools of Europe tend to turn out more generally cultivated graduates.

CA: You observed filmmaking abroad for several months in 1964. Did you observe anything on that trip that has since had some significant effect on movies?

Kauffmann: I saw the beginnings of some young talents, and some that were coming along were pointed out to me in various countries that I visited. I learned something about the intrinsic conditions of filmmaking in a number of countries in both Eastern Europe and Western Europe, and I got some smell of the universality of problems—that was one of the more interesting things I learned in those months. For example, I had assumed that the difference between Eastern European filmmaking and Western filmmaking was the difference between capitalism and communism. That was not true. The difference between them is more a matter of detail—both sectors are interested primarily in success and operate to that end, generally. There's not the blitheness about profits in the East that I thought there would be.

That's the gloomy side of it. The other side of it is that I saw in Eastern Europe and in Western Europe a kind of film education that was really marvelous. The best-integrated film schools are in Europe, and there is more connection between those schools and the profession there than there is here. One sees the fruit of this: there are still European films by new people coming along to some degree even in this strangulating economy. I've just had a notice from the French film office in New York that there's going to be a showing at the Museum of Modern Art in New York of a dozen films by new people which can't get commercial release here.

CA: Is that quite a problem?

Kauffmann: Yes, that's a problem for all filmmakers throughout the world. It's roughly equivalent to writing a symphony and not being able to get it performed. There is, I ought to add—I get angry letters about this every once in a while—a whole other terrain of filmmaking in this country and elsewhere: the independent filmmakers who usually work in nonfiction, documentary form. It's a highly active field, and those filmmakers are not looking, for the most part, for conventional theater release. But they have a very difficult time getting their films shown. There are filmmakers who make films and then pack them in suitcases and travel around the country from campus to campus and show them, or have to find special means of distribution. Occasionally one such film will break through to national attention. You may have seen a film called *Best Boy* that won an Academy Award last year. A year or two before that there was one called *Harlan County, U.S.A.* That was made by Barbara Kopple, a young woman who was determined to make her film. There was a fiction film by a young woman named Claudia Weill called *Girlfriends* that was made the same way. It's a whole large area that the public at large doesn't know much about. Just as the public assumes that if you write a book it gets published, so they assume that if you make a film it gets shown.

CA: Do you think there should be subsidies for this kind of filmmaking?

Kauffmann: It's very easy for me to say yes, I think so, but it's ridiculous to talk about it in the atmosphere of today. This is the only country in the world that provides no kind of subsidy or financial encouragement for film-making. Every other country has some way of assisting films. Either they do it through direct grants or through tax remissions or by contributions to the industry or by prizes that are given by the government a year or two after the film has been released if it has not made its cost back. In any case, there is some way of helping the filmmaker substantially.

There's a day-and-night difference in this country, and it cuts through all the arts. For four years I was on the theater advisory panel of the National Endowment for the Arts. We met five or six times a year and debated how to allot throughout the United States of America a total budget of—at its highest—almost three million dollars. At the same time the city of Hamburg, Germany, was giving its opera house six and a half million dollars a year. That is only one of many examples of the difference in government attitudes toward the arts, here and abroad. To talk about American subsidy for films in any useful way is a joke at the present moment because films have become so expensive that if we asked for help in any way that really made a difference, Congress would just faint.

CA: What are the greatest obstacles you face in writing the kind of film criticism you wish to write? As a film critic for a magazine such as the *New Republic,* does one have time to mull over a film in his mind before writing a review, or is there more pressure? For example, does your publication require delivery of your copy on a short deadline after only one screening, limit the space available for your reviews, or dictate which films you should review? How difficult is it for you to keep up with all types of film releases?

Kauffmann: There are no obstacles of any kind in my writing for the *New Republic.* Any limitations are my own. It is not difficult for me to keep up with all sorts of films because I don't try. I choose to see those films that seem possibly rewarding in some way. Of course, life being what it is, I'm often disappointed; or sometimes I find out that I've ignored a worthwhile film, in which case I try to catch up with it. But, in general, instincts and experience are good guides.

As for time, there's usually plenty of it. For me, plenty of time is a couple of days, though often it's longer; it depends on when I see the film in relation to when I'm going to write about it. Sometimes I have a week or two weeks. I don't like to wait too long because then details become fuzzy. Anyway, when I see a film that is of some texture and depth, I almost always try to see it again before I write about it. I wouldn't dream of reviewing, let us say, an Ingmar Bergman film on one viewing. You've only got to see a really interesting film a second time to be scared by the thought that you might have written about it on one viewing. It frightens you to see what you've missed.

CA: What qualities make for a memorable film critique? Do you think such critiques tend to be positive or negative in tone? Is discussing a film's social or political aspects as important to you as treating its cinematic qualities and value as art or entertainment?

Kauffmann: The essentials are perception and style, perception that freshens, style that breathes and lifts. Negative or positive tone depends entirely on the instance. For much of the last century a critic, of film or anything else, was thought serious only if he was mostly negative, if—as the phrase went—he said no to America's yes. This seemed to me as formulaic as the reverse, just as facile and (sometimes) cowardly.

A film's social or political aspects are inseparable from its cinematic qualities if it's a good work. The more separable a film's cinematic qualities are, the less good it is likely to be.

CA: Do you ever see a film or a play you find difficult to write about?

Kauffmann: Yes. That's particularly true in the theater, where there is a kind of art growing called "performance art," which doesn't deal with plays and scripts in the conventional sense. They do theater pieces, more than plays, which really don't deal much in traditional structures or characters, that are really, one could say roughly, attempts to incorporate the modes of ballet and painting into the theater. Some of the people who work that way are Richard Foreman and Robert Wilson. Their work is extremely difficult for me to write about with any helpfulness because the vocabulary of dramatic criticism doesn't really accommodate it in a useful way. One has, if one can, almost to evolve a separate aesthetic for each one of these art forms.

There's a production in New York now, for example, by Richard Foreman, called *Penguin Touquet.* I don't think I'm going to review it because the *Saturday Review* has given me limited space and there are other things I must write about. But if I had to review it I would really have my work cut out for me. Most of the reviewing of such a piece, for me, turns out to be description with some pretense at comment thereafter. The reader has no way of telling what you're talking about, no reference points, unless you describe the thing in considerable detail.

CA: What do you consider the weaknesses in film and drama criticism?

Kauffmann: The chief thing that's wrong, I think, is that it's still generally thought that anyone who can write can do film or theater criticism. We have plenty of instances in both fields of people who write reasonably well who are doing just such criticism and who are really betraying to me—and I'm glad to say to a few others—that they have neither the informational foundation nor the quality of perception the critic needs; and more, if I may put it this way, the moral rigor—a commitment to the art, a passion to see it improve, a disregard for any kind of popularity.

CA: How would you characterize the relationship between film critics and the film industry? Do you think film critics could be more influential in this relationship? How?

Kauffmann: The relationship between the film critic and the film industry is, or ought to be, of interest only to the industry. If filmmakers care about a critic's work, for whatever reason, it will influence them without his giving any thought about it.

CA: What is your current opinion on film festivals?

Kauffmann: Unchanged. I wrote my first piece on the subject in 1965, and nothing in the last sixteen years has changed my opinion. What I've seen is mainly the New York Film Festival—though I have been to three or four others. I have no wish to travel to film festivals anymore. I've seen through the years at the New York Film Festival a number of films that I would not have seen otherwise, and I'm very grateful for that. On the other hand, my opinion on the form of film festivals and the hoopla about them is unchanged. They give the false impression that they are dealing adequately with international production, and they do it in a jam-packed way that makes seeing films a marathon instead of a pleasure. I said then and I say again that there should be—as I believe there still is in Sweden—a way of importing foreign films under bond so they don't have to pass customs and no import duty has to be paid, which is possible if they're going to be shown only in selected club situations to members. It would take some time, but it wouldn't be hard to set up around this country a thousand such cinema clubs at universities. Films could be imported to be shown all year long at those places. There could be in the course of a year more than a hundred films from abroad shown in that way, and it wouldn't impair the commercial possibilities of those films, if they had any, because they would not have been reviewed and would not have been shown for profit.

CA: In your years of writing criticism you've followed a number of actors whose early work you thought promising. Have any of them notably fulfilled that promise?

Kauffmann: Not yet, no. The trouble with both film and the theater is that almost all the ingrained factors militate against seriously pursuing an acting career. I can think of one exception to that, Meryl Streep, who comes from the Yale School of Drama, where I teach (though I was not her teacher). She seems to be holding to a fairly rigorous line, doing good films when she can get them and trying to do good things in the theater. There are other people whose efforts I admire, like Christopher Walken and James Earl Jones, but nothing has yet come to a point where I can feel that anyone of that generation is fulfilling his promise. Jane Fonda—I was one of the first ones to take her seriously and was hooted at for it—seems to me to be fiddling around.

CA: In *Albums of Early Life* you wrote about your work as an editor of comic books and about the brief period in 1954 when you became "Terry Kirk" long enough to write a Western. Is there anything different from your present life you'd like to try?

Kauffmann: If I had the chance, I'd like to direct a play or two again. I occasionally get an offer to do a little acting, but I haven't been able to do so because of the pressures of my work. As it happens, I did a reading last night from *Albums of Early Life* at a theater club in New York, and someone there suggested I do a part in a play there, which I would like to do but don't have time. And—this is pure fantasy—I think that in the right circumstances and with the right material, I wouldn't be a bad film director—but there's no point in thinking about that now. I'm not a frustrated film director. I'm not abnormally frustrated in my present life; I'm doing a lot of things that I really enjoy and that are worthwhile. I have five jobs. I teach at the Yale School of Drama two days a week; I go up on Thursday and come back on Friday. I teach on Monday afternoons in the theater department of the City University

Graduate Center in New York. I write a weekly film article for the *New Republic* and a monthly theater article for *Saturday Review,* and I do a bi-monthly article, usually on television actors, for the *Dial,* a good new magazine sponsored by public-television stations.

CA: Do you feel at all optimistic about the future of the arts?

Kauffmann: Having said so many gloomy things about the prospects of film and having *not* said some almost equally gloomy things that I might have said about the current state of playwriting, I ought to say that I think some art in this country is thriving. Poetry in this country is very good, there's some good fiction being written, and, as far as I can tell, some good painting. My wife, who is a ballet enthusiast, tells me there's some wonderful dancing. So it's not a philistine desert.

CA: Do you have any pet peeves or personal frustrations that you'd like to address? Or would you like to share your critical credo or a favorite maxim about film criticism from a forerunner?

Kauffmann: I'm too far along to address my frustrations. Without forsaking a hope for alertness and self-discipline, I'm pretty much stuck with myself as I am. If I have a credo, it is that the criticism of film, or of any art, can be literature in itself. The reader can be enlightened by the best criticism and, additionally, can be glad that the art in question has brought about a corollary art.

Studs Terkel Interviews Stanley Kauffmann

Studs Terkel / 1985

Transcript of radio interview conducted on WFMT, Chicago, 5 March 1985.

Opening: "The Ballad of Mack the Knife," excerpt sung in German by Kurt Gerron.

Terkel: You recognize that—"Mack the Knife"—known as Mackie Messer. And that voice you hear—that nasal, nasty sort of voice—is that of the original Macheath, Kurt Gerron. And the reason I'm playing that now is because my guest is, I think, the most perceptive of drama critics in the country. He is a superb film critic, too, for the *New Republic,* and, at the moment, drama critic for the *Saturday Review.* And his name is Stanley Kauffmann. Stanley Kauffmann has covered theatre for a good number of years in his own incisive way, and on hearing that original "Mack" of Kurt Gerron, I'd like your thoughts after having seen a number of later productions of the work from which it's taken, *The Threepenny Opera.*

Kauffmann: Well, the first thing I think of is that voice, which is like the quintessence of the German—the Berlin, not German—1920s. This voice sounds the way Brecht's face looks. It has encapsulated in it, enclosed in it, all the bitterness that was going to explode in several different directions shortly thereafter. This man . . . if you want to go into this man's story—

Terkel: Go ahead.

Kauffmann: —the tragic story, of Kurt Gerron. Many people are familiar with him, though they may not know it, from the original *Blue Angel* film with Marlene Dietrich. He is the stout man who's the head of the vaudeville troupe of which she is a member. And he fled Germany when Hitler came, went to Holland, thought he'd be safe, was captured there by the invading Germans, and taken to a concentration camp; there he was ordered to direct a film to show how wonderful concentration camps are for visiting Red Cross officials; then, after finishing it, Gerron was immediately shipped out and incinerated at another camp.

101

Terkel: One of the questions that comes up in thinking about *Threepenny*: Germany in the '20s, pre-Hitler—*Berlin,* I should say—may have been the most artistically exciting city in all Europe.

Kauffmann: I'll tell you an odd, bitter story. I met a well-known rabbi, a German-Jewish rabbi who had lived in Berlin in the '20s, and he got out by the skin of *one* tooth, after almost being burned up along with his family. He knew everything that you or I could possibly tell him about Germany and more, because he'd seen it first-hand. And in conversing with him once, I said, "If you'd had your choice of the range of Western history, where and when would you like to have lived?" He said unhesitatingly, "Berlin in the 1920s." Unbelievable.

Terkel: Yeah, yeah. Of course the question always comes up—how come? Because here was the Germany of Piscator, of Reinhardt, of Kandinsky, of Klee—just to name men from a few of the art forms, not to speak of music composers—and the question, again, is, how come? That's the nub of the matter, isn't it?

Kauffmann: Well, "how come" is the result of the '20s with the bubbling up of what had been happening in Germany for almost 200 years before that.

Terkel: Yes, and that's not accidental. Then when you see some contemporary productions of *Threepenny* that receive rave reviews, you have to insert another view and say, "Wait a minute, something is missing."

Kauffmann: Well, *The Threepenny Opera* is, for me, a gigantic work. Not in size, obviously, but in implication, in resonance. And one of the ways it's gigantic is in its use of *seeming* vaudeville to take apart the corrupted spirit— not just of a city, not just of a country—of a *continent.* And it does so with little razor cuts.

Terkel: Yes, that's right.

Kauffmann: I haven't seen that many productions, but I'll tell you about a funny one I saw. An odd one, I mean. I haven't seen that many, but by far the *best* I saw was in Rome in 1956 done by Giorgio Strehler. He brought his company down from Milan—

Terkel: *Teatro Piccolo*—

Kauffmann: *Teatro Piccolo di Milano*; he brought that company to Rome to do *Opera da tre soldi.* And it was a magnificent production. In fact, I learned much later that this was the production that Brecht himself had seen in Milan about three or four weeks before, and, shortly before his death in the same year, he revised his ideas about his own work because of it. That production was the thing in itself. But then, once in Athens about ten or twelve years ago, I read that it was playing somewhere in a theater—and it would be for us the equivalent of a neighborhood movie house, but it was a theater—and who directed it? Jules Dassin! Do you remember him?

Terkel: Of course.

Kauffmann: He lived in Athens, or did live in Athens—

Terkel: Married to Mercouri—

Kauffmann: Married to Melina Mercouri, right. I think that she had been in it, but she left the cast before I saw it. And there were a lot of nice housewives on their way home from shopping at a 5:30 or 6:00 performance, sitting down and filling the place with their shopping bags next to them, sitting through a performance of *Threepenny Opera,* and then going home to make dinner and take care of their families. *(Laughs)*

Terkel: But, you see, I suppose what you find objectionable or lacking in some of the contemporary productions that have been praised for technique or design is the lack of that hardness, of that bite.

Kauffmann: Yes. It's possible to do *Threepenny* the way—although I think he's a wonderful singer—the way Frank Sinatra sings "Mack the Knife." I mean . . . his version has nothing . . . it's devoid . . . it might as well be "Lola the Flower Girl." After all, this is a song about a killer who kills because the world had left him murder as the *brightest* of options.

Terkel: Yes, true. Talking to Stanley Kauffmann and thinking of theater, let me just reflect.

Kauffmann: Fine.

Terkel: You once wrote about two great actors of theater, about Ralph Richardson and John Gielgud working together on a Pinter play. And you spoke of something they *do,* each one.

Kauffmann: The play is *No Man's Land,* a play that I think is underestimated in itself to begin with. I'm a great Pinter enthusiast. I think he has written two or three plays that are genuinely and unassailably great. I don't think that's true of *No Man's Land,* but still, to me, an interesting play because I see it as a *Cubist* work—a play that tries to take different planes of time and put them before you simultaneously. And, here were these two old actors—actors renowned, and justly so, for careers in the traditional or classical theatre—you might say venturing forth into brand new territory at quite advanced ages. And doing it like . . . like experienced navigators in very strange seas. *(Laughs)* And acting the play beautifully. But what was particularly wonderful about it for me was that one saw here, at least, three things in conjunction. One saw, or heard, Pinter's writing and what lies underneath Pinter's writing, which is his own uncanny sense of *acting. Acting.* Pinter's plays are based on *acting.* And these two men, from an entirely different generation and tradition, were communicating with Pinter as *actors,* with a writer who knows how to write for *actors.*

Terkel: Writing for acting or actors helps explain Pinter because he writes about illusion, in a sense.

Kauffmann: Yes, he's writing about what cannot be *said.*

Terkel: You point out something in your review. At the very opening of this play, *No Man's Land,* one guy is visiting the other guy at home—

Kauffmann: Yes—

Terkel: —and says, "Let's have a drink." They have a drink. And as Richardson is pouring a drink for Gielgud there are three words: "As it is?" And you wrote—quoting Kauffmann on the Richardson interpretation— "Richardson [puts] his vocal 'hand' firmly on the audience, determinedly *beginning* the play with three separate utterances. 'As. It. Is?'" And that also sets the play up, doesn't it?

Kauffmann: Yes. He sort of . . . uses those three words—or used them—in the way that the three blows behind the curtain of the *Comédie Française* start the play.

Terkel: Oh, when the guy backstage or off to the side bangs the stick upon the floor.

Kauffmann: Richardson said, "As it is?" and the play *began.*

Terkel: Yeah.

Kauffmann: There's one . . . may I tell one other—

Terkel: Of course—

Kauffmann: —story about an actor responding to the theatrical. There's a story in John Lahr's book about his father, Bert Lahr—

Terkel: *Notes on a Cowardly Lion*—

Kauffmann: *Notes on a Cowardly Lion.* Its chief detriment for me, if one can call it that, is that I'm jealous of John Lahr. I wish Bert Lahr had been my father. *(Laughs)* He tells a story about Bert Lahr reading *Waiting for Godot.* Now, Bert Lahr—wonderful, wonderful comedian and theatre *animal* that he was—didn't have much brains, despite his theatrical expertise. But he read this script, *Waiting for Godot,* and he read it before the professors had written the books, before there was any explication of the text; before there was anything to go on, someone put a script in front of him. And instead of being *Getting Gertie's Garter* or *Up in Mabel's Room,* it was *Waiting for Godot.* He read it the way he read any script, and it didn't make any sense, given the way he was used to reading scripts. And John Lahr tells the story about—he quotes at length—his father getting on the telephone to the father's agent and saying, "I read this play, and I don't understand a blankety-blank word of this play. I can't . . . I don't know what it's all about. But there's something there for me to *do."*

Terkel: He knew that.

Kauffmann: That's what I'm saying about Richardson and Gielgud vis-à-vis Pinter. There's a certain *meta*-language of theatre that real theatre people respond to.

Terkel: And they get it. Since you mention *Waiting for Godot*—Beckett, of course—I suppose the greatest living dramatist—

Kauffmann: I wouldn't want to argue about that—

Terkel: O.K. But Beckett: do you have reflections on him? You saw a German *Godot.* Suppose we hear about the American director closest to Beckett—

Kauffmann: Schneider.

Terkel: Alan Schneider. And Alan Schneider is talking to me about Beckett, about his bleak outlook. Beckett's landscape seems bleak. I ask Schneider, "Is he possessed by pessimism, or is it something else?" Here is what Schneider says:

Schneider and Terkel on tape

Schneider: Of course, the situation is basically very serious, very tragic, but he finds the humor in the *human* predicament. And that's what Beckett ultimately finds—the human predicament.

Terkel: This is what Beckett finds. On television—I didn't see it in the flesh, I wish I had—but on TV, I saw Irene Worth doing Winnie in *Happy Days.* Now

Winnie is a woman who is up to her neck in a sand pile—that's it! What is the opening line of that play?

Schneider: "Another heavenly day." *(Laughs)*

Terkel: What can you say? How can you say the guy's pessimistic? "Another heavenly day." *(Laughs)*

Tape fades.

Terkel: That's it, isn't it? So Bert Lahr, of course, as Gogo—

Kauffmann: —was perfect—

Terkel: —was funny—serious, of course—but at the same time hilarious.

Kauffmann: But that's . . . you see, to me . . . two of the greatest playwrights who ever lived in the Western world are Beckett and Bernard Shaw. And it's just civilization's good luck that they're both Irish. Because when wonderful Russain writers, or French writers, or American writers look into the heart of the universe and find it empty, it depresses them. When an Irishman looks inside it, he *laughs. (Laughs)* It's *funny* that there should be nothing at the heart of the universe.

Terkel: By the way, Stanley Kauffmann is in Chicago, at the moment, under the auspices of the Court Theater, to talk about Shaw in conjunction with one of the Court's productions. And now *we* come to Shaw.

Kauffmann: Oh, *good.*

Terkel: And I hope before our talk is over, we can get in some references to a very moving memoir Stanley Kauffmann wrote called *Albums of Early Life*—his own reflections on, and memories of, theater and offstage life as well, which Ticknor and Fields published. Oh, by the way, his theater criticism is published by *Performing Arts Journal*—

Kauffmann: —*Publications.*

Terkel: *Performing Arts Journal Publications.*

Kauffmann: It started as a journal, and then its publishers developed a book line. And I'm going to put in something about them, if I may. May I?

Terkel: Oh, of course.

Kauffmann: This is a husband and wife, Bonnie Marranca and Gautam Dasgupta, an Italian-American girl from New Jersey and a man from Calcutta, who started a small publishing firm that is now the best theater publishing firm in the country, and one of the best in the world.

Terkel: Isn't it funny? It takes small publishing houses these days to issue a book like yours.

Kauffmann: They just insist. They just insist on doing it, and they do it.

Terkel: And so you write in *Theater Criticisms,* which Marranca and Dasgupta published, of a certain production of *Saint Joan.* Of course, that's got to be one of the great modern plays—

Kauffmann: A pinnacle, a pinnacle.

Terkel: Yes. Suppose we hear—this is years ago, it was 1963—Sybil Thorndike, one of the doyennes of British Theatre—

Kauffmann: The first English Joan.

Terkel: I think Shaw wrote the part for her, though it was first performed by an American—

Kauffmann: —by the Theatre Guild. A woman named Winifred Lenihan actually did it first, but that was a contractual mess—

Terkel: But this is Sybil Thorndike. She's about eighty-five when I'm interviewing her. It was in Brighton, where they had some try-outs. And she was making her début in a musical—would you believe it, at eighty-five? It was a take-off on *Becky Sharp,* the dramatic adaptation of the novel *Vanity Fair.* And in the dressing room in Brighton I was asking her about some things: what interests her in the world and how that affects her acting. At the time, she was against the Vietnam War and that affected her playing of her role in *The Trojan Women.* And then I asked her about *Saint Joan,* and this is what she said:

Thorndike and Terkel on tape

Thorndike: Well, Saint Joan was the greatest thing that ever happened to me, theatrically—the greatest thing that ever happened to me in the theatre. And in my own life, too, because she said and did so many things that I felt so *deeply* about. And I think that is probably why Shaw chose me to be his . . . why he wrote the play when he found that I could do what he wanted.

Terkel: What is it about Joan? There are so many things, you feel, that Joan expresses on the stage.

Thorndike: She was an extraordinary creature, wasn't she? Her *passionate* faith, her *passionate* Christianity, and yet she was this amazing general. I mean, I've got no sympathy with her in violent, military matters. But she was a pioneer in her age. As one of the generals of the time said, "She wants to use artillery in a way we never thought of before." But it's the way they use it now. She was a great military inventor as well as a mystic and a saint.

Terkel: Was it the passion of Joan that caught your fancy because of your own fervor for life?

Thorndike: I think it was. In a way it symbolized everything I'd felt. I mean, she was such a great person, but I felt that to get inside such a person would give *me* an enormous stimulus to do things.

Terkel: I must ask about Shaw now, your memories of him. He produced *Saint Joan.*

Thorndike: Oh, he produced it. He produced every one of his plays that were done for the first time. Always. And he was wonderful, wonderful. And he could act all the parts better than any of us. He was a wonderful actor.

Terkel: In reading through the play for the first time, say, he would act out all the roles?

Thorndike: Yes, he did! And do you know—it's an extraordinary thing—he knew the tune of every sentence. It was like conducting an opera. I could go through some *Joan* now and know the exact tune of every sentence: where he made his pauses, where his voice went up, his inflections; he knew exactly. And he wouldn't pass a line by until he got what he wanted.

Terkel: It's interesting that you say he knew the *tune* of every sentence as though it were part of a musical.

Thorndike: Well, the theatre is a musical thing. And I look upon it awfully musically. I'm a musician myself. . . .

Tape fades.

Terkel: Isn't that interesting? Shaw knew the tune.

Kauffmann: That's a word which has some history in a director whom Shaw admired and who preceded him: William Poel. He was a great Shakespearean reformer—whom Sybil Thorndike knew—who used to talk about "the tune." But what this reminds me of is that in 1956 my wife and I were living in London for six to eight months, and that was the year of Shaw's centenary. There was a great luncheon in his honor at the Savoy; he, of course, had been dead six years. The Master of Ceremonies—they were called "Toastmasters"—was St. John Ervine, playwright and critic, who also wrote a good biography of Shaw. And *she* was one of the speakers, Sybil Thorndike. And I remember her saying—she's a very passionate woman, as you could hear. I mean, if she were to ask you to pass the salt at the table, she'd knock you off your chair. *(Terkel laughs.)* But I remember, at the end of her short talk to this huge ballroom full of people, her thanking God that she was born to live at the same time as Bernard Shaw.

Terkel: You know, in your review of a production of Shaw in 1978, you quote a line from Bishop Cauchon, a Shavian line: "Must then a Christ perish in torment in every age to save those that have no imagination?"

Kauffmann: You see, if you had to pick *one* line in all of Shaw—which would be stupid, but if you had to do so at the point of a gun—which summed up what he was about, that's it! Because it contains the idea of progress, the idea of the obstacles in the way of progress, and it contains the key word in his entire intellectual and artistic being—*imagination.*

Terkel: Imagination. You know, if ever there were a play that is contemporary now, in 1985, it is *Saint Joan* with this line as its fulcrum.

Kauffmann: Shaw said that the greatest imagination is the capability to imagine things as they *are.*

Terkel: As they are. Isn't that funny? I think of Pinter. Shaw's opposite, in a way. "As they are." "As it is."

Kauffmann: Suppose we could read the newspaper today with the imagination to see what's *really being said* there on the front page. The whole country would be up in arms.

Terkel: Of course, the banality.

Kauffmann: And the contradictions and the cruelty.

Terkel: It's exciting talking to you about theater, because it goes on off-stage as well. I clipped and framed a little communiqué from Bangkok, Thailand, and it says, "In a fight last night several people were killed as the policemen disguised as bandits were attacking a group of bandits disguised as policemen." This is an actual news item.

Kauffmann: *(Laughs)* Sounds like Genet.

Terkel: Yes, doesn't it? *(Laughs)* It is Genet. It is *The Balcony.* It is everything. So this is what we're talking about. And brilliant theater reflects this reality.

Kauffmann: Yes. What I'm particularly happy to see, as clearly as you do, is that Shaw gets more modern every day.

Terkel: He does, doesn't he? We have to talk about Eugene O'Neill also. You've reviewed a good number of revivals of O'Neill's plays. We have to come, I suppose, to the Father of Modern American Theater.

Kauffmann: Well, yes, I guess that has to be said. Yes, he is the Father of Modern American Theater, yet he gets his seed from abroad. *(Laughs)*

O'Neill is, in every way, a fascinating man, I think. Everyone knows the encyclopedia clichés about him, that his last three or four plays were his best ones. We all know them: *Long Day's Journey into Night, The Iceman Cometh, A Moon for the Misbegotten,* and possibly *A Touch of the Poet.* And we tend to slough off much of what he wrote in the preceding years. A lot of it is pretty difficult to take seriously, particularly after you know the late, great plays—almost by common consent the best plays written on this side of the Atlantic. But what has always been interesting to me, peripherally—but not peripherally about O'Neill—is that all through his life—a man of intense, burning, Strindbergian commitment, a man who lived to put his life on the line for what he was writing, even when it was terrible—he was moving towards the ability to write about himself and his family.

I'm sure you are familiar with his biography, that he was the son of a very famous, old-fashioned actor. We know about that at least from *Long Day's Journey.* He *hated* his father's theater, his father's style of acting. As a boy, he had to be an extra in his father's acting vehicle, *The Count of Monte Cristo,* and it disgusted him. He used to get sick, literally, from having to be on the stage and listen to that stuff. He went as far away from it as he could towards everything that was going on—and a great deal was—in the new European drama, which is what he thought he was destined to create in American form. The curious thing is that, having absorbed what he could from Europe through his long, *hard,* utterly committed working life, he came back to his father's theater in style, in essence. Everyone thinks, or many think, that *Long Day's Journey* was delayed in production because he didn't want to hurt people's feelings, his father's and his family's feelings. Not so! He couldn't find an *actor* like his father.

Terkel: That was it. He needed an actor like his father.

Kauffmann: As Shaw said, "a brass-boweled roarer" to do the part. *(Laughs)* So, at the end of his life, he found himself aching for the techniques of the theater he had turned his back on. In his last plays, there is a kind of marriage of all that was *best* in the nineteenth-century theater—much was rotten in it—with what he could bring to it from twentieth century-thinking: Freudian psychology and so on.

Terkel: Then there is the conflict of cultures, the Irish and the American.

Kauffmann: That's a key word—Irish. When he got the Nobel Prize, of course he got thousands of messages and telegrams from all over the world congratulating him—you know he's always been very big in Europe, Scandinavia particularly.

Terkel: Scandinavia, I suppose, because of the Ibsen/Strindberg influence on him.

Kauffmann: Yes, that's right. And also because they say he gains in translation. *(Laughs)* Anyway, he got a message from the Irish Embassy in Washington congratulating him on winning the Nobel Prize. And he told all his friends that that message from Ireland meant more to him than anything else. And for me, *Long Day's Journey* is about America vs. Europe. It's about what happens to pure Irish Catholic faith when it lands in this country and gets absorbed. What happened to the father, who was in some ways a noble man? He got buffeted into a commercial life, a *successful* commercial life— I'm not saying there's no such thing in Europe, I'm talking about what happened to him here. But what's even more pertinent is the mother's role. For me, she is the protagonist of the play. She is the heroine of this tragedy, which consists of her whole movement—the dynamics of the play—in relation to the Catholicism she feels she abandoned by marrying this handsome actor, who obviously had more than just physical attraction for her. That twist of abandoning faith made her a drug addict, made her lose herself to dope. And the last line of the play, when she is far off in dreamland, is, "Then [. . .] I fell in love with James Tyrone and was so happy for a time."

Terkel: I suppose *A Touch of the Poet*—
Kauffmann: Well, that's literally about Ireland and America, about European panache trying to survive by running a little hotel up in New England.

Terkel: There's this character who dreams of a battle in which—
Kauffmann: —he fought as a member of the British army.

Terkel: But he's faced with a tough, young daughter who's more the realist.
Kauffmann: Yes. She's America.

Terkel: She's American. That's it, yes.
Kauffmann: That's really what I was trying to say before. You brought it out better. There's a movement in O'Neill's life away from all the European influences he absorbed and, in a way, tried artificially to reconstruct—as in *Strange Interlude* and *Mourning Becomes Electra*—to this facing of the fact that he was really the American son of Irish immigrants. The two great plays

about immigration—I mean, not schoolbook plays about immigration; fundamentally, what's underneath them is the entry of European culture into a new setting—are *Long Day's Journey into Night* and *A Streetcar Named Desire*.

Terkel: *A Streetcar Named Desire* brings us, of course, to probably the second greatest playwright in American theater.
Kauffmann: The only one who comes close to O'Neill.

Terkel: And that's Tennessee Williams.
Kauffmann: Yes.

Terkel: He was a guest on this show about three or four times. The last time it was a celebration, if you will, of his seventieth birthday. And I was asking him how he felt about himself now that he had created such a body of dramatic literature, and would create even more to come. Listen to this:

Williams and Terkel on tape
Williams: You must remember that you're now talking to a man who has gone through what Blanche went through. I've been in the asylum, and I've survived. *(Laughs)* I came out. *(Laughs)* Whether or not I'm a crackpot—I said in an earlier interview that I was not. But I think I'm a man who has the San Andreas Fault built into him. *(Laughs)* I'm not confident of the future.
Terkel: I was thinking, you're the artist who creates. But are Blanche DuBois, T. Lawrence Shannon, Alma Winemiller, and other Tennessee Williams characters, are they so different from you as a person? Or is it that their sensibility is such—fragile, like so many of us—that at the time of some brutishness, they break down? I've had more than my share of friends, among the most sensitive, who have had nervous breakdowns, to put it mildly.
Williams: So many people you wouldn't expect to crack up, they do suddenly. They live behind a façade, you know, which is what society expects from them, and they manage to maintain that façade up to a certain point. Then, suddenly, a pressure shows how thin that façade is, because it cracks wide open.
Terkel: Is there such a thing as a complete person? What makes a complete person, if there is any such animal?
Williams: Oh, perhaps one could be a complete idiot. *(Laughs)* I don't know whether the form of completion is offered to humankind.
Tape fades.

Terkel: Your thoughts on hearing Tennessee Williams?
Kauffmann: It was very moving to hear him. And to hear him so soon after our speaking of O'Neill reminds me of something that is absolutely true

about both these men, so vastly different in so many ways: their lives con-
sisted, fundamentally, of commitment or subscription to the idea of being an
artist. No swimming with one foot on the shore—plunge right in! A novelist
once said to me—a man of some talent who didn't fulfill his talent—he said
to me, "I know the secret of being a great writer. It's not hidden; it's easy.
You have to have talent, of course, but then you have to give your *life*."
O'Neill did. Williams did. However ridiculous or silly the latter might have
gotten from time to time in his personal life, or even in his writing, there was
always that feeling of complete commitment. He wanted to do nothing else
in life but write well. Nothing else mattered!

A few months ago, there was a small sort of—shall we call it a celebration?
Can you celebrate a death? There was a memorial service—I hate that
term—in New York for Williams, and I read—different people read different
things—I read my review (collected in *Theater Criticisms*) of his memoirs.
It is a book that people should read, extravagant, bloated, overdone, hyperfer-
vid as it is. Still, it contains the essence of this committed man. What was
much more interesting than my review, I thought, was the passage about
Williams that the poet William Jay Smith read from his autobiography. They
had been young men together in St. Louis. Smith able to go to the university,
Williams not, or not yet; he was working in a shoe factory at the time. So
they knew each other, and Williams was always around the university hob-
nobbing with the young writers there when he wasn't working at the factory.
And these men formed a poetry society. From his earliest days of cognition,
of sentience in the world, there was nothing Williams wanted to do but to
respond to experience—mostly inner experience—with some kind of formu-
lation in words that would reproduce, heighten, and comprehend that experience. That's very moving. That deserves every respect, I think.

Terkel: Also, I suppose, he wanted to understand the fragility of the
human make-up. Somewhere in my last conversation with him, I referred to
his defrocked preacher in *The Night of the Iguana*—
Kauffmann: Lawrence Shannon—

Terkel: —and Blanche and, for that matter, Laura Wingfield; they're always at the end of their tether, these characters. That's a phrase he used, and
that's exactly it. A certain person at a certain critical moment, and—
Kauffmann: Yes. It's what they call in classical dramatic analysis "the
late point of attack." You start at the nearest point to the end of the tether.

Terkel: We've been talking about relatively gigantic figures in American theater today. But there are some plays written by considerably lesser playwrights that have moved you deeply, such as *The Elephant Man.*

Kauffmann: That's right. I think *The Elephant Man* is actually a kind of hybrid. I liked it much more than the few other serious critics in this country—there are not so many. I'm not the least bit reticent about putting the matter that way—this play is a kind of hybrid. The man who wrote it, Bernard Pomerance, is an American. But he had spent so much time in England, and had worked so much in the English theater, that he wrote it with a kind of English *astringency*: understatement. It's not just that *The Elephant Man* is about an English subject. It's written with a—oh, well, let's use it, an easy word—*minimalist* approach. And it seemed to me to combine that minimalism with the symbolism of the Elephant Man himself; and the church model that runs all through the play itself was very poignant, touching, keen. Moreover, there was—simply because of the church model—a kind of reflection on the infinite questions about God and His infinite wisdom.

Terkel: And the illogic sometimes of that wisdom. Or the random aspect of this character's fate. Unlike a cathedral that he would build—

Kauffmann: Yes, that can be designed—

Terkel: That can be *designed.* Fascinating. You know, how can we talk about theater, contemporary theater, without talking about the novelist Dickens. And we come to *Nicholas Nickleby,* don't we?

Kauffmann: Well, that to me is a wonderful subject: Dickens and the theater. There's an excellent book by a man named Robert Garis called *The Dickens Theater.* And this is not about what you might think—the theatrical characters in Dickens, or episodes of theatrical activity in Dickens. Garis's thesis, which he demonstrates very beautifully, very movingly, is that Dickens's "theater" is his *prose.* His *prose* is his theater. If you've read Dickens's biography—I'm sure you have—you know that he wanted to be an actor. He had an audition set at one of the big London theaters but developed a bad cold and couldn't turn up for it. And the next audition was going to be in six or eight months, and he had to get a job. So he took a job as a Parliamentary reporter. I don't say that he would *never* have been a writer. Who knows? But the fact is that his mind was set *early* on the idea of theater. Garis makes the point, not biographically but intrinsically, that the theater was sublimated into the way Dickens thought about the English language.

In my recent collection, *Theater Criticisms,* I have taken off the titles of the reviews as they appeared in the *New Republic,* and just put the title of the play at the top of each piece. Once in a while, I regret that I have established that custom for myself because in this book is my review of *Nicholas Nickleby.* And the title I use on that piece in the magazine, which is not in the book, to me sums up this work completely: "Dickens Comes Home." *Nicholas Nickleby* seemed to be born of, to be generated through, a theatrical sensibility. Garis talks about a certain passage in *Nicholas Nickleby* as epitomizing this theatrical quality that he's trying to describe and isolate.

In the production of *Nicholas Nickleby,* there's a moment at the beginning of the second act when Nicholas and Smyke return to London after having been away. And the production faked a carriage—they didn't have real scenery, they just pushed a basket along with these two sitting on top of it on chairs. Nicholas and Smyke were surrounded by fifteen to twenty actors who recited in perfect unison Dickens's paragraphs of descriptive narration about Nicholas and Smyke's return to London: how London looked, what they saw, what they smelled, what they heard, how it affected them. That prose was so *enveloping,* so *wonderful,* so *aromatic.* I just wished they'd kept on doing *that* all evening.

Terkel: You know, as you're talking, I'm thinking of the only other critic of today—he died recently—of whom you remind me, or he reminded me of you. That, of course, is Harold Clurman.

Kauffmann: Yes. I knew him.

Terkel: I know. I'm talking about his and your enthusiasm for theater. That's the aspect about the both of you which I like. It's coolness or distance in a critic that disturbs me a little.

Kauffmann: Clurman certainly had none of that. You wouldn't have had to ask Harold many questions if you had ever had him on this show. *(Both laugh.)* If you just said, "Good morning, Mr. Clurman," you were *off.*

Terkel: Very often, his shirttail would come right out of—

Kauffmann: He once said, "I've always been a disruptive person." *(Laughs)*

Terkel: We've got to talk about a couple of other playwrights whom you like—the British dramatists David Hare and Howard Brenton.

Kauffmann: I like David Hare very much, and I believe he's also a gifted director. I did think, however, that *Plenty*—as I say in *Theater Criticisms*— had severe shortcomings. But it's clearly the work of a man who understands how to use the theater instrument, both as a writer and as a director. Howard Brenton, to me, is special, someone to cherish. Particularly in light of a particular play of his called *Sore Throats,* which I saw first in London, then read and worked on with student actors at Yale. I gave it to the editor of the Yale magazine called *Theater,* who liked it himself and published it. I also gave it to a young director who was just graduating, a woman named Jan Eliasberg. She loved it. She got a job at the Repertory Theater of St. Louis, and they eventually committed to do this three-person play there with Eliasberg directing. I went from New York to St. Louis to see the production and I wrote about it. *Sore Throats* was supposed to come to New York, but, as often happens, it never made it. I am confident, though, that this play will come into its own.

Terkel: That was your longest review in *Theater Criticisms.* I noticed.

Kauffmann: I think so. Yes, you're right. Because the magazine for which I wrote it said they would pay my way out to St. Louis and back only if I wrote a piece twice as long. I was happy to do so . . . I would have written it three times as long.

Terkel: As you describe it, it seems incredible, Brenton's insight into human behavior.

Kauffmann: Well, this is a play about a man and a woman and therefore—if it's any good—about men and women, in London today. I'm not going to tell the story, but let me put it this way: I felt convinced that this was the epilogue, the contemporary epilogue, to Strindberg's *Dance of Death. Sore Throats* is about the difficulty of being a man with a woman and a woman with a man, seen right through to greater torment because you know how wonderful such a relationship can be. It's an agonized play, done in understated, terrible terms—terrible for both of them. It isn't a play about a man's abuse of a woman or a woman's utilization of a man. It's a play that tries to find some way that a man and a woman can really *live* together with more than sex—I'm not discounting sex—with more than sex, more than affection, more than tedium: in friendship.

Terkel: And, of course, the agony is there because of the conflict.

Kauffmann: Yes. It's a wonderful play, and I hope those in your audience will get *Sore Throats,* and read it.

Terkel: One aspect of David Hare's *Plenty* that struck me in your review was that it's a political play. Did you say this, or did Hare say it? "One of the reasons for the theater's possible authority, and for its recent general drift toward politics, is its unique suitability to displaying an age in which men's ideals and men's practice bear no relation to each other."

Kauffmann: That's Hare's statement, yes. He says somewhere else in the essay from which I quoted these words, that what he likes about the theater is—this is apropos of this quotation—the fact that while a man can be talking nobly about this or that sitting next to a woman, his hand can be going up under her skirt. *(Laughs)*

Terkel: Yeah, that's funny.

Kauffmann: That's what the theater means to him.

Terkel: "It's clear that *Plenty*"—this is Stanley Kauffmann writing—"is about scarcity—scarcity of convictions in the midst of material plenty. I can't recall an age when, in Hare's terms, men's ideals and men's practice *have* borne much relation to each other, but he has chosen an age [the 1950s and early '60s] in which the disparity between ideals and practice was particularly painful." There's *no* relation between the two. There's nothing but lack of conviction at a time of such seeming plenty.

Kauffmann: And the theater is a very good place in which one can enunciate the ironies of this difference, this opposition.

Terkel: If I could come back to Eugene O'Neill for a minute.

Kauffmann: Surely.

Terkel: O'Neill said he couldn't find an actor of the stature of his father, James O'Neill. I suppose someone approaching such size today would be George C. Scott.

Kauffmann: Very close to it, yes. As close as we have in the American theater, I think. That's the kind of actor O'Neill meant. The kind of actor—there's no point crying over spilt talent—but the kind of actor that Marlon Brando could have been. One of the qualities—this is not a cheap tag, although it could sound like one—one of the qualities that distinguishes the really exciting actor from the many very good ones (whom we need and should cherish) is *fright*. They frighten you. The best actors—men and women—always frighten you because you feel that you don't know exactly what's going to happen. There's a panther in them that may strike—you're always seeing a characterized panther if what we're talking about is a good actor. The panther of that particular person they're playing. Even for such a civilized actor as John Gielgud, this is true. The panther is sometimes not aggressive, just frightening. You listen to the recording of John Gielgud's Lear, the last speech of Lear when he talks about . . . well, I'm not going to do Lear's last speech for you. I don't want to put Gielgud to shame. *(Both laugh.)* But a different kind of something bursts out there, of surprise that frightens you because, in a certain sense, although you're listening to an actor or watching an actor in order to be moved, you're almost afraid of the emotion when it occurs to that degree. You're like a child who wants to see over the ledge, but, my Lord, I didn't know we were *that* high up. That's the sort of thing Gielgud can do for you.

Terkel: You feel fear and, I suppose, astonishment.
Kauffmann: Yes, "étonnez moi." Astonish me.

Terkel: John Barrymore might have been someone—
Kauffmann: Absolutely! Absolutely. I've seen, I guess, almost every film he made. I saw him on the stage, too, late in his life. He had that quality of flirtation with insanity. Robert Shaw had it, too.

Terkel: The playwright is the overall creative spirit, but the actor has to be able to astonish you, to scare you.
Kauffmann: Yes. Well, let's not oversimplify. I'm not talking about Boris Karloff in *Frankenstein*—I'm talking about the sense that the great actor can give you of the hidden aspects in the human spirit.

Terkel: That's what theater may be about, too, of course. We haven't talked about your *Albums of Early Life*. This is a collection of memoir pieces by Stanley Kauffmann, and they're terribly moving.
Kauffmann: Thank you very much.

Terkel: In a way, *Albums of Early Life* concerns theater—well, a lot of theater is in it, but the book also concerns what led you to an interest in theater. For instance, the drama in seemingly uneventful lives, like those of the farmhands you observed.
Kauffmann: Boy, you have put your finger on what *Albums* is about. I tried to find the drama in relatively ordinary or commonplace things that happened to me—I never shipped out to sea, I never went down a coal mine, I never went over Niagara Falls—like working on a farm, which, through the people I met there and elsewhere, opened up aspects of life to me.

Terkel: Stanley Kauffmann is my guest. I know that we could go on talking for several hours, but for the moment this will do. Stanley Kauffmann is here in Chicago under the auspices of the Court Theater, but you can read his reviews in the *New Republic* on film, and in *Saturday Review* on theater. *Theater Criticisms* is a collection of his reviews that's available from Performing Arts Journal Publications. And *Albums of Early Life* is published by Ticknor and Fields. Thank you very much, sir.

Kauffmann: I'm greatly obliged to you for having me.

Stanley Kauffmann on the Unknown Shaw

Jane Ann Crum / 1986

From *Shaw* 7 (1987), 31–44. Interview originally conducted on 9 January 1986.

Mr. Kauffmann first studied Shaw at New York University in the early 1930s under Randolph Somerville, who had himself studied with Louis Calvert, the English actor prominent in the Court Theater seasons of 1904–7. For ten years (1931–41) Mr. Kauffmann was a member of a repertory company, directed by Somerville, that specialized in Shakespeare and Shaw and for which he was stage manager of, among others, *You Never Can Tell, Misalliance,* and *Androcles and the Lion.* Outstanding in his Shaw memories is the centenary luncheon, July 1956, in London—which was chaired by St. John Ervine and at which Sybil Thorndike spoke.

Jane Ann Crum: In our original conversation about this interview, you expressed an interest in discussing Shaw as "avant-garde." Since this term has already been used by Stanley Weintraub, could you comment on your particular use of it as applied to G.B.S.?

Stanley Kauffmann: "Avant-garde" is as useful a phrase as any other. It has a lot of colorations, but I use it to mean two things in relation to Shaw. The first is advance in ideas, the most commonly ascribed aspect of his work; the second, and to me equally interesting, is advance in dramaturgy. That, I think, is the aspect of Shaw's work that is usually skimped. Not, however, by Weintraub.

JAC: By dramaturgy, do you mean primarily his craftsmanship?

SK: Not just craftsmanship, but ideas of form, ways to enlarge or focus or advance theatrical energy in the theater. Shaw is usually taken to be a playwright who concentrated especially on the dramatization of ideas. I think he also concentrated on the idea of dramatization and that he was as dissatisfied—and increasingly so—with dramatic form as given to him as he was with the political, religious, and economic ideas and all the other ideas, as given to him, with which he meddled and tinkered all his life. In short, even though he sometimes specifically denied it, Shaw was as much a conscious exploratory artist as he was anything else. Certainly as much so as many other dramatists who did a great deal of public theorizing on their advances in art.

You can divide Shaw's playwriting career into two periods. The watershed mark is usually taken to be 1900. Roughly, his first decade—in the 1890s— reflected, in a nicely ambivalent way, his attitude toward the theater he had loved as a boy. He adored the Victorian theater, and he used that adoration to help him explode it. You can say in an overall, inclusive way that the plays he wrote, from *Widowers' Houses* to *Caesar and Cleopatra,* were plays in which he took forms and modes that had prevailed in the English-speaking theater for a century and used them in a new and shocking manner. From about 1900 on he was much less interested in taking forms from the Victorian theater and much more interested in devising new dramatic shapes. One can say, then, that there is the Shaw who took what he loved and used it in ways that it didn't know it could be used, and then there is the Shaw who exhausted that interest and delved into new dramatic territory.

JAC: So what we see as we go through these very different shapes (using your words) of dramaturgy, is an artist who has put aside a form he has mastered and is very consciously trying to make new forms.

SK: I would say the same thing just a bit differently—that we see a genius mature. Like another genius, Beethoven, Shaw started by utilizing forms at hand which he loved, but he grew impatient with them and moved on to the completely original. It isn't so much a question of exhaustion as of matura- tion. And that means, when you're talking about any artist, let alone a genius, self-discovery.

But this leads to an even larger and infuriating subject, which is that, of all the famous dramatists in Western history, Shaw is the least known. More people speak authoritatively about Shaw without knowing what he has writ- ten than any other dramatist on earth, including Shakespeare. Statements are made, for example, about Shaw and sex, or Shaw's addiction to facetious- ness, or Shaw's lack of passion, that are so easily swept away by direct refer- ence to the plays that you know the speaker or the writer is pontificating out of catch-phrases rather than investigation.

The only qualification I add is that Shaw wrote so much in play form and other forms that no human being could keep all that he wrote in the forefront of his mind, including Shaw himself. I am continually rediscovering things in Shaw that I had forgotten. But given that qualification, there is no famous dramatist who is less known, less really read, than Shaw. There has been a special antipathy toward him in the last forty years because he has been taken as a "cheery Victorian" who had no idea of the depths of despair in the human soul. As one very well-known critic said to me, "Shaw is irrelevant after Auschwitz." That seems to me no more or less true than saying "life is irrelevant after Auschwitz." Concerning Shaw, this claim is best answered by the last section of Alfred Turco Jr.'s *Shaw's Moral Vision,* entitled "The Tragic Optimist."

JAC: Do you think this antipathy toward Shaw occurs because, unlike Ibsen, Strindberg, and Chekhov, his career took him well into this century?

SK: Shaw wrote so much, talked so much, appeared so much, and made himself so present throughout his life that he humanized himself as those men did not. He made himself a public person in a way that Ibsen, Strindberg, and Chekhov did not. It is impossible to find any analogy today for the presence of Shaw in the world I was aware of from the early 1930s until his death in 1950. In those twenty years of my life there was no writer in the world who was equally famous, no writer so much quoted, no writer so much consulted. If a president was elected here, or a king was assassinated there, some reporter went to Shaw for an opinion, and Shaw gave it to him. I would make a rough guess that in those twenty years Shaw was quoted in the *New York Times* on some topic at least every fourth day or so. After all the work Dan H. Laurence has done in collecting Shaw's letters, here is an entirely separate volume—*Agitations,* which he edited with James Rambeau—of more than 150 letters to the press that Shaw wrote between 1875 and 1950 on topics that range from whether one should stop after hitting a dog with a motorcar to how to settle the First World War. In an intellectual world that thinks a man who is humorous and vivacious cannot be first-rate, he militated against himself to a certain degree.

JAC: We've chosen *You Never Can Tell* (1896) as our first play for discussion. It is rarely performed and rarely mentioned in even the major critical studies of Shaw, yet I know that it is one of your favorites.

SK: I think it is the greatest high comedy in the English language after Sheridan. If I were making a bouquet of high comedies in English, I would pick *Much Ado About Nothing, The School for Scandal, The Rivals,* and *You Never Can Tell.* (I omit *The Importance of Being Earnest* because it's sui generis.) The fact that Shaw's play is a scintillating high comedy has (again) militated against it in many critical minds. I've had the experience in my Shaw seminar at Yale of students picking up that play reluctantly and coming back with dropped jaws about several of its kinds of mastery. The first is fundamental: *You Never Can Tell* is a high comedy. Shaw takes the summery comic romance, a staple of nineteenth-century theater, and lets you think this is going to be just one more—and then subtly, but rather quickly, he changes it into something else. The play takes place in summer and in one day. It starts in a verbal atmosphere of music and dance. You can't speak the opening dialogue in any other than a sparkling way. And it moves in four acts to a final dance with music. It is a humming dynamo of progress dramaturgically. I think that's its first mastery. If you could make a computerized graph of its dynamics, it would have an amazing consistency of oscillation in sound.

Secondly, the play is wonderfully skillful in symmetry and form with the idea of letting the audience understand what is going to happen *just before* it happens, so that they are co-conspirators with the playwright about the fate of the characters. In other words, instead of being dully predictable, it is engagingly predictable. For example, in the first act, we know before it is revealed that Crampton is the missing father, but instead of spoiling matters, it just whips up our appetites for the confrontation to come.

Shaw seems to me here very consciously writing about the turn of the century, not as a calendar date, but as a time when certain social and political ideas are going to change. Mrs Clandon is an antecedent of Roebuck Ramsden in *Man and Superman,* which is coming along soon. Both think they're tremendous progressives, but they find out that they're clinging to progressive positions that are thirty years old. Mrs Clandon thinks she has seen the future, but she hasn't seen much into her children's lives. For me there's a tremendous sense in what would otherwise be a seaside butterfly romance, of changing attitudes toward sex, pursuit, courtship, and candor. Others have noted that the romance of Gloria and Valentine is a prediction of what will happen with Ann Whitefield and Jack Tanner in *Man and Superman.* That's true, but I don't think it's a rough sketch; rather, it's a different approach to the same subject.

JAC: I think you see more similarity between Ann and Gloria than between Jack and Valentine.

SK: Yes, much more, but the idea of an alteration in the courtship pattern as times change is common to both plays.

Lastly, there's the character of Crampton. Shaw will not let this be *only* a

pleasant play. Instead of making the estranged husband a Pantaloon, an old
fogy with a walking stick, Shaw makes him a man who has suffered greatly
because of his inability to express his feelings. He is a man who was brought
up to crack nuts in his teeth and brush his teeth with soap. He cannot understand why everyone isn't as rigorous as he is. Out of his incomprehension of
anything that is not rigidly Victorian, he is prevented from asking for or
giving the love that he has wanted all his life. He did do the things that his
wife accuses him of. He did buy a whip to beat his children. But he's the
victim of that more than they ever were, and has been all his life. Shaw
created such a character to run as a kind of dark ostinato through the lighter
configuration of love and romance. This, I think, was for Shaw an act of
intellectual necessity. Old Crampton is the one in the play who personifies
what they are all moving away from. But it's also an act of dramaturgic
daring, esthetic daring, to have him in that play—not losing one iota of grim-
ness, isolation, and loneliness, yet fitting him perfectly into a comedy. I call
that dramatic genius.

JAC: The scene I always come back to in *You Never Can Tell* is the dinner
with the comic waiter, William. I don't think it can be appreciated on the
page. A complete meal is served, and whenever there is the slightest hint of
tension or trouble, William is there with "Salt at your elbow, sir."

SK: And how easily Shaw synopsizes a long meal into a few pages and
makes it credible. I'm glad you raise the subject of William. Martin Meisel
makes the point that he derives from the comic waiter of nineteenth-century
farce. But again Shaw wanted to take something familiar and use it in a way
it had never been used before. William acts as a benign spirit, a kindly old
angel disguised as a waiter. It's as if he's a guarantee to the audience that
things will turn out well because he is a delegate of Providence, smoothing
out things, assuring us that everything will be reconciled. If you want to be
fanciful about this—about spiritual messengers and so on—you could say
that the waiter not only keeps things in perfect balance, it's his son who
brings about the final settlement.

JAC: His son, Bohun, is the basso, the bottom register in terms of the
musical analogy you were talking about. The play begins in the high registers
with the pitter-patter of Dolly and Philip, and by the end Shaw adds the
pedals of the organ.

SK: Yes, Bohun provides the resolution of the chord. He is decisive, with
his "You think you wont, but you will."

JAC: Which seems to be a restatement of his father's final line, "You never can tell."

SK: Exactly.

JAC: *You Never Can Tell* is usually classified as a farce. William Archer described it as such, and Shaw's rebuttal was sharp. I gather from your comments that farce is not a word you would apply to this play.

SK: I know it's often called a farce, but I think that's a misapplication of the term. Farce is a genre based on plot or action more than on character. There is certainly a good deal of plotting, of carefully articulated design in *You Never Can Tell,* which I think has misled people into thinking of it as a farce. But the play resides so thoroughly in character, in ideas treated lightly but nonetheless treated as ideas, that the term farce cannot accommodate it. I don't know of any play that I would call a farce, even the best works of Feydeau, that has the texture of *You Never Can Tell.* Besides, there is another simpleminded test: comedy tends to aim toward amendment and change, and farce does not. Farce, as Eric Bentley has told us, operates fundamentally out of fear and the gratification that we are not in the danger that the characters are in.

JAC: Also, in relation to your comments on Crampton, another quality of farce is that there is no real pain, yet there is very genuine pain in Crampton.

SK: I agree with you and think that, in a nonparadoxical way, the true pain in the character of Crampton proves that this is comedy, not farce.

JAC: I read a review of *Misalliance* in your *Theater Criticisms* and was struck by the fact that you described it as a genre unto itself. Could you talk about form in *Misalliance?*

SK: First of all, it's the second of a pair of comparable plays, with *Getting Married.* I much prefer it to the earlier play simply because *Misalliance* lives more theatrically. Its characterizations are vivid, and it relies on an absurdity of circumstance that underscores the seriousness of what it's about. *Misalliance* (1909) is the first major occurrence in Shaw of a subtext that runs to the end of his career—the idea of absurdity. There are two forms of this absurdity: the first is the "absurd" as we use the term philosophically today; the second is the absurdity of the theater itself. Being a master of theatrical form, a prestidigitator of theatrical moments, Shaw was able to be dissatisfied and impatient with what had been done before with "good form."

He submerged this dissatisfaction a great deal of the time in his larger works and used it instead to create a series of one-act plays which occur at intervals between his major works, and which are absurd in the best sense of the term. With them, Shaw seemed to be saying, "Yes, I wrote *The Doctor's Dilemma,* but consider *Annajanska;* that's another way of looking at the theater." This attitude comes to full flower later in Shaw's life as his view grows that some absurdities in existence need to be more forcefully matched by absurd theater forms.

In *Misalliance* there is a gross disproportion between the cogency of the ideas presented and the likelihood of the circumstances. This disproportion is quite deliberate, and this is the first time it happens in a long Shaw play. Later on in his career, it happens more and more. It's as if he were saying: "You're sitting at a play. Actors are pretending to be people. We know that this is false. Let us agree that this is false by having a woman say she wants an airplane to fall from the sky. Then it does fall and everyone survives. But after we've signed our pact of artifice and reciprocal belief in disbelief, let us use the occasion for serious ends. Let us not become so committed to the idea of realistic illusion on the stage that it saps our energies. Let us take the circumstances of the play simply as 'occasions.'"

In one regard I think of the plot of *Misalliance* as some eighteenth- and nineteenth-century composers thought of librettos. What happens between arias and duets is just something that enables the arias and duets to occur. Even in the most serious of such operas, there is a complicity between us and the librettist/composer so that we can appreciate the beads that come to us on the string without being too worried about the string.

JAC: In terms of your description, do you see the whole play as working toward Lina's final "aria" demolishing Johnny?

SK: Yes. And nothing that I've said should be taken as a stricture on the seriousness of the ideas of the play. *Misalliance* takes place in a rich man's home. . . .

JAC: And, connected with *You Never Can Tell,* a summer home, with people on holiday . . .

SK: In one day. But its intent is less toward facsimile of life than *You Never Can Tell. Misalliance* is a kind of pressure cooker; everything is condensed and intensified in terms of time. People change fiancés, engagements, and even alter their lives in stage time—without much pretense that it is real time, as it *is* consistently pretended in *You Never Can Tell.*

The play can also be seen as a convocation of different currents in the

Western world of this time. Hypatia is a young woman going mad with energies for which she has no channel. Tarleton is a man who has made a fortune
but, in his own view, has wasted his life. Mrs Tarleton is upset by living in a
new world where drainage is discussed by ladies. Joey Percival is shocked to
discover that his fellow passenger is a woman. Gunner, who takes his ideals
from Victorian fiction, is willing to die for the sake of these false ideals. Yet
this all happens in the course of a merry summer's day.

I stage-managed a production of *Misalliance* many years ago for a repertory company and saw about twenty-five performances of it over the course
of some months. And it was possible after all those rehearsals and performances to hear that the play is really built musically, that it exists in large
phrases. One episode leads to another, like variations on themes. There are
very few plays by Shaw in which his background of musical training and
sensibility is more patent, operative, and beneficial. It's another play that
suffers from misunderstanding. One critic called it a "hodge-podge." To
which, in Shaw's words, I can only respond, "Why was I born with such
contemporaries?"

JAC: If *Misalliance* is a "hodge-podge," perhaps the best segue into *Androcles and the Lion* (1912) is that here is a play, amazingly enough, that is
often treated as if it were children's theater.

SK: Well, *Gulliver's Travels* is often taught as a children's book. *Androcles* is one of the most moving religious plays written in the twentieth
century. That it should be taken as a children's play because it takes its title
and enclosing fable from what has become a children's tale . . . well, to put
it gently, I see it differently. I don't want to belittle the charm of the play,
because it *is* charming; but it seems to me a very serious play, and not just
because of possible martyrdom and words like "Christ" and "Christianity."
For me, it is a drama enclosed in its subtext. Androcles, the simple human
being of pure love and trust, suggests the transition of the Western world into
Christianity.

JAC: This is interesting to me because most views of this play pretty much
dismiss Androcles as any kind of "idea" within the play. The common opinion is that the play is about Lavinia and the Captain, or Ferrovius. . . .

SK: Of course it is, *but* as seen within this broader idea of perfect love, of
charity and humility. Androcles, through these qualities, is the savior of all
these people at the end. He is unafraid in the Prologue—not because he is
brave, but because he is compassionate.

JAC: This seems to be the same kind of insulation that Shaw is using with William in *You Never Can Tell* in that he is our guarantee that everything will work out. Androcles, then, is the outside that allows us to deal with the inside of blood and death.

SK: That's an interesting analogy. William can be seen as a suggestion of Divine Providence; but in this case, Androcles's initial act of Christian charity is also the final resolution.

Enclosed in this gentle tale are other stories of transition, a matter that occupies Shaw time and time again, moments of change in people's lives and the world around them. Shaw takes this tremendous subject—the introduction of Christianity—and encloses it inside a child's fable, and within that enclosure gives us several portraits of different kinds of courage and desperation. A Roman noblewoman cannot put a pinch of incense on an altar because she would betray herself. A Roman captain swears that if she dies he will kill the emperor and then cut his own throat. He is a believing man; although he doesn't believe in Christianity, he believes in honor and love. Androcles is the connective tissue between them. There is a false believer, Spintho, who is using Christianity as insurance to have a good time on earth and pay for it on his deathbed. Also there is the warrior—Ferrovius—who would like to believe, but has not yet grown to that spiritual point. We also have the mockers, who crop up again in *Major Barbara* and *Saint Joan.* All are handled with an economy that is staggering. All these gradations in the spectrum of the advent of Christianity are enclosed in the simple story of Androcles—a man who has no intellectual life but is simply, by nature, gifted to be a Christian.

Because of the brevity of the play, I've always thought it should be paired with the dialogue between Pilate and Jesus from the Preface to *On the Rocks.* When asked why he didn't write a play about Jesus, Shaw responded that it was impossible to write a play about a man who didn't fight back. But then he wrote this dialogue. If it were played as a curtain-raiser to *Androcles,* it would give us not only, in the utilitarian sense of the word, a "full" evening in the theater; it would also give us an overture that would state the themes that *Androcles* would then dramatize.

JAC: I find it interesting that you see this play as being so tied to Christianity. I have a tendency to disregard Christianity and see it much more as a new religiosity replacing something that has become habit. Lavinia seems to be working on impulse ("It is not in the nature of my hand to touch a mouse") rather than rationality.

SK: Well, I agree and disagree with you. *Androcles* is, in a general sense, a play about the impact of freshness on habit. It is about the shaking of spiritual lassitude—to the point of giving your life in order to find out what God is. But the instance that Shaw has chosen is Christianity. His love/hate affair with Christianity runs all through his life. As he says in the Preface to *Androcles,* he has considered the world and its problems for over fifty years and doesn't know any way out of those problems except that which would have been found by Jesus if he had undertaken the work of a modern states-man. The vitality and necessity of Christian doctrine were always pressing Shaw, even though he couldn't stand organized religion. He objected to it as his later creation, Joan, did: it stood between himself and the spiritual. The question is less Christianity in itself than as an example of why it is necessary in Shaw *to be something,* to be willing to give your life for something.

From that, here is my own extension: I don't think there's much difference between the noble Lavinia, perfectly willing to take the consequences of Christianity, and Dubedat in *The Doctor's Dilemma,* who is a cad, a rogue, and a scoundrel, but perfectly willing to take the consequences of what *he* believes in. Shaw makes a good case in his life and work for something Kierkegaard said: "We must live as if life had meaning." The emphasis, for Shaw, is not on the "as if," but on the "*must.*"

JAC: When you've seen *Androcles* on stage, how real were the pain and the blood, the death and dying? After all, the underpinnings are quite gory—Ferrovius kills six armed men, Spintho is eaten. . . .

SK: It's played the way death is played in comedies. It's not visible, never seen. And after all, we know Spintho; his death is ironic, not tragic. When Ferrovius enters with a bloody sword crying "Lost! Lost for ever!," it's funny that a man who has conquered all those gladiators comes in ashamed of himself. In many farces and comedies, death is frequently an offstage pres-ence. There is nothing imperatively gruesome about death. It depends on how one sees it.

JAC: As we begin to talk about *Too True to be Good* (1913), I just want to comment that this play is pointed to as proof of Shaw's final pessimism.

SK: Shaw did himself a bad turn in the Preface of *Too True* because he said that the play is about the strictures of capitalism on the rich. It is not. That's just the comic premise with which the play begins, and then it goes off in several directions.

After World War I, Shaw wrote *Back to Methuselah,* a gigantic work that is an almost conscious effort to regain balance and sanity. Then comes *Saint Joan* (and I'm not going to argue with anyone who calls that his greatest play, although I have no "favorite" Shaw play). All Shaw's plays that followed World War I seem to combine two factors: (1) a recurrent, almost hysterical desperation that he was approaching the end of his life without having bettered the world, and (2) impatience with the forms of the theater. We see this latter element in other great dramatists' later plays as well. *When We Dead Awaken* is a prime example of a genius saying "This form, this theater, is not enough! I want to go beyond that, yet that's the only thing I know how to do, to work with people speaking words on a stage." In a certain intrinsic sense you can feel this same thing in *The Tempest.* "Language is not enough for my spirit," seems to be what Shakespeare is saying in the text. I'm not really comparing *Too True* with *When We Dead Awaken* or *The Tempest,* but I feel something of that same impulse here and in other of Shaw's later plays. He refuses to be bound any longer by the design that operated in, for example, *You Never Can Tell.* He begins to think, as Richard Gilman once said, that the well-made play, in a certain sense, reflects a well-made world, and that therefore one must not write well-made plays. (I'm adding that last bit myself.)

JAC: But, you're right: there are no more symmetries. . . .

SK: Yes, *Too True* follows intellectual impulses; the consistency of the play comes from Shaw's unconscious rather than from a plan. There's a theory of modern art, *The Hidden Order of Art* by Anton Ehrenzweig, related to the painter's unconscious. I don't think *Too True* is stream-of-consciousness playwriting, but I do think Shaw allows one idea to summon another from its depths. He does that because he does not want to do otherwise anymore. In other words, he is saying to the theater: "I've served you long enough, now you serve me. Let me have my little game because my games are serious."

It occurred to him to use his friend T. E. Lawrence as a model for Private Meek, but that was merely something that suggested itself. I've read about the play that it was Shaw's tribute to Lawrence. That is simply not true. Meek is there as one comic character.

JAC: He's not a major focus, although he is related to the idea of British colonialism. . . .

SK: And also a jocular commentary on the idea of finding one's vocation and sticking to it. But *Too True* is not a play about T. E. Lawrence; nor is it a play about the confinements of the rich, their incapacitation by wealth; nor is it antimilitarist. All these are simply ideas that occur. What we finally get in this play is the question, "Are you there, God?" Aubrey says before we meet his father that the old man was an atheist and therefore a strict moralist. The Elder turns out to be that atheist. The play ends with the son, who has inherited his father's preaching ability, speaking to us at length because speaking now is all he knows how to do. That's possibly desperation. It's also possibly fulfillment. People are always telling us that Shaw is saying at this point, "I feel useless. All I can do is go on talking, and I shall go on talking." I think that's reductive. Speech as expression of thought is the highest achievement of the human race so far. The ability to speak as Aubrey speaks at the end of the play is a pretty good example of that high human faculty at its highest. So, it could be that, instead of empty articulation, the last speech is a verbal/ aural banner proclaiming that Armageddon and catastrophe may be upon us; but at least as we go down (or go up), Shaw is going to demonstrate that the human race achieved something on this earth by putting thought into words that are well chosen and that evoke music and response. In other words, I think that last speech, even if somewhat desperately insistent, epitomizes the idea of the "tragic optimist," less by what it says than by what it is. "How dare you," says Shaw, "say that talking is mere talk? So far as we know, we are the only sentient beings in the universe who can speak. If we're going to blow up, let's do it while we're speaking."

JAC: I've always been struck by the landscape of *Too True.* It moves from the sickroom to the bathing area, to that very strange third act with rough-hewn rock arches and people wandering around on sand dunes. For me, it is a Beckettian landscape.

SK: I certainly don't think that Shaw is a symbolist, but there are settings in his later works, like *The Simpleton of the Unexpected Isles* and the last play of *Back to Methuselah,* that are more or less placeless and are Beckettian in that they are realizations of mental attitudes. And within this (let us call it) "symbolic landscape" there are human beings who seem to me to be less characters than disassociated sensibilities. I think of them as sets of nerves that have been extracted from different human beings, then sentenced to wander.

JAC: A good experiment in what you're describing would be to compare, say, the Elder with Crampton. The only thing they share is that they represent

an age whose time has passed. But there's nothing about the Elder that creates the emotional connections we feel for Crampton.

SK: You can't say that Shaw had abandoned ideas of character, because
eight years later he wrote *"In Good King Charles's Golden Days,"* which is
pretty well characterized. But there is a strong recurrence in him (especially
in his last twenty years) of this impulse to have personages on the stage rather
than people. Collections of attitudes and views, rather than people with birth
certificates and insurance premiums. Neither are they allegorical; they are
patterns of thought or response liberated from corporeality and set free on
the stage to bombard each other with their different molecules.

JAC: Do you think that's a function of the bacillus called "The Monster"?
That from the very beginning Shaw is showing us another kind of being?

SK: Yes, I think that idea fits quite well with my view of *Too True.* I also
have dissatisfactions with this play. Tallboys is a bit of a cliché. Some of it is
more arbitrary than spontaneous. I don't feel as keenly about the ignoring of
this play as I feel about *You Never Can Tell.* I think that ignoring *You Never
Can Tell* is an outrage. I think that ignoring *Too True* is a loss.

My chief interest in *Too True* is that it brings to the foreground Shaw's
impatience, his need to defy everything that's expected of a respectable playwright and to create something vivid and incisive at the same time. He had
confined this feeling pretty much to his one-act plays, such as *The Inca of
Perusalem, Augustus Does His Bit,* or *Passion, Poison, and Petrifaction.* But
toward the end of his career it occupied more of his time—*Too True, The
Millionairess,* and *Buoyant Billions.*

Some people—Stanley Weintraub, Brigid Brophy, for examples—have
marked especially well this idea of the avant-garde or absurd that runs
through Shaw. Not enough attention has been paid to it, however. It's a kind
of counterpoint to the miraculously well-organized work through most of his
life. Perhaps by the end of his life Shaw felt he had earned a kind of freedom
from the niceties of traditional dramaturgy.

There's so much silly boring talk about Shaw as a didact—that all his
characters are versions of himself. Shaw the preacher, Shaw the talker. It
makes one feel weak to have to counteract that nonsense. One reason it *is*
nonsense is that it takes no account of Shaw the playful. And to be playful in
a range from eating plaster off the ceiling in *Passion, Poison, and Petrifaction*
to the ending of *Too True* is a considerable range of frivolity.

JAC: I keep trying to go back to what you said about finding the shapes
of Shaw's dramaturgy. I see the pattern of *You Never Can Tell* and *Androcles,*

which both have, as we've said, a providential figure as a guarantee for the audience. And in *Misalliance* and *Too True,* I see a different pattern—two plays that are moving through to a final aria, Lina's and Aubrey's. . . .

SK: In a way I wish you hadn't said that because I would like it to be true that the more neglected plays of Shaw fit into a pattern. But as you've just said, they do not. There are the well-designed, traditional plays, and there are those that are the efflorescence of a darting spirit and a mind never at rest. One can't say that either type is ignored more than the other.

In my view, the chief reason for the ignoring of the plays we've been discussing today links with what I said earlier—that Shaw is famous and unknown. I'm not arguing against the majesty of *Major Barbara* or the Dickensian splendor of *The Doctor's Dilemma* or the lightning dazzle of *Pygmalion.* I'm simply saying that for the slothful, it is easy to settle for those plays that are better known.

One of the signs of greatness in an artist is that he or she can imbue seemingly endless perspectives. I'd like to close with one anecdote about myself and Shaw. When Shaw was ninety an anthology was published called *G.B.S. 90,* which is a series of essays about his work in various fields, each essay written by a specialist in that field. There was a critique of Shaw's work in economics by an economist, of his work in theology by a theologian, and so on. And each one of these men who wrote about him had some really stringent criticism to make of Shaw's work in his field. When I was halfway through the book I thought, "Well, maybe this man isn't as titanic as I thought he was." But by the time I was three-quarters of the way through, I thought, "Idiot! Here is a man who is so huge that twenty people, who did nothing else but their own specialty all their lives, have to take him seriously when he touches their specialty."

The trouble with talking about Shaw is you can't find a place to stop. . . . (*Laughter*)

Writing about Movies (and the Theatre): An Interview with Stanley Kauffmann

Robert Boyers / 1991

From *Salmagundi* (Spring/Summer 1993), 113–27. Interview originally conducted in July 1991 at Skidmore College under the auspices
of the New York State Summer Writers Institute.

Robert Boyers: Start off in whatever direction seems useful, Stanley.

Stanley Kauffmann: Film is the art—leaving all hierarchies out of it for
the moment—where America has made quantitatively, without any question,
the greatest contribution in history. It can be said in fact that America gave
film to the world. I don't mean technologically, in terms of invention. There
are at least three other countries—Germany, France, and Britain—which
have substantial claims to having invented the actual machinery of film. But
in terms of formulating the art, giving it some sort of shape and aesthetic
viability, America has taken the lead since the beginning. There's a case to
be made that the idea of film editing was first crystallized by a man named
Edwin S. Porter. There's a very strong case to be made that what is called
the "language of film" (a term now in thorough disrepute) was organized
first by D. W. Griffith. There's plenty of testimony to Griffith's influence on
others. Eisenstein is one example. But what's more important to my argument here is that before the First World War—or until about 1915—American
films, through their intrinsic quality and also through American organiza-
tional industrial genius, occupied 90 percent of screen time around the world.
That situation, of course, has greatly altered since then. But still, the one
country whose films dominate the rest of the world is ours.

From that follows another proposition, which is: on the first day that the
first film flashed on the screen, the double life of human beings intensified
astronomically. That double life had existed since the origins of the rudest
forms of art. I'm not talking about the unconscious and the conscious—the
Freudian division—I'm talking about the *conscious* double life, the life of
external actions, choices, movements, divisions, and the privacy of fantasies,
self-knowledge, and self-ignorance. Every art had at some level addressed

the binary state of each human being. Film intensified that matter dramatically. Dreams and fantasies and external actions as well were influenced by movies. I'll give you one example from my own experience. When I was in high school I took a girl to a dance—sweet Rosie Schultz—and when it came to saying good-night at her front door, sweet innocent Rosie Schultz gave me a kiss—and as she kissed me I saw her become Joan Crawford. As I thought about it, the transformation became clear to me. Who was going to teach her how to kiss—her mother? If that example can be amplified to represent the experience of generations of film-goers, I think it can be said that American film artists have done more to influence the private lives of human beings than artists in any other form. And the influence on European directors of American filmmakers was enormous. When John Ford died, Satyajit Ray wrote a long piece about his indebtedness to him. I cite Ray because he seems so remote from Ford.

RB: You've been writing about movies in the *New Republic* for well over thirty years. The association between you and the magazine must affect what you write and the way you think about your work.

SK: I can't imagine how it could be otherwise. If you write regularly in one place for a number of years, you become—you feel—fused with that place and that function in an almost metabolical sense. And, if the readers of the publication you write for are particularly responsive—whether or not they approve of what you've written—then you feel you occupy a privileged and responsible position. Writing under such conditions, you find that your reviews are not solo efforts, that they are part of a continuous, even kinetic pattern, and that they nourish a relationship. That sense of the thing also helps a reviewer to feel that when he writes has some consequence in relation to the art that's being talked about. And if you can't have that sense of consequence, why bother to write regularly about a particular art? It's really very different from writing an occasional review.

RB: I recall your having at one time cited Oscar Wilde, who said that criticism is the highest form of autobiography. Is your film writing a continuous autobiography?

SK: In an important sense it is. But I suppose I think less about that than about all of the ways in which I've been nourished by my conviction that film is itself an important art and that I am responsible for helping to connect that art to the best possible audience for it.

RB: Have you always believed that in the end what matters most is your capacity to decide, on plausible grounds, whether or not a film is worth taking seriously?

SK: I know that some people often disagree with my judgments, but I have to assume that it matters to them and to me whether a film is good or bad or something that can't quite be expressed in either of those words. Most of us, I think, want to feel that things matter. Movies matter, moral choices matter, the way we live matters. To take something seriously is to feel that it is possible to make a judgment about it.

RB: I'll say simply that virtually no American film that I've seen in the last twenty years seems to me to have been made for grown-ups. The best American films are fun, and grown-ups like to have fun. But they like also to think and to have obstacles of one sort or another set in their way. The American films that are made with "serious" intentions seem to me to be pompous and empty, and I would include among such works even films of a gifted director like Terrence Malick, whose *Days of Heaven* and *Badlands* have been celebrated in this very magazine.

SK: There's a school of criticism—very serious and intelligent people with whom I happen not to agree—who believe that what you're describing as entertaining films are really very serious work, who take the polished works of Howard Hawks with utter seriousness, analyze them endlessly. The name of Racine is frequently evoked in these commentaries—and I don't cite that for a laugh. It's true. This view is not a small or parochial view; in fact, it's held more strongly abroad than it is in the U.S. These people are interested more in cinematics than in subject matter or character development, and so find American films worthy of their very serious scrutiny. In terms of achievement in film there is a very strong world view that rates names like John Ford, Busby Berkeley, and Otto Preminger as equivalents of the great names of European film. How can you prove that they're wrong? I don't happen to agree with them, but there is more than one way to talk about the art of film. The fact is that many serious people take American film very seriously.

RB: You know, more than opinions are involved here. I don't think the critics you refer to *are* serious when they write about American films. I say this because they make allowances for them that they would never think of making if they were writing about a novel or a book of poems. Isn't it a fact that many book-review critics writing for daily newspapers use more rigorous standards to evaluate and judge a novel than most of those critics would use or invoke to judge a film?

SK: Yes, that's true in comparison with the novel, but it's not true in comparison with the opera. And there perhaps is where you should look to accept in part at least what many film people say: that American films look just fine when they are seen from the point of view appropriate to film. You don't ask the plot developments in many important operas to be "adult" in the way you would with novels. Why shouldn't the same distinction be allowed for film?

RB: Some would say that all this talk of judgment is bunk, that finally our preferences simply express taste. Now I know that you don't hold with this view, or with the idea of taste as a merely "personal" predilection for certain things as opposed to others. But I think you'll agree that it is sometimes tempting to speak of someone—a film critic, for example—as having good taste. What would that mean?

SK: Aestheticians love to debate the relationship between taste and judgment. Of course it's impossible to think about taste without considering a person's experiences. A person who seems to you to have good taste will seem to have had experiences that made good taste possible. But I suppose there is one fundamental way of thinking about taste I can endorse. When you approve of someone's criticism you feel there's a certain degree of congruency between you and what you read, between you and the critic. You feel that this person lives on the same planet with you, has seen the film in question somewhat in the way you did, or would. I'm sure you yourself, Bob, have often had the sensation, when reading criticism, that you don't know what the critic is talking about—not that you don't agree, but that you don't understand what the hell the critic is talking about. Good taste entails the sort of understanding we learn to miss when we feel the critic doesn't know what he's talking about.

RB: You've written, and spoken, with enormous admiration of George Bernard Shaw. And I take it that you admire his criticism quite as you admire his plays.

SK: Very few critics leave you in their debt as Shaw does. Others will occasionally show you something you'd missed, or inspire you to feel that you'd all along thought what you hadn't been able to articulate. But Shaw is really a special case. You read him today and you realize that he's writing about singers and performers long gone, artists almost no one alive has heard of. But you feel that he is talking to you about experiences you have had, telling you things about yourself in relation to music as if he were inside you correcting your vision, enlarging your scope. When you're in his company you almost feel that you're equal to handling the issue of good taste, that you can say with confidence that it's more than a tendency to be outraged by new art.

RB: Suppose we have a look at a contemporary film artist whose movies inspire a wide range of judgments, some of which may have more to do with taste than with anything else. Would you agree that Woody Allen inspires wildly different responses and that some people readily concede they "just" like, or dislike, the kind of thing he does?

SK: I think that's true, though I'm not sure it wouldn't be true in other cases too.

RB: Granted there are other comparable cases. But Allen may serve our discussion of taste better than the others. I thought about this recently when I reread your piece on Allen's film *Manhattan,* a piece in which you write of its desire "to stay cool" as an objectionable affectation or ambition. Would you talk about that criticism?

SK: Implicit in a film like *Manhattan* is an assumption about the contract between film and audience. The contract has it that the hip viewer of such a film will have progressed past a violent emotional response to the material presented, that he is above such a response and need not for a moment doubt his superiority to those who are not above it. You don't have to live in Manhattan to feel that you belong to the chic "cool" world depicted in the film. Allen's film makes two-hour Manhattanites out of everyone who sees it. What is fabricated is a kind of spurious elevation. You get a version of this in Hemingway, who allows people in Des Moines and Saratoga Springs to feel that they have sat in European cafes and felt the feelings of a so-called lost generation. No effort is required to participate in these feelings. And this effect of Hemingway's writing seems to some of us objectionable even as we're willing to make a case for him as a great writer. How much more objectionable this sort of thing seems in Woody Allen, who is not a great director. I'd go so far as to say that there is a smug Jewish cosmopolitanism about *Manhattan.* I know about this, as I'm a smug Jewish cosmopolite myself, and I can recognize something unsavory in the type when I see it. The assumption underlying films like Allen's is that anyone who knows anything worth knowing about today lives in a big city and probably wishes he were

Jewish. The movie provides its own version of a vicarious thrill, allowing those who really aren't "cool" at all to believe that they are. To be sure, there are other kinds of coolness, genuine and not genuine, but Allen's is a recognizable variant. It's different, for example, from that of David Lynch, who did *Twin Peaks* and represents what I'd call gentile Texan coolness. But both of these are spurious, suggesting that viewers can leave the confines of their desperate little lives and be coolly bored—with Woody or David or whomever else.

RB: Would you agree that a certain inveterate aversion to the chic and the cool may be said to inform, perhaps even to determine your criticism of Allen's film? That your "merely personal" taste is very much at issue in your response to a work you do in several respects very much admire?

SK: I can admire Allen's film as filmmaking without believing that it's good enough or that its stance is morally acceptable.

RB: But would you agree that your criticism of the film in terms of its spurious coolness is more a reflection of taste than your criticism of its realism?

SK: I'm not sure about that at all.

RB: Why don't we look at the critique of Allen's realism, then.

SK: Fine. As I recall, I saw Allen's film as an increasingly typical piece of mimicry, not much interested in getting at the truth of its material, but satisfied with reproducing the surfaces of a milieu.

RB: You quoted Allen, to the effect that, if people a hundred years from now see his film, they'll know something about life in New York City today.

SK: About how many films would it not be possible to make some such claim? Even the most ordinary films offer something of the look and the customs of a particular place and time.

RB: No doubt. But I'm not as ready as you are to conclude that, in the best of Woody Allen, what we see on the screen is "indistinguishable in texture or depth"—these are your words I'm quoting—"from the life in the lines outside the box office." And how, after all, do you make such a case with conviction?

SK: You make it, I suppose, by pointing out what is lacking. You ask what might have been done with the material, and you wonder why it has not been done.

RB: I like especially your observation that what is missing in *Manhattan* is "any true sense of dissatisfaction." What would you expect the film to be dissatisfied *about*?

SK: Well, I don't want to dictate to Allen what he should or shouldn't feel about his characters, but I think it's fair to object to a kind of self-love that issues from a film of this sort. When the characters demand a sharply critical or satirical treatment, and the filmmaker seems unwilling or unable to follow through with that, you ask what prevents him.

RB: You don't feel that the display of neurosis is itself potentially a valuable thing, that in exposing to us the vulnerability and self-delusion of his characters Allen is, at least implicitly, performing an act of criticism?

SK: That act of criticism is, I don't say wholly, but largely, invalidated by the self-love that excuses everything by demanding only that we be proud of ourselves and acknowledge our failings. I don't call that an acceptable moral posture. And it certainly doesn't make for moral realism, whatever the hype surrounding Allen and others like him may want us to believe.

RB: Do your objections to Allen extend more generally to most of what passes for realism?

SK: I say nothing new when I assert that realism has been central to the art of the last hundred and fifty years. This belief has been a background for movements that take it as a primary goal to oppose realism. It is, of course, not only an approach to representing things, but a view of the world. But it is fair to say that in no medium has this view been so cheapened as in film. In film you can excuse anything, exploit anything, fake anything—you can get away with anything—simply by calling it realistic. And it would be misleading to claim that only persons of an elevated kind are susceptible to this cheapening. Recently I went to see a film called *Die Hard II,* a film popular with many different audiences, or so I hear. It takes place within about five hours in and around an airport. The hero, played by Bruce Willis, goes through a whole series of beatings and fights. He is shot at, he jumps from great heights, he goes through things that would hospitalize Arnold Schwarzenegger within five minutes. But the hero persists, and all of the fantasy— it's the sheerest fantasy—is passed off as realism, because the setting seems to be a real airport. Bolts and nuts are discernible. The whole thing is more fantastic than *The Arabian Nights,* it's in fact low level comic book material. But—and this is my point—comic books at least don't pretend to be real. The realism of contemporary film is not only at odds with, it actually subverts the original purpose of the great realists, which was to present the facts of our experience so that we could also see beneath them. We never feel, when we read Flaubert, that he shows us only what we would have seen for ourselves if we had lived in the time of his characters. But in the realistic films of our time we get mostly commonplace data, even when it's dressed up—as it is occasionally in Woody Allen—with wit. Harold Rosenberg once wrote that if you look closely at the new realism you see that it's mostly decor. I like that remark, and it helps me to recall what I like about films that are more than decor, that know how to put their realism to use. I think of D. W. Griffith's film *Broken Blossoms.* Griffith was no hard and fast realist, but there is a strong element of realism in his work. In *Broken Blossoms* there is a scene in which the Lillian Gish character is locked into a closet by her father. She becomes hysterical, and we see that Griffith has every opportunity to turn the whole thing into a piece of sentimentality, or to offer a standard psychological insight such as we associate with an easy realism. Instead, he resists the inclination to produce merely a superior realistic document. Suddenly, he moves the film towards difficult insights, working that father's incestuous feelings towards a kind of revelation you know instinctively to be altogether different from the familiar goals of realism.

RB: You speak of knowing things "instinctively," and though we're taught nowadays to be suspicious of instinct, suspicious of the very idea that we can just know anything with a real conviction that it's true, I often find myself believing in just that sort of valid instinct. And yet I wonder. Sometimes I see a film I know "instinctively" to be wonderful, only to find that my friend Kauffmann doesn't at all see it that way. He has little patience with Wajda's *Man of Marble,* though I can't help regarding it as the most searching and honest portrayal of worker communism I can imagine—and a magnificently lively and inventive film as well. Or he has but modest praise to spend on Istvan Szabo's *Mephisto,* which my instinct tells me is about as commanding a film on its general subject as I can recall.

SK: We disagree about some films.

RB: Not as often as we agree. And of course I often learn more from you when we disagree, when you show me that my own sense of what a film is after is deficient.

SK: But don't let me interrupt you. You were saying about the matter of instinct that it's often unreliable, or misleading.

RB: Yes, and if I may I'll refer to a film we've argued over on two or three previous occasions. I bring it up, again, because the business of instinct bears upon our disagreement—as I suppose it bears upon most disputes of a similar nature. Years ago you published in the *New Republic* a review of Bertrand Blier's film *Going Places,* a film with Gerard Depardieu, Patrick Dewaere, and Jeanne Moreau. It's a very disturbing film, as you well know, and yet it seemed to you fine, stirring, enlightening. To me, not often given to puritanical squeamishness, it seemed revolting, offensive. "Instinctively" I knew when I saw it that my friend Kauffmann would, like me, find the daring elements in the film an expression of a willed, almost sophomoric transgressiveness.

SK: You were not alone in feeling that way. When Martin Peretz became owner of the *New Republic* he phoned me, by way of making my acquaintance, and at once asked how I could have liked *Going Places.* My review of that film was on his mind when he met Irving Howe one day and asked him if Kauffmann wasn't a good deal younger than Peretz had thought possible.

RB: So Peretz was also stunned by what he took to be the temporary failure of an instinct he'd long had reason to trust. Is it conceivable to you that a viewer who's responded to *Going Places* as Peretz did will be brought around to another sense of the film by reading you?

SK: I don't know. These things are not easy to judge. You and I certainly agree that there is a place in film for what strikes us as disgusting. We don't object absolutely to any depiction of sex. We object when we feel that what is shown is superfluous. If I feel that I am being enlightened I don't want to object. It's possible that a viewer with Peretz's response—or yours—will appreciate the case I've made for the film's merit without getting over the feeling of revulsion.

RB: Fair enough. But then we have to get into what does and does not constitute enlightenment. In *Going Places,* when we watch two young men joyously assault and demean an attractive young woman on a train, we are disgusted not only by the assault—though that would be quite enough—but by the film's resolutely upbeat and enthusiastic handling of the thing. Would you agree that the film offers nothing like a critical perspective on the behavior of the two rambunctiously predatory young men?

SK: I'd agree, but I'd argue that there's enlightenment in that as much as in anything else we learn about a certain kind of young man.

RB: But isn't it a bogus form of enlightenment? I might be more willing to go along with you here if Blier did not go so far, not only as to make the young woman submit, but to make her submit—after her initial reluctance—with pleasure and with gratitude. That seems to me not only revolting but plainly false. And I don't see how what is false or misleading can be enlightening.

SK: We are enlightened about a way of regarding things that runs counter to our own moral instincts. And if the film seems to support the amoral stance of the young men, that is a fact we are asked to think about and to learn something from. I don't see that this is dishonest or exploitative, even if I agree with you that the behavior of the young woman in the scene you describe is not typical of women generally.

RB: We've a fundamental disagreement on this, and if we looked at the film together I suspect the disagreement wouldn't go away.

SK: Probably not. And you're right to wonder how reliable instinct can be when two people who agree about so much see a film like *Going Places* in such different terms.

RB: If we leave the question of instinct behind and focus on the rather different issue of sex in film I expect we'll find more common ground.

SK: It seems clear to me that the treatment of sex in most contemporary films is exploitative and unnecessary.

RB: Maybe not unnecessary from the point of view of selling tickets to film audiences.

SK: That's a troubling question, but a different one, even if in the end it's not separable from the issue I'm raising. And of course you can't really think about it at all without remembering Hollywood's earlier handling of sex. For many years there was no sex on screen. You had to supply for the filmmakers what they were unable to put in their films. In the James Jones novel *From Here to Eternity* the hero goes to a brothel near Pearl Harbor and meets a young tart whom he likes. In the film made from the novel the young man goes to what looks like a sorority house, and the girl, played by Donna Reed, at the end of their conversation, to indicate that intimacy is in the offing, takes off one earring. The viewer is supposed to read the rest.

RB: And would you say that, apart from the sanitizing of the brothel, the representation of intimacy in the offing is about as much as any viewer needs to get the point?

SK: Of course.

RB: And would you agree that even a superior commercial film today would seem coy or evasive or downright inadequate if it were content to offer such a token?

SK: It would certainly seem inadequate to much of the filmgoing audience brought up on contemporary films. I can remember noting, when I saw the film of *Who's Afraid of Virginia Woolf?*, that the Elizabeth Taylor character actually said on camera the words "son of a bitch." And that was in 1966! By now the changes in what is customary have been so drastic that there is almost nothing to be surprised by. The result has been exactly what you would expect it to be. There haven't been many D. H. Lawrences around waiting to express the truth about sex—or about anything else—on the screen. But there have been lots of exploiters waiting around for serious people to bring down the bars and allow the exploiters to do what such people will do. And even good filmmakers have been badly affected by the climate.

RB: Are you saying that even good filmmakers use sex in exploitative ways that have little or nothing to do with the purposes of their films?

SK: That's exactly what I'm saying. And I say it, though obviously I would hate anyone to believe I was advocating censorship, which does not seem to me to be the answer to anything.

RB: And would you say that good filmmakers are routinely guilty of exploitation—not just occasionally?

SK: I'd go so far as to say that I can think of only a few steamy bedroom scenes that seem to me essential to the films they're in, where, if they weren't present, you'd feel that something essential was missing. Among recent films I think of *Enemies,* made from the Isaac Bashevis Singer novel. In that film it's essential that we see the violent sex, because the participants are both concentration camp survivors, and you have to see them relishing, and affirming, and reclaiming in effect what had been taken from them, in order to understand what is actually a part of their characters. The sex scenes seem very much a part of the milieu and the tenor of the film. But of how many other recent films can you say that?

RB: And why is it that one rarely comes upon such distinctions, or objections, in responses to recent films?

SK: To say such things in print on anything like a regular basis is certainly to give aid and comfort to the enemies of art. And those enemies do exist.

There are bigots and there are those who want to censor books and paintings and films. And of course you don't want to help them.

RB: Nor, I suppose, do you want to offer serious readers the impression that this is what seems to you most important about the films you review.

SK: It isn't the most important thing about them, or not always, but it is a symptom of other problems.

RB: Are you thinking of, say, violence in film?

SK: That's a problem, no doubt, but it's another kind of problem, though it does bear on the whole issue of aesthetic utility we've been talking about.

RB: For one thing, literature and film have long portrayed violence without routinely resorting to the kind of obliquity deployed in the treatment of sex.

SK: That's true, though in recent films the violence has become extreme in a way that suggests a significant change. I'd like to have a penny for every bullet that's fired in *Die Hard II*. And of course it's hard to take a film seriously when virtually all of its characters are involved in the violence, when all but the hero are shot and killed.

RB: But you were saying that the violence is another kind of problem. In what sense?

SK: In the sense that the actual visceral response to violence is different. For most of the filmgoing audience the response to the violence is not as participatory.

RB: Many sociologists dispute that.

SK: I know they do, but I think they're wrong. The average filmgoer watching a violent episode in a film isn't identifying with the participants, imagining what it would feel like to kill all of those people. But the same filmgoer, watching the nude body of an actor going through the motions of sex, thinks, "oh, that's what x or y looks like when he or she is having intercourse." The viewer feels that he is privy to the private experience of the actor, and identifies with one or another participant in the lovemaking. While it's impossible to take seriously the violence in most violent films, audiences take very seriously the sex scenes.

RB: And would you say then that the distraction from everything else that might matter in the film is greater when the emphasis is on explicit sex than when it's on violence?

SK: That may be. But in any case, there are visceral differences. With violence you might also say that, given how much of it there is, it's almost impossible for audiences to respond to the real thing when they're confronted with it. Not many viewers feel the difference between the unbelievable violence in *Die Hard II* and the extreme but authentic violence in a film like Sam Peckinpah's *The Wild Bunch.* That film calls to mind the writings on violence of Antonin Artaud, who sees in certain kinds of theatrical violence a refuge and hope. I don't say that is exactly what I feel about Peckinpah's work, but at least it's possible to entertain such a thought when you see his film.

RB: Are you comparably impressed by the authenticity of the violence in the work of Martin Scorsese?

SK: Scorsese is a very serious man, though not always a successful artist. I don't think I would ever accuse him of using gratuitous violence, but in a film like *Taxi Driver* he seems a little sophomoric in his conception of violence. This is not the case in *Raging Bull,* where the violence—there's a lot of it—is absolutely essential, and not at all a matter of a concept to which the director is mostly unequal. Even the slow motion violence, which is usually exploitative and objectionable, in *Raging Bull* is acceptable. You see through it all that Scorsese is really making a film about immigration, about one immigrant population in the United States, how it's been trying to fight its way into the warp and woof of American society. The violence doesn't distract us from that, it helps us to understand the struggle, which is not only about becoming a boxer, but about getting out of the immigrant ghetto. All of the flying blood and aggression are in the service of something more.

RB: Why do you think so many people are turned on by the grotesque images of a film like Peter Greenaway's *The Cook, the Thief, His Wife and Her Lover?*

SK: It offers a fake sophistication and an easy symbolism. What could be easier—more childish, really—than those pictorial symbols of maggots on meat, or people making love surrounded by hanging food? It must seem very "advanced" to think about the link between sexual appetite and other kinds of appetite. The film treats in a seemingly sophisticated way really banal high school insights into human behavior. And like a high school boy, the director lays on the disgusting details as a proof, apparently, that he's got a mature vision, that he flinches from nothing. He's the sort of fellow who thinks he's really getting at the nitty gritty when he shows sex taking place in the stall of a toilet in a ladies' room. This is his version of what he'd no doubt call basic animal instinct. He must think we'd otherwise not get the connection between human sex and sex in general.

RB: I'd love to spend an afternoon with you studying the similarities and differences between the Greenaway film and *Going Places.* Much that you say about the one seems to me largely applicable to the other, though I'd never accuse Blier of the sophomoric indulgences you cite in the Greenaway. Is the popularity of the more recent film, and other ostensibly serious films like it, a sign that there's not much hope for the future of the medium?

SK: You know as well as I do that there's not one single logical reason why there should ever be another good film made. The conditions of film-making, in this country and in others, are now so stringent that it would seem almost impossible to predict that good films can emerge. And yet they do. There have been many more good American films during these last years than there have been good American plays since, say, 1925. And that has been so in spite of the fact that, to make a profit, films much reach audiences many times larger than the audience for even a successful play. I can't explain that, but it's so. You think of recent films by David Mamet and Sam Shepard, and you might almost forget that the overwhelming number of recent films are straight, mainline, factory produced, and stupid.

RB: Would you say that the situation is much the same elsewhere?

SK: The economics of filmmaking are always, or almost always, very important in terms of what is likely to get made. But the conditions vary, obviously, from one place to another. And there are times, too, when one or two people can temporarily change things. You think of the legend of Godard and the French new wave of the late fifties and early sixties. The legend has it that Godard made his first feature film, *Breathless,* for $1.98, with a lot of talented people chipping in their own money because they were so enthusiastic about the project. Included in the legend—this sort of thing received a huge amount of publicity—was Godard's inability to secure a travelling camera, to afford a dolly and other kinds of equipment. And so Godard put his gifted cinematographer into a supermarket shopping cart and had him holding onto his camera while his legs dangled over the edge and Godard wheeled him about. From this stemmed all the talk of Godard's enormous virtuosity, his improvisatory courage, his creation of a really wonderful revolutionary atmosphere in which it was possible to make something entirely new. Such antics were associated in legend with the pre-1968 era leading up to the cultural revolutions of the late sixties. And of course the people associated with that era did produce several wonderful films.

But *Going Places* appeared after 1968, after the failure of the revolution and the waning of the spirit of the era. The opening sequence of the film has Gerard Depardieu sitting in a shopping cart being pushed around by Patrick Dewaere. But they're not making a film. Their object is to pinch the behind of a woman who's running away. This was, to me, a clear statement, to the effect of "So much for your revolution." And once you recognize the semi-private in-joke, you see that for a new generation Godard is old hat, the revolution is old hat, not much more than a joke, and all that lies ahead is outrageous hedonism, which is required to fill the vacuum left by the departed hopes of an earlier new wave. That opening sets the tone for the entire picture to follow, for all of the outrageousness and exploitation. For these people in *Going Places* one thing is like any other, what they do to women they do because it gives them pleasure and no apology is necessary. When they break into a house they do what comes naturally: they eat the food, they drink the wine, they look about for a woman, and when no woman appears for them to have sex with, they have sex with each other. Warm bodies, that's what they're after, and there's not much difference between one warm body and another. It's just this kind of iconoclasm as fate that is established right from the opening shots. Now the spirit of *Going Places* is obviously very much at odds with the spirit of Godard, and yet it's clear to me that both Blier and Godard defy the conditions of filmmaking that seem so insuperable to others who make films. And that's what I mean when I say that, though there are no general reasons for the continued appearance of good new films, we're likely to have more of them in the future.

RB: D. W. Griffith—speaking of the movies—once said that "Hollywood made an industry of what should have been an art." Do you see any developments in the film industry that will allow us—once and for all, or not simply in a minor key—to take the movies away from the technocrats and give them back to the people who need and live through them without merely having that recovery process turn into an archival process?

SK: I have to quarrel a bit with your question because it has a sort of "lost paradise" suggestion about it. There are film historians who feel that the U.S. was ideally suited—apart from technological and industrial advantages—to become the dominating country in film because it had a short history and no aristocracy, and because it was founded and continued as a democracy. And since film began and was promoted as the working man's theater—that's what it was called—it spread like wildfire throughout the world. Let's say that's a demotic reason for the growth of film in this country as against others.

At present there are discernible at least three important streams of film-making. The first one is the most visible kind, theatrical filmmaking, which is a capitalistic enterprise and in the cause of which many of those works that we love have been made. Then there is the stream for which there are several names—avant-garde, underground, whatever—gallery films as opposed to theatre films which address the opportunities, challenges, and rewards that have been traditionally handled by the graphic arts. Some of the filmmakers associated with this stream, including Stan Brakhage, are people who have tremendous unrecognized reputations based on a record of genuine achieve-ment. There are numerically few enthusiasts who work for these people and champion their work. My conditioning is theatrical. Those films mean less to me than others, though I get rewards from some of them. The third, possibly least known kind of filmmaking might be called personal or documentary filmmaking. There are lots of individuals and small teams—most of them politically impelled—making films on tiny budgets all over the country, packing them into suitcases and carrying them from campus to campus. One surfaces into the theatrical world once in a while. A particularly noteworthy one was made about five years ago—by a Canadian named Jerry Bruck—and was called *I. F. Stone,* a thrilling documentary about a troublesome, cantan-kerous, independent man. Another film of this kind surfaced recently and got an academy award—*Harlan County, U.S.A.,* a picture made by a young woman named Barbara Kopple. The two latter kinds of films—gallery films and private documentaries—are two kinds of film which are responding to the possibilities you talked about, Bob.

RB: I want us to go on with this, but I do think we should hold off long enough to say a word or two about theatre in America. Maybe it doesn't belong in an interview mostly devoted to film, but you at least have managed to write about both arts with some regularity.

SK: When people ask about theatre in America, what they usually mean is, "Is there any good playwriting going on in America?" My opinion of American playwriting is very, very low, and I've tried to fight the kind of Chamber of Commerce "Let's keep the Theatre Alive" hoopla that goes on in the New York press all the time. Still, I've served for four years on the theatre advisory panel of the National Endowment for the Arts. The first time I went to review applications I felt a little sad about American theatre, even though I teach prospective professionals at the Yale Drama School. For several years I read several thousand grant proposals from theatre groups all over the country. Theatre in this country is in a very vital state. There's lots of it and of great variety—not much of the first rank, but still it's alive. To me there's an analogy here with publishing. A publisher has to keep a house going so that if a great book comes along, he'll be ready to publish it. These theatres have to keep going so that if a great playwright comes along, or at least an exceptionally promising new play, they'll be there to employ the talent to produce it. The only thing that obscures the state of theatre in this country is the vast, overwhelming presence of film.

RB: Let's follow up a little on the question of theatre in America. Is serious American drama at present still largely imitative of European models or are we developing a serious tradition of our own? I have my own views on the question, but I'd like you to handle it.

SK: That's a complex question. I—like a lot of people who go to the theatre—am bored to death by a lot of talent. Harold Clurman said America is lousy with talent. He meant that America has assumed a distinction between talent and work. If you show talent, you're OK: you can get grants. You can go on for fifty years and never write a realized, satisfactory work of art, and still make a very good living. America is full of playwriting talent. I deal a little with it, tangentially, at Yale. American theater is very low right now, and one of the reasons is that you can't find—particularly among the much boosted work talked about in Section II of the Sunday *New York Times*—any distinct cultural voices. Good works are almost always rooted culturally. There is a stunning group of contemporary, young English playwrights (like Edward Bond) who are writing out of their country's dilemmas and agonies—very personally, not didactically. They are rooted in a history that leads to *them*. That kind of personal summation of a national anguish or joy is not present in the work of any American playwright with the sole exception of Sam Shepard.

But there's something else that's happening in theatre all over the world. Theatre is occupying itself with more than the traditional business of taking a script, learning the lines, and delivering them with verisimilitude. There are artists working in this country like Robert Wilson and Elizabeth Swados who are trying to find within theatrical instrumentality a way of compensating for—indeed of overcoming—the fact that plays are not being written. They recognize a kind of authorial bankruptcy among writers today, a result of all sorts of things including cultural and spiritual desolation. Writers aren't writing well for the theatre these days, so Wilson and Swados are doing something to use the wonderful means of theatre, not just in compensation for, but in triumph over this state.

RB: The trouble with our discussion of film and drama is that it has stopped short. What are we supposed to be serious *about?* The question of content has been evaded. Maybe some of us think that the question of content *has* to be avoided. It's hard to talk about it, and some think we're not *supposed* to talk about it. It seems to me that there is a distinct contrast between the arts and sociology and history. The people in social science seem to take for granted that sociology, philosophy, and history are not disciplines primarily about themselves, but are disciplines which have something to say about American life, that engage specific ideologies that have specific political implications. The people in the arts have studiously avoided all such considerations.

I'll be more specific. Susan Sontag, in her excellent book *On Photography,* discusses the implications of the democracy of seeing and begins to say something significant about what photography has to say to us. Her book on photography is not a formalist book, it's a book about the world. I agree with Susan Sontag that it's a waste of time to talk about content unless you are concerned about the specific way content is embodied in particular works, but it's also disastrous to pretend there isn't any content to discuss. When you, Stanley, speak about the absence of a certain kind of national anguish in American films, I wonder what exactly you have in mind. What attitudes do we have in place of national anguish? Somehow we haven't gotten to that. I believe that people concerned about art have to ask the same sorts of questions that political and social scientists ask about their disciplines, even if this means being so vulgar as to treat artistic events historically.

SK: Let me sidestep your challenge to discuss "content" in the arts, in film, and say something I can't imagine anyone disputing—believe it or not. The happiest thing about American films is that they have nothing to do with art. I think we get into trouble in Hollywood only when the people who are producing begin to think that they are creating art instead of a commodity which is to be sold to the public. The anecdote which comes to mind is the classic argument which took place between Samuel Goldwyn and George

Bernard Shaw over filming *Pygmalion*. Shaw finally said to Goldwyn, "The trouble between us, Mr. Goldwyn, the reason we shall never agree about how to proceed, is that you think of nothing but art, and my only concern is money." When Francis Ford Coppola thought of nothing but money he made marvelous films. When he began thinking about Joseph Conrad and T. S. Eliot, he made schlock.

A Coupla White Guys Sittin' Aroun' Talkin': A Conversation with Stanley Kauffmann

Jonathan Kalb / 1992

From *Free Admissions: Collected Theater Writings,* by Jonathan Kalb (New York: Limelight, 1993): 98–102. Originally published in *The Village Voice,* 1992.

Jonathan Kalb: I've been asked to chat with you about what is or ever was valuable in the Off-Broadway and Off-Off Broadway theaters. Do you detect a slightly funereal aroma in this?

Stanley Kauffmann: I see the Off-Broadway and Off-Off Broadway theaters operating in the garments of legacy. There is a sense of continuing rather than propelling. In the earliest days of Off-Broadway and Off-Off Broadway—they started within seven or eight years of each other—there was a sense of bursting creativity, of things rushing into life. Some cheery souls even called it a new Elizabethan age. Those theaters blossomed for something over twenty years. The original impulses have long since waned, have been diluted by various factors, and there isn't much sense of pioneering about those theaters anymore. There's a sense of continuance, a feeling of persistence, and perhaps that's where the funereal aroma comes from. I have to add that I don't go to those theaters as much as I used to, but I get that feeling from reading the *Voice* and from conversations with people like you.

JK: What was the most valuable contribution these two kinds of theater made?

SK: The shift in values they brought about. When I was growing up, when I first began going to the theater before the Second World War, there were no such things as these theaters. There was some activity in Greenwich Village—the Provincetown Playhouse and the Neighborhood Playhouse, although these had withered—but anyone who wanted to work in the theater had only one place to aim toward, and that was Broadway. The latest, smart, commercially minded playwright aimed there, and Eugene O'Neill aimed there, too. That was all there was. The rise of these two other theaters brought a widening of the spectrum and a pluralism in opportunities so that a change of values could be put into effect. Before Off-Broadway and Off-Off Broadway arose, you might have decried and despised Broadway, but that was it. Now there were other options. Of the two most prominent American playwrights of the last twenty-five years, David Mamet never had a play produced on Broadway until very far along in his career. Sam Shepard not yet. Their goals were elsewhere.

These other theaters made possible the crystallization of different kinds of ambition—one of the most important crystallizing forces, incidentally, was Joseph Papp. Before the war you really had the feeling that there was a high, glistening steel wall around the theater, and only by luck could some people get over it or find a crack in it. By what he instituted, Papp made every young person interested in the theater feel: "If you have ability, you will find a place to use it." He changed what seemed to be a jealously guarded preserve into a field of open possibility that depended more on you than on approval from guardians on high.

JK: Could you name some specific high points for you during the heyday of Off- and Off-Off Broadway?

SK: Something that's been overlooked is that their greatest achievements were not a result of jobbing around but rather the work of institutions like the Living Theater and the Open Theater. In the Living Theater, in its early days, you felt that a new kind of blood had flowed into the body of the theater, a new kind of enterprise, a new reason for being. One of the best-directed plays I've ever seen was *The Brig* in the early 1960s, done by Judith Malina, which gave me a glimpse of a vitality that wasn't available anywhere else in this city at that time. *The Brig* was the kind of production that you came away from with a sense of replenishment and a kind of surprise. The Open Theater's *The Serpent,* directed by Joseph Chaikin, still lives in my memory. I thought I was going to hate Andrei Serban's *Fragments of a Trilogy,* which he did with his La Mama company, but it was a transformative experience. I went back about eight times in the succeeding years. Serban would be waiting there when I came out to tick off the number on his fingers: "Number five!" "Number six!" That was one of the best things that ever happened to me in the theater. I thought that that company under Serban was going to be an exemplary force in the American theater. As I understood it, he went off on jobs and the company waited on unemployment insurance for him to come back and continue working with them, but he stopped coming back and they disbanded. I consider the disappearance of that company the greatest sin of

the non-Broadway theater. This past January I went to France to see Mnouchkine's production of three Greek plays, and it was absolutely thrilling in
every serious sense of that word. But it was also sad, because I thought, "This
is what the Serban company might have been if it had worked together under
one leader for as long as the Mnouchkine company."

JK: People of my generation can admire certain achievements of those
years, through books, films, or other sorts of reports, but we have trouble
believing a lot of the lofty rhetoric. The communalist ethic, the sensualist
ethic—it's all very hard to swallow after the fall of the Berlin Wall in the age
of AIDS. Furthermore, whenever I hear the Off- or Off-Off Broadway theater
described as a haven of cozy laboratory experimentation I have to laugh,
because I've worked in some of those theaters and I know it's anything but
safe or cozy there.

SK: Yes. I'm sure that's true. Although some of them still talk about "the
right to fail." How I hate that phrase.

JK: So let me ask you: what was real and what was rhetoric in all those
claims about using the greater intimacy between audience and stage to develop a new sense of community?

SK: It's right for you to entertain doubts, because reminiscence is always
tinged with a kind of ego. "You missed it; I didn't." But if I may reminisce,
egotistically, it seems to me that there *was* a real sense of community
there—a community derived from a simple proposition: there exists a hateful
middle class which owns the commercial theater and we're here to uproot it,
dynamite it. That simple war doesn't exist anymore. No one's revolting
against Broadway anymore. In sheerly artistic terms, no one's revolting
against the middle class anymore. I mean, what more trite kind of theatrical
enterprise could there be today than to do something that exposes the Rotar-
ian aspects of society? It would bore the avant-garde itself, let alone anyone
else. Our vital theater is trying to find ways to be healthily aggressive, healthily purgative, and the battlefield lacks terrain. Instead of fighting to cure this
or that, most people are fighting to find out what to fight about.

JK: Maybe you're right, but I don't feel that the problem is lack of talent.
I know some extremely talented, even brilliant, people. A more important
factor for me is that New York City has become a place where the sort of
people who once supported this art can't survive. It used to be possible to
maintain a bohemian lifestyle in the Village, working at odd jobs and so on.

Now the ostensibly "alternative" scene is filled with people so busy scratch-
ing the rent together they barely have time to think about art, NYU students
shooting film, and an army of recent college grads with rich parents willing
to support their desire to act bohemian. For those not born to privilege it has
become too harsh and unforgiving a place to concentrate on anything. I once
said to Jim Leverett that people my age always had the feeling of arriving
just after the party ended. He shot back, "Make a new party, Jonathan." I
should have answered, "That's easy for someone your age to say."

SK: You've put your finger on something very important. New York in the
1950s was more or less what it had been in the preceding part of this century—that is, a white, middle-class city. And Greenwich Village was what it
had been historically in the days of O'Neill and Edna St. Vincent Millay,
only brought a little up to date. We now live in a radically changed city,
racially and in many other ways, and New York is really trying to find out
what it is. In the midst of all this turbulence and turmoil there's no possibility
of anything like a bohemian life. The demographics have changed, and consequently so have the cultural obligations.

JK: Can we talk about those obligations? The word for all this is multicul-
turalism, which many people think should ideally involve a form of affirma-
tive action, since certain people, even whole classes of people, were
previously excluded from being heard. What do you believe?

SK: Here's the time for a large pronouncement. I certainly do believe they
were excluded and that something should be done about it, provided—and
this is a heavy proviso—that artistic standards don't get lowered. Why
shouldn't every racial group, every sexual group, every political group have
cultural representation? These people have the energy to counteract the funereal air we were talking about at the start; they're greatly beneficial so long
as they aren't praised just because they are of whatever race or persuasion
they are.

JK: Are you saying that you see a relaxing of standards for the sake of
inclusion?

SK: I certainly do, in education, in the theater, and everywhere else. We
won't go into the subject of hiring faculty people by reason of gender and
color of skin, because it inevitably sounds as if I'm against the other gender
or certain colors of skin—which is not at all what I mean. It's a given that
there's no going back for society. We're not going to return to a completely
white, completely heterosexual (on the surface) city. What we have to do is

go forward, keeping the *best* of what we've learned from the past in operation for the benefit of everyone concerned. Otherwise there's no point in the theater existing. Put the money into bridges and hospitals if we're not going to do this. The theaters must exist at their best according to the best of our tradition.

JK: But you know the problem here. Whose standards are to be used in determining what is "best"? Those of white male Stanley Kauffmann or white male Jonathan Kalb?

SK: No, it's myself and yourself as two of the inheritors of a world tradition that's funneled down and crystallized through centuries of the European American tradition. Of course, I'm not saying there are absolute standards of good and bad, but surely there's not much question about the areas of art in which the highest standards operate, where they come from, what they tend toward. When a group with a specialized interest says that other standards must prevail, they know they are rejecting the tradition, which has been growing for at least 5000 years in the Western world and which made them possible. The standards of X theater, which says that it is not going to be dominated by white, heterosexual, European inheritance, are consciously disruptive of a historical line, which I hope will always be open to growth but which I take to be fundamentally nourishing. It's very difficult to talk about this without sounding prescriptive, but any man or woman of whatever ethnic background or sexual persuasion who is cultivated in the Western tradition at its broadest, most humane, most liberal, most helpful, understands what this is about. And when they choose not to engage that understanding, they are often doing it for non-artistic reasons. And I think the theater is a poor place to do things for nonartistic reasons.

JK: I marvel at your courage in defending the Western tradition so unrestrainedly. I guess you don't have to worry about being called "old." Lately, I find myself increasingly forced to answer questions like this in the most unfriendly circumstances. So many people my age or younger, white by birth, "of color" by conviction, believe that the Enlightenment is necessarily something imposed from above and enforced by institutions with exclusive policies. How do you respond to, say, a graduate student who believes he or she is of a revolutionary state of mind?

SK: If you want to indulge in the twentieth-century pipe dream of revolutionary explosion, then you're bound to end up at an impasse. I think that's just a form of narcotic. I think it's been woefully proved to be so. Our world may disappear, but I doubt that it'll be through that kind of political explosion. Look, this is very large, very inclusive, very sweeping, and I suppose ultimately ridiculous, what I've just been saying, because it's so easy to ridicule. But in art it seems to me that the real triumph for all those groups—Asian people, black people, brown people, homosexual people—is not to splinter away from the best of the past but to enter into it, reshape it, renew it. This is obviously—I hope obviously—not to say that there shouldn't be black theater, Jewish theater, Asian or homosexual or feminist or any other kind of theater, each with its own thematic agenda. It's only to say that the artistic progress of those groups, in my view, is not in fragmentation. It's in taking possession of what there is to take possession of.

JK: After centuries of abuse, though, it's perfectly understandable that disadvantaged groups would jump at real chances for power and hegemony, and the real chance for power in the theater lies in the smaller institutions of Off- and Off-Off Broadway. The non-Broadway theater world is as preoccupied with power struggles as with aesthetic struggles, and that situation shows little sign of changing. What is it that you and I think we're upholding in such an environment?

SK: Nothing about the power struggle—anyway, not as far as I'm concerned. But a good deal about the aesthetic struggle. We want the disadvantaged to have the best of what they've been shut out of, to add to it, not diminish it, to give to it and get. To serve their causes by, so to speak, beating the mainstream at its own game. To take a foreign example: a woman who wanted to shake the theater awake, to dramatize political and social views, and who shamed the orthodox theater by beating it at its own game, Ariane Mnouchkine.

The Film Generation and After: A Conversation with Stanley Kauffmann

Bert Cardullo / 1992

From *South Atlantic Quarterly* 91, no. 2 (Spring 1992), 459–97.

Cardullo: How has the academicization of film—in film courses, film departments, and film criticism—helped to shrink the audience for serious film? You brought that up in your "After the Film Generation" article, it fascinates me, and I tend to agree with you: the compartmentalization of film has done something to hurt students' interest in film. I'd like you to comment on that if you will.

Kauffmann: It's a paradox—the educational activities in film, the positing of film in college curricula that went on furiously from about 1960 on. At first, the effect was to make film more important, more necessary, more feverishly acquirable for students. I suppose that's still true of people who are film specialists, but I think the situation has changed for those who are just generalists about film, who are interested in film only as one of the increments of their cultural life. And this has a certain parallel, I think, with what happened long ago in literature. Let's assume that there were once people who read, read with pleasure and freely; then literature became for them a straitened, compartmentalized, curricular activity. At the beginning, I think the teaching of literature in colleges and universities helped people—I'm speaking always about the general person, not the specialist. But later, I think, it became for them a means of, in their minds, finishing with literature. "I've read my great books, now I'm free."

Cardullo: Let me just add, to back you up, that I know I felt this way after I graduated from college, and I've talked to friends who have said, "After I left college, I didn't read a book for a year."

Kauffmann: That's conservative, a year. "I've read my books," a lot of them feel. I think that happened with film. I don't mean that people stopped going to films after they finished their film courses, which they took on their way to becoming doctors, lawyers, or just general good citizens. But that their interest in any kind of expansion or extension of themselves as the result of film experience, in taking any kind of trouble to see films, was something they associated with the moribund past, with note-taking, exams, and papers.

Cardullo: Well, as a college student in the early 1970s, I never took a film course, and I like that. What we felt then, I and my friends, was that we were discovering film along with frontline critics like you, and once film became part of the academy, it was as if that process of discovery had disappeared. It had been taken over by establishment academics.

Kauffmann: And in a certain sense, mummified. Going to a film was no longer a question of experience, but of visiting a tomb. That's of course regrettable for literature, for art history, for any art that gets studied systematically in the university.

Cardullo: I think that for a while, this academicization of film hurt my interest in it—to see film being written about in third- and fourth-class journals, to see certain canons being established that had no business being established, was dispiriting.

Kauffmann: Once film got established as part of the curriculum, that meant people were teaching it, then that meant they had academic careers. They had to work for promotion in their departments, they had to please their deans, etc. I don't mean to disparage en bloc, with a grand gesture, all the people who are teaching film and writing about it in this country; we're speaking in the most broad, general terms here. You and I both know people whom we admire very much as individuals who are teaching film and writing about it from academic positions, but, in general, the most of anything is humdrum, and the most of film teaching and writing is humdrum. What does the humdrum person do when he is teaching film and needs to gain a certain stature for himself? He resorts to vogue, to critical vogue. It's easier to subscribe to a critical theory than to operate independently as a critical mind and talent. Again, it would be somewhat presumptuous of me to dismiss the great minds of critical theory who've been operating in our time: I'm not talking about them.

Cardullo: I know what you mean, you mean the epigones.

Kauffmann: Yes, there are plenty of little epigones, less than epigones— mobsters, let's call them. Faculty mobs need to come under the shelter of some giant critical or theoretical wing because they can't fly on their own.

Cardullo: This leads into a subject that I've thought about a lot lately and that I'd like to bring up because you've been a part of it: the controversy over film as popular art versus film as high art. Often if you're an academic in a university looking to make your name, you attempt to "discover" certain directors, to induct them into the pantheon, and, in my view, and I think in yours, certain directors have been elevated in status, directors whom one would normally consider "popular," such as Frank Capra. You've been criticized in your career as being a literary or "highbrow" film critic, and in a recent letter to you at the *New Republic*, the writer brought up the fact that you have always stood strongly for the distinction between popular and high art in film. I'd like you to comment on that, because I think it is related to this whole issue of the academicization of film.

Kauffmann: Well, it's amusing because, depending on the day of the week, I get a letter berating me for this schism in my thinking, telling me that I'm snobbish toward pop film, or I get a letter applauding me for this schism but at the same time berating me because I seem to have become less snobbish of late toward pop film. I'm told, in the latter case, that I'm trying to please the yuppies who would rather rent *Ghostbusters* instead of any Bresson film. Of course, this is always strange to me—finding out how people read, what they find in you that you have no intent of putting there. I have never, in any way, taken a stance about film in terms of pop or high art. The distinction used to be posed in terms of American versus foreign films. It never was that way for me arbitrarily, categorically. What happened was that, if, in the course of a year, I reviewed fifty films, I discovered when I went over the list at the end of the year that forty of the ones I'd liked were foreign films. It's retrospective rather than prospective for me. The foreign versus American distinction got translated into the distinction between high art and pop art. I don't know how far we want to explore that now; it's been much belabored in the last thirty years. I certainly believe that there's a difference between the two. I'm not in favor of eradicating the difference, as some rather highly placed thinkers are; I certainly am not. I think that the differences are discernible and that those differences ought to be in the mind of the critic, ought to be in the mind of the intelligent viewer, without being prescriptive. And the matter is further complicated because—and this is where it becomes really muzzy because I seem to be coming to agree with the pop elevators— there are some pop films that are more than good entertainment, that become fine works of art. The first example that always comes to mind is *Some Like It Hot*. I think that *Some Like It Hot* is a great film, by any standards.

Cardullo: Well, the elevation of *Some Like It Hot* comes in tandem with the elevation of farce in dramatic literature to higher status than it has heretofore had.

Kauffmann: Yes, it's true that there has been a terrible, snooty prejudice against comedy as being lesser. There is a very fine book on Beethoven by J. W. N. Sullivan that I read when I was a college student, and he prefers the first, third, fifth, seventh, and ninth symphonies of Beethoven because the second, fourth, sixth, and eighth tend to be jolly. Well, you just extend that principle artibrarily, and you end up in a cement bag with the cement hardening. It's fundamentally in the brightest people that you see this attitude—and it's a stupid attitude, to be prejudiced thus against comedy. I'm willing to stake a good deal, for example, that Richard Lester's marvelous film comedy *How I Won the War* is one of the most important pictures of the 1960s. What you've raised is pertinent, but the final distinction between the comic and the serious is not between the low and the high, because there are people on both sides of this pop-art, high-art schism who take comedy very seriously. And what we come down to, finally, is what we want a film to be and to do, without derogating the film that pleases us but that doesn't do those things.

Cardullo: Let's clarify our terms briefly. When students ask me what the difference between popular art and high art is, I say, "Popular art more or less *reflects* what's going on in society at a particular time, whereas high art *examines* and sometimes criticizes what's going on."

Kauffmann: That's a perfectly tenable and useful distinction. Another distinction, connected with what you've just said, is that popular art is made to make money.

Cardullo: Right.

Kauffmann: *All* films are made to make money, but pop art is made *primarily* to make money. And serious films *hope* to make money but are made primarily because they say something for the people making them. Yet another distinction is between the impersonal, committee film that's cooked up by—

Cardullo: By the Hollywood studios.

Kauffmann: By a *lot* of people around filmmaking, sometimes quite cleverly, and the film that is the project of one or two people who must make it, who want to make it, and who will do anything to make it.

Cardullo: Say, a team like Zavattini and De Sica.

Kauffmann: Yes, there are many such examples, as you know, and there are lots of Americans who are trying to do that kind of thing.

Cardullo: Let's take a relatively recent, contrary example, *The Untouchables*. *The Untouchables* could not be regarded as a serious piece of work in the terms we are using here, but it's entertaining.

Kauffmann: *The Untouchables* was directed by a man consecrated to pop, Brian De Palma. The film was originated by a producer who was smart enough to get David Mamet to write the screenplay. And then they, as I understand it, engaged De Palma to direct it because he is adept at the making, the exaltation, of genre films—and most genre films are pop films. What they did was to take a 1935-type film, a gangster picture, "colorize" it, expand it in every conceivable direction—not just in screen size, but in tones of character, in quality of acting, in subtlety of camera work and editing—and thus make it an apotheosis of a 1935 film. It's as if someone took a 1935 automobile and restyled it for the late 1980s in such a way that it fit the 1980s but still bore visible and enjoyable vestiges of the 1930s. We got into all this because I'm using *The Untouchables* as an instance of the film made for no other reason than to be a hit.

Cardullo: And those who have trouble with it, like me, are people who went to it, based on the reviews of some critics, expecting more.

Kauffmann: Yes. Immediately that such a film gets made, it's idolized, iconized.

Cardullo: And that often happens with De Palma.

Kauffmann: It happens with many directors, many of them better than De Palma. Rhapsodies follow upon their work, so ecstatic that they are misleading, and you become disgusted with the result when you see it. That's another subject, however. I picked *The Untouchables* as an instance; every one of us would have different instances. The basic point is that the serious critic, the serious viewer, who can't enjoy what to him is a good entertainment film, is lacking in full capacity for enjoying the best film, I think. Ingmar Bergman once said that he loved the idea that his films are shown on the same screen that showed Bob Hope the night before.

Cardullo: I'd like to address the corollary of what we've been talking about, and that is the insistent criticism over the years that your film reviews have a literary bent. I understand why people make this criticism of you, but I don't agree with it; I think it has to do with this distinction, again, between high art and popular art. And I'd like you to address this subject, if you would.

Kauffmann: Well, I've always been amused, because my critics don't know what my chief defect is. It's a defect I hope I've amended in the course of time—it was certainly there when I began. My defect wasn't that I had been writing novels; I think I published seven before I ever wrote film criticism—six, and the seventh came out later. It was that I approached films from the *theatrical* point of view, not from the literary one. I was educated for the theater, I worked for ten years in a repertory company, I'd written plays, I'd done some other work around the theater. Through these years I had always been going to films and loving them, but I always thought of them as secondary.

Cardullo: As something a stage actor did when he couldn't get a New York theater job.

Kauffmann: Yes, when he, or a director or a writer, couldn't get work in the theater. I thought that it was wonderful to have films around, but they were like the vegetables around the roast: the roast was what mattered. And through a series of accidents, I became a film critic. And when I look back at some of those early reviews of mine, what I see is a theater person going to films.

Cardullo: A theater person who read, and reads, books.

Kauffmann: I can't help that. I'm sorry. And I also review books quite a lot. My aesthetic objection is to the idiot-savant approach to film—the idea that one can and should know only one thing and that the arts don't enrich one another. I simply disagree. My own conditioning, training, and interests—strong interests, I presume to think—are to write about three fields: theater, film, and literature. And I can't see any more logic in my being debarred from film criticism because I review books than vice versa. I know a good many distinguished literary critics and not one of them has ever said to me, "Oh, you're a film man, you shouldn't review books." There's a certain nervousness in the film world which doesn't obtain in other fields. There's a certain eagerness to preempt territory and sometimes the person's sole claim to preemption is that he doesn't know anything except film. That's pretty slim qualification for film criticism, I think, as nothing but theater knowledge would be slim qualification for theater criticism.

Cardullo: Your theater background is certainly clear in your analysis and criticism of acting.

Kauffmann: I hope that's true, I've wanted it to be, and I hope that it hasn't diminished. But I hope also that, through the years, I've learned more about film and about film values as such. I'm very anti the auteur theory, you know, but I owe the auteur theory a debt. It made me look at films as films. And the auteur critics made me make the examination of purely filmic values part—not by any means the primary part, as it is with them, but certainly *a* part—of my criticism.

Cardullo: It's interesting that you say you're against the auteur theory. I'm against it *and* for it because, on the one hand, as you suggest, it is good to look at film as an autonomous, unique art form. Please explicate the other side.

Kauffmann: The other side is summed up in one word: priorities. I can't be expected, I as an individual, can't be expected to leave at the door of the film theater all my experience of life and art, and concentrate only on what the film has to offer me. I can't be expected to leave at the door my knowledge, insofar as I have it, of psychology, of acting, of structure, of stories, of depth of theme, of political relevance, of social weight, etc., and say, "But ah, look at the way he panned across that room and then segued into that beautiful long shot."

Cardullo: Max Ophüls is the prime example.

Kauffmann: Max Ophüls, yes. I can't be expected rationally, aesthetically, to substitute that sheerly cinematic value for all the other things that I've been asked to check at the door.

Cardullo: And what you say connects with what we said earlier about the academicization of film, in that film critics and supporters have felt the need to justify films *as films* as opposed to films in comparison with literature and paintings and music.

Kauffmann: That is true. They've had to plump for, to campaign for the sheerly cinematic as a raison d'être. In my opinion, again a matter of false weight.

Cardullo: The other aspect of the auteur theory that you might comment on is this idea that you can't view an auteur's film in itself, you have to view it as part of his entire career. Auteur critics do this with John Ford all the time—looking for stylistic signature in every film and becoming ecstatic when they find it, apart from its connection with the rest of the film.

Kauffmann: I agree with this idea as a principle; it's the ostentation of it that seems to me odd. Hitchcock directed a film called *Stage Fright,* which is surely by anyone's standard, including Hitchcock's, one of the worst films, mystery films, that he made or anyone has made. But it's seen as virtually equivalent with the best Hitchcock films because it's by Hitchcock.

Cardullo: It has the Hitchcock tics.

Kauffmann: Yes. On the other hand, it would be impossible, and in a sense cruel, to come to *Stage Fright,* just to keep that as an example, without keeping Hitchcock's whole career in mind. It's slavishness to doctrine that one objects to, not necessarily to the doctrine itself. The auteur theory is a doctrine that has contributed a lot, I think, to film thinking. Recently, by the way, Harvard University Press published two collections of material, edited by Jim Hillyer, from *Cahiers du cinéma.* The first one deals with the magazine's earliest years and therefore is concentrated on the auteur theory. *Cahiers* has since become a structuralist, Marxist magazine; it was in its first ten years or so thoroughly auteur. I wrote a long review of that book for the *New Republic* and I tried to identify the auteur theory with the post–World War II surge of *happiness* about the film as such. This theory originated in France, and it was just happiness that film existed as a fresh art for a new generation that wanted to be rid of the trappings and moral debts of the past. This feeling was conveyed in the course of time to America in a different context. I'll give you a wide analogy: it's like communism coming to this country from another country in which it had some pertinence and application. People gathering to overthrow governments in the Balkans are a little different from people gathering in Union Square here to overthrow the forces of the White House, which they used to do—talk about—in the 1930s. Likewise, transported auteurism became a very different item here. It ceased to be the reclamation of the future by the young and became in this country a mode, a vogue, an academic imperative for a time. Of course, by now, it's quite démodé, auteurism.

Cardullo: You yourself have several times quoted Bazin's line, "Auteur, yes, but of what?" Auteur critics don't like to think that Bazin had this attitude. But in translating some of his reviews, I've had it reemphasized for me that he knew the differences between films—by the same director and by different directors—knew that some were better than others.

Kauffmann: But he also saw, as I read him, the value of the auteur theory, which was to make us look at the virtues of the text. People have said—I have said, others have said—that there is a certain parallel between the auteur theory and the New Criticism, which was a corrective of the biographical, psychological, and Marxist criticisms that had taken over literature. It said, "Come, let's look at what we're talking about here, which is the text on the page."

Cardullo: And it did its job.

Kauffmann: Yes, and auteurism, I think, helped in the same way.

Cardullo: There's another side of auteurism that we haven't discussed yet and that you've brought up numerous times in your reviews. In fact, I think you wrote an article on this very subject. That is, crediting the various aspects of a film—cinematography, editing, casting, etc. Which is to say, you may have an auteur, but often he's not the auteur of everything you see— obviously he cannot be the auteur of everything you see. A great cinematographer can make a filmmaker, as Sven Nykvist has, in part, made Bergman, and a great screenwriter can make a director.

Kauffmann: *Matewan,* directed by John Sayles, speaks to this point. The triumph in that film for me is the cinematography of Haskell Wexler, or, to take an earlier example that more people will know, a film by Howard Hawks called *Twentieth Century.* Now everyone says, "Oh, Hawks," and tries to find virtues in Hawks's work in that film. Of course he's a highly gifted director, that's not arguable, but for me the auteur of that film is John Barrymore. Hawks could auteur six ways from Sunday, but the film wouldn't *exist* without Barrymore. The same thing is true, at a higher level, of Dreyer's *Passion of Joan of Arc.* Who'd care for all of Dreyer's miraculous art—and it is marvelous—if it weren't for the central miracle of Falconetti's performance? Of course he helped her with that, so in part you could say that his auteurism reads through her, but she did it.

Cardullo: Another example is Ted Post's *Go Tell the Spartans.* Post's screenwriter, Wendell Mayes, transformed Daniel Ford's novel, he significantly improved it, and without that script, there'd be no *Go Tell the Spartans.* So the auteur theory is always—was always—suspicious.

Kauffmann: The latter-day auteurists, insofar as that's still a tenable term, have tried to make up for this shortcoming by talking about other kinds of auteurs who operate in film, about the actor or screenwriter or cinematographer as auteur. But centrally, we know that the idea behind auteurism was essentially "the director as auteur."

Cardullo: I'd like to get back now to the negative description of you by some people as a literary film critic, and I'd like to talk about how that criticism of your work is a product of the kinds of criticism being written today. Why do critics—not daily or weekly critics but academic ones—feel this way about you, why do they describe you as such?

Kauffmann: Well, I don't think that they do, so much. The academic critics today, and there weren't that many when I began writing, think of me as an impressionist, just as they think of, to pick a name out of a hat, Irving Howe as an impressionist. That's not to equate myself with Irving Howe, necessarily, although I'm happy to be linked with him.

Cardullo: And you say it's the film buffs who look at you as a literary critic?

Kauffmann: Yes. The academic critics think of me as an impressionist, because I—now I'm putting this in my own terms—deal experientially with film, deal with it analytically in terms of a highly personal set of ineffable standards. That is, I could not possibly codify for you what my beliefs are about film; it's a matter of instances rather than precepts. I don't suppose that we should dampen our ambition for absolute standards in art—we just have to be very careful not to arrive at any. It would be very nice if we could say that X was faulty in liking that element in that picture because we know that element is capital-B Bad. But nobody knows—nobody knows whether that element is capital-B Bad. One can only say that in the light of his own experience, his own psyche, his own pair of eyes, his own experience from his moment of birth until that moment when he saw that film, it struck him as bad and he can explain with internal consistency, at least, why he thought so. That's the most that anyone can say. Of course, if we pursue this to a ridiculous extreme, it would mean that everyone is a good critic. But the way you tell good from lesser critics—for yourself again, only for yourself—is through an experience with them, an experience either that shows them corroborating what you feel or establishing differences which you can respect, but never establishing absolute, die-stamped standards. The academic critics, by contrast, could tell you what their doctrine is, what their standards are, to a great extent; I could not, and to them that's a defect.

Cardullo: To me what they do is a defect because they stifle sensibility when they let doctrine dictate response.

Kauffmann: Again, I'm speaking in a brusque way about a lot of bright people, but I have often thought that for the non-bright who are doctrinaire, doctrine is a substitute for talent. And if I'm anything, I'm a critical talent, and I don't think that's a factor in their thinking at all—intellect and erudition, yes, but not talent. I've read more than one book in which I've been mentioned as someone who was a factor in the author's coming to film and taking it seriously and whom, by implication, that author has now passed, outgrown. I don't mind that in the least, I hope it's true, but I don't for a moment subscribe to the idea that the kind of criticism I practice is outmoded or passé.

Cardullo: I would have to say that the kind of criticism you write, in my experience, is the kind in history that survives, because it has what some would call the impressionist element, what I would call the personal element.

Kauffmann: I agree with you. Eric Bentley, too—the best drama critic we've produced in this country—feels the same way about criticism. That's not to allocate immortality to myself, but I agree with the principle you've stated. Although, of course, when we speak of history, we're only speaking of what has happened up to now.

Cardullo: And George Bernard Shaw, as you know, made the same point about criticism. It has to be personal.

Kauffmann: Well, we both would have thought so, but personality now sometimes evinces itself just in the way an individual handles a well-thumbed deck of cards, critical cards, that have been handed to him by colleagues.

Cardullo: Is there a critical theory ascendant today in film studies and what is its effect?

Kauffmann: Well, there are three theories that are said to be dominant in criticism generally today in this country, three approaches: feminism, Marxism, and structuralism. And I know by looking at journals that, if these three approaches don't prevail in criticism, they're plentifully visible. I have nothing to say against any of them as contributors to enlightenment. It's like being asked to militate against Freud—who wants to? The intelligent person who is alive today and doesn't know Freud isn't exercising his intellect to the fullest extent. I happen to have strong sympathies with feminism, if the feminists care. Marxism has affected me as it must any person, certainly any person my age who's lived through the things I've lived through, and structuralism is an enlightenment in itself. But I simply can't find an intellectual reason or an emotional propellant to make me adopt any one of those approaches as the sole or even primary series of tenets in judging a work of art.

Cardullo: I've always shied away from such theories because each seems to shut off a whole other world of experience.

Kauffmann: Only when you go in and close the door behind you. Not if you take something out of that particular theoretical experience and move on. And that isn't to trivialize the matter, either. I grew up in an age when what are now called macho attitudes were *the* set of attitudes. But I've learned a lot from young women who have been my students at Yale and at the CUNY Graduate Center. That hasn't made me—I will use the phrase—a parochial feminist, but I hope I'm a more understanding human being and critic.

Cardullo: A recent film obliquely on this subject is *Working Girls.* I think that those who have praised the film too highly, feminists among them, are blinded by their own critical theories. I myself didn't care for *Working Girls* because I thought that in many ways it was artless. I know that you saw virtues in it and I'd like you to comment briefly on them.

Kauffmann: Perhaps I should explain that it's a documentary-type fiction film about an expensive brothel in New York, and that its protagonist is a woman who has a master's degree from Yale and works as a prostitute in this brothel. I liked the film, allowing for its odd gallery of male characters. All the males who visit the brothel are eccentric in one way or another—no one is what you would call, if there is such a word, normal; maybe the steady customers of brothels are all eccentric. Aside from the peculiarities of the males in the film, however, what I liked about it was that it was not in the least bit polemic; it dealt with the lives of these girls during the day—I'm using the word "girls" because that's the word they used and that's used in the title. It simply detailed what goes on for them every day and night in this brothel, and that in itself is supposed to carry its own weight. I thought the film, for all its extravagance of characterization in some regards, had a certain reticence in this way. It was for me much stronger than, for example, a Dutch film that came along very soon afterwards, Marleen Gorris's *Broken Mirrors.* Gorris's film was sentimental and lurid; *Working Girls* tried to make its point, and for me in some good measure did make its feminist point, simply by detailing the lives of the women who worked in this brothel.

Cardullo: I think that feminism has been at its worst in exalting this film and making it out to be more than it is. But, then, feminist blinders are what Lizzie Borden had on, to judge from an interview she gave on the CBS television program *Nightwatch,* and I think that's what led her to caricature most of the men. It's a two-way street: theory and practice feed off each other, and both, in this case, are insidious and inane.

Kauffmann: I'm always hesitant about using an interview as a factor in the judgment of a film. I don't think it's fair. I've read interviews that made good people look foolish and I've also read interviews, like many of Bergman's, that add a dimension to the director's work. But one can't use interviews as a factor any more than one can use events off the set as a factor. Does it matter in your judgment of Antonioni's *L'avventura* that he went through hell to get that film financed? Do we like it because of that? Obviously not. It's a great film in itself. What we learned later about Antonioni's difficulties in getting it made increased our admiration for him but was basically irrelevant.

Cardullo: Yes, but all that I'm saying is that I saw the men being caricatured when I saw the film, and Borden's comments in the interview helped to account for the almost contemptuous attitude she had toward the male customers of the brothel.

Kauffmann: I concede the point, and I certainly wouldn't maintain that I've never done that sort of thing in my life—have the resonance of something that was said about a film affect what I thought about it.

Cardullo: Could you talk a bit about the structuralist, as opposed to the feminist, enterprise before we move on to another subject?

Kauffmann: Well, like so much in film criticism, it's trying to be like Daddy. Literary structuralism anteceded it and is much greater in every sense—to begin with, it has a greater body of work on which to operate. And film critics are trying to be like structuralist literary critics; the only way they can prove they are adults is to behave like Daddy, in the approved magisterial fashion. Again, I don't want to adopt a tone that sounds dismissive of a lot of serious and intelligent people, but not all structuralist film critics are intelligent, and even those that are seem to me to some extent blinkered, which I would also say of Marxist critics. Structuralism in film studies has a particular application and use because of the operation of the term "genre." In a certain sense structuralism is more pertinent to film than to any other field because genre is a more potent force in film than it is in other arts. It's obviously discernible in drama, literature, and painting, but it has more potency in film, I think, than it has in the other arts. And by its very nature genre is analyzable by structuralist standards because it is a mode of art in which structure is the chief cause for being.

Cardullo: And structure, for the structuralists, connects ultimately with the structures of society.

Kauffmann: As does genre.

Cardullo: Right, and one of the problems I have with the structualists is that, as we suggested earlier, they flatten all works of art, popular and high, and examine them as artifacts of the society in question.

Kauffmann: Yes, it's finally, if not primarily, a non-aesthetic enterprise. But the more rounded critic can, again, learn from the structuralists. What I have been saying through our talk makes it sound as if I favor a series of co-optings—the embracing and defanging of one opposing theory after another—but this is not what I mean.

Cardullo: No, you're not talking about defanging, but about taking the essence, the best, of a particular approach and blending it into your overall approach.

Kauffmann: Of course, the teaching of the kind of criticism I try to practice is very difficult compared with the teaching of doctrinaire approaches.

Cardullo: Well, if I may say so, if a student doesn't have critical talent—not the ability to learn, but *talent*—that student will find the going rough in a class of yours.

Kauffmann: I hope that, in a progressive sense, what you've said is true, that I've helped people to refine their talent. But, as a teacher yourself, you can obviously see that teaching doctrine is easier than developing talent.

Cardullo: Never having had such a teacher, I've always been puzzled about what staunch Marxist and structuralist critics say in the classroom. If they are as doctrinaire and arcane as their criticism, I just wonder how they communicate with undergraduates about film. Do undergraduates really comprehend their arguments?

Kauffmann: I can't answer that question because I've never attended such a class, although I've heard Marxist and structuralist critics speak at conferences and I've read articles by many of them. But my guess is that they're very effective teachers, that they give all their students, undergraduates as well as graduate students, some sense of acquisition, some sense of insight, in reasonably accessible form. Revelation comes more easily through the doctrinal approach than through the generalist approach.

Cardullo: I guess such teachers are particularly successful at schools like Yale, where you would find the sort of student susceptible to the new, the fashionable, in criticism and theory. I'm not sure that their approach works at any but the most cosmopolitan universities.

Kauffmann: That's impossible to pronounce on.

Cardullo: I'd like now to discuss a subject that you've brought up a number of times in your writing. I quote from "After the Film Generation": "In recent years, for reasons too complex even to dabble in here, both the flood of serious foreign films and the stream of serious American films have dwindled pitifully." What do you think are the reasons?

Kauffmann: This has to be answered very carefully, because one can give an answer that's too simple or that's ludicrously broad.

Cardullo: Let's set the stage first by saying that we're comparing what's going on now with what was going on in the halcyon days of the late 1950s and early 1960s, when directors whom you esteem, like Antonioni, Bergman, Kurosawa, and Truffaut, were doing what many considered their best work.

Kauffmann: Fine. The short answer, which doesn't tell you nearly enough, is economics: everything in film has become more expensive to do, and money is hardly irrelevant to filmmaking. Orson Welles once said that the man who talks about films and doesn't mention money is a jackass, and I would try not to be one. But the economics are connected with other, social factors, I think. One of them is the very success of films. The impact of films has been so strong that, to a certain degree, it's turned people away from films. It's seduced young people into intellectual sloth. The success of film itself, generically, has made many young people feel, first, that merely by going to a film, they're indulging in a cultural act—that to put their behinds in a film theater is to be seated in a wagon to Parnassus, no matter what the film happens to be. Second, the success of film has, I'm convinced, vitiated literateness to some degree. Fewer young people these days are as passionate about reading as they used to be. I think the person who is passionate about reading is passionate about films; and when the act of filmgoing turns you off reading, you also lose your interest to some extent in serious films. Because you begin to associate serious films with laboriousness, with enterprise, with collaboration, audience collaboration with the work being projected on the screen. I think that it's a very serious charge against film that it has in a certain sense vitiated passion for itself, vitiated the very passion that it once aroused in people.

Cardullo: But how did it do this?

Kauffmann: By making people intellectually slothful, by making them feel that by going to a film, they were taking care entirely of their cultural life, no matter what the film is. You're taking care of all your obligations to culture by going to see the latest *Star Trek,* and if anyone challenges you,

you can say, "Well, look what X said in the so-and-so quarterly about *Star Trek.*"

Cardullo: I remember that when I was an undergraduate, a professor of mine chastised me for seeing too many films; he said that filmgoing was too passive an enterprise. This clearly pertains to what you've been saying.

Kauffmann: Filmgoing is certainly in some degree a passive enterprise, but it doesn't have to be too passive a one.

Cardullo: He said that the conventional filmmaker did everything for me, did for me what I had to do for myself when reading.

Kauffmann: He overstates his case, but his wariness is appropriate—wariness at how film allows you to lean back and have your popcorn and let the images wash over you at the same time that it allows you to feel that you've engaged in the great cultural enterprise of the day. That film allows both these feelings is harmful to it in the long run as an art form.

Cardullo: I see what you're saying, that film lulls you into thinking you've paid your cultural dues, lulls you into intellectual laziness, so that eventually literary culture itself declines—the very culture that, together with the theater, produced a critic like you. Very interesting.

Kauffmann: Let me add just one more thing if I may. I don't know anything about rock music, but I'm told by people who do that rock speaks to them and for them in ways that film may once have tried to do but doesn't anymore. I'm talking now about people of fine intelligence, not just punks.

Cardullo: We'll get back to the subject of why film is in the state it's in, but what you've said about the dangers of filmgoing is related to the subject of literary culture. For the most part, this culture doesn't exist the way it did in the 1930s and 1940s. A man with your aspirations today has to go to the university; there is no real literary culture to nurture and support him. He has to teach in order to eat, so he usually has to leave a major city like New York, and I think that this may have a deleterious effect on him. I myself feel that, having left the New York area, I'm in danger of becoming too compartmentalized, of separating myself from all different kinds of people and associating with only one kind. I think that, at worst, this is what breeds sterile, academic film criticism. If I may say so, I think you were very fortunate to have grown up in literary New York.

Kauffmann: Literary/theatrical New York! All of what you've said is true. One difference between us is that I graduated from college in 1935 and you finished graduate school in 1985—I didn't do graduate work. Half a century, very neat. When I went to the university to study theater and drama, the idea of studying criticism in that field didn't exist; it wasn't ludicrous, *it didn't exist*—it wasn't there to sneer at, even. Criticism was something that sportswriters did when they failed as sportswriters and were assigned by their editors to the drama desk, or it was something that failed playwrights or failed directors did as a balm for their wounds. The idea of planning to be a critic and devoting one's self to education for that profession was past even contempt or mockery, let alone aspiration. There's no need to go into all the changes in attitude that have occurred.

Cardullo: Changes in attitude that brought about all the graduate and undergraduate programs in theater.

Kauffmann: And the acceptance of film into the curriculum on the graduate as well as undergraduate level, and the acceptance of criticism as an important vocation in all the arts. Of course, it achieved that respectability last in theater and film, and long before that it was an honorable profession in literature, painting, and music. By the time you came along, not only was criticism taken seriously, as something to which a sensible person could devote himself, there were methods of education for it. And the upshot of that, it seems to me, is that this very process of education brings about the situation you've just talked about in which in order to go on as a critic, you have to become an educator in order to support yourself as a serious critic. I'm not speaking of this as a defect in a virtue—I don't think it's a defect—but it is a result of a virtue.

Cardullo: Well, in your day, to judge by what you've done for a living, aspiring writers and critics often became editors.

Kauffmann: I've worked at a lot of jobs, including editing, and many a time during those years, I wished I could have taught, but one thing I did not have to do, to sound very parochial: I did not have to leave New York. And in our profession—film criticism, theater criticism—New York is still, alas, the center of activity. We all know that there is theater in other parts of the country, we all know that good films are shown outside New York, especially in film societies, but by sheer weight of numbers—the number of critics, the number of readers and viewers—if not other merits, New York is still the court of hearing.

Cardullo: I'd like to get back to the reasons why fewer and fewer serious films are being made. I'd like you to continue with the point you made about the reciprocal effect filmgoing has on film and literature: the act of filmgoing at once turns a person off to reading and makes him feel that he has paid his cultural dues, with the result that interest in serious literature and serious film declines, serious thinking in general declines, and consequently fewer and fewer serious films get made.

Kauffmann: There's a sort of creeping lichen or moss, I think, in our cultural scene at the present time that's affecting standards. What you quoted of mine about the dwindling number of serious films, both American and foreign, could, with slight changes, be said about book publishing—it has been said. And this is due to the growth of this lichen of sloth, of passivity, which is the result of several factors. I'm now going to make some very broad, possibly ludicrous statements, but they run through my mind on this matter. Culture, as we have understood the word, means less to young people now than it used to, as a force in their lives, as a necessity in their lives, and film has, in a sense, fed that apathy by its very ease of absorption. It provides an escape from the world.

Cardullo: It's almost the only culture for some people.

Kauffmann: When we go to a film, you and I, the film certainly envelops us no less than it does anyone else, but within that envelopment we discover things; within that envelopment many young people think of nothing. This leads to some very large issues, which I hesitate to mention because what I say will verge on intellectual buffoonery. The decline of culture is connected with malaise in our time, which is connected with theological crisis, which comes home to roost in the existence of nuclear weapons.

Cardullo: And in the loss of trust in political leaders and in the future. The malaise has to do with the question, "Why bother?"

Kauffmann: "Why bother?" or "Let us live from day to day," not in an existential way, but in a hedonistic one.

Cardullo: Exactly, hedonism is the word I would use.

Kauffmann: It's easy to controvert this by talking about individuals we both know who work with energy and initiative to make something of their lives. But broadly speaking, they are the exceptions, which leads me to something positive in the general film situation. In view of the somewhat disastrous experience of filmgoing these days, we must realize that we live by the exceptions. In the film world, the American film world, the situation is such that a film made at the highest technical level, a feature film, now must take in fifty to sixty million dollars to break even. It used to be forty million about eight years ago; I assume it's gone up 20 percent. How much flexibility and adventure can there be if you have to please that many people? One could conclude from this that no good films would ever be made again, but the startling fact is that they come along insistently—I won't say regularly, but insistently.

Cardullo: And let's not delude ourselves into thinking that most of the films made in, say, 1960 were good. They weren't—most of them were bad; but 1960 still produced more good films than 1986.

Kauffmann: Right. We're talking about proportions here. And when you idolize foreign films, you have to remember that, in any year, most of them are so bad they never even get to this country. And half of the ones that do come over are not very good. The inexplicable fact, to speak again of American films, is that *Tender Mercies* comes along. The inexplicable fact is that Jim Jarmusch's two films, *Stranger than Paradise* and *Down by Law,* come along. The completely baffling fact is that a very pleasant, delicate little film like *Roxanne* comes out of Hollywood with a Hollywood star. These things cannot be explained. They are the result of human stubbornness triumphing over the dismal state of film production in particular and cultural life in general.

Cardullo: Let's talk further about some exceptional American films. I resaw *Tender Mercies* recently, and it's even better than I thought. I think one of the reasons it's so good is that its production values are simple. Unlike most films, this film is not overproduced. I have not liked Horton Foote's other work for film and for the stage, but he certainly hit the jackpot with *Tender Mercies,* perhaps in part because of Bruce Beresford's direction.

Kauffmann: I think one of the reasons it succeeds, besides its chasteness in production, is that it fits a definition I recently read in a book called *The Classical Hollywood Cinema,* by Bordwell, Staiger, and Thompson, a very good, very important book. That definition is of what they called "the art film," simply because they had to call it something; and the art film for them, as opposed to the commercial film, is a film that faces the effects and tries to look for the causes. It's not content to accept things as they are, to reflect what's going on in society, in your words; it must analyze and explore. *Tender Mercies* analyzes and explores what's going on in one person's life. Here's a man who finds himself in a baffling and despairing situation, which I won't detail, and fights his way out of it by looking for the causes. And why the film triumphs for me—I'm talking about it thematically now, not cinematically—is that he doesn't find the causes, the reasons. But he knows that he was right to search for them, and that the search is what reclaimed him as a human being—to the extent that he is reclaimed.

Cardullo: And he's not even convinced at the end that matters will continue to be as good as they have been.

Kauffmann: You're right. He doesn't believe in anything. He says that, even though he's fallen in love, has married, and is resting as from a storm in the shelter of this woman's affection, which he repays with his affection, he doesn't trust happiness.

Cardullo: I like the fact that in this scene with his wife, he keeps on hoeing his small vegetable garden the whole time he is talking. He doesn't stop once. In a lesser film, this man and his wife would have had a very maudlin conversation, after which they would have embraced and he would have resolved to trust his happiness.

Kauffmann: In Foote's other work that I know, people *are* glowingly reconciled at the end and they *do* find answers. This film, *Tender Mercies,* in its quiet way, is stark.

Cardullo: And the vast Texas landscape in which it takes place contributes to that starkness.

Kauffmann: There's a line in *Agamemnon,* spoken by the nurse, I think: "I have looked into the hand God, and in it, nothing." That's always seemed to me to be profound, because there's not nothing, there's *the hand of God,* and *in* it is nothing.

Cardullo: And Duvall has come to that perception by the end of the film. Let's talk a little bit about him, because just as *Twentieth Century* wouldn't exist without John Barrymore, *Tender Mercies* wouldn't exist without Robert Duvall.

Kauffmann: I can't imagine the film with anyone else, although it is possible that George C. Scott could have done the role.

Cardullo: Maybe Jon Voight, too.

Kauffmann: But that's not to detract in the least from Duvall's performance. We've both seen Duvall in a lot of things, and I have a very serious grievance against him, which is that he could be acting great roles, greatly.

Cardullo: On the stage?

Kauffmann: On the stage and on film. If Steve McQueen could make a film of *An Enemy of the People,* why can't Duvall do one of *John Gabriel Borkman?*

Cardullo: He certainly has the influence to get funding for such a project. But I think he actually said once that he preferred the anonymous roles that films afforded him.

Kauffmann: Yes, I think anonymous is a good word. The roles he creates can be associated with no one but him: they're not like the well-known, highly sought after roles in the theater repertory.

Cardullo: That's one of the virtues of film: you do the part and it's done, forever—except in the case of remakes!

Kauffmann: I have seen Duvall in the theater and he was wonderful. Not in the so-called classics, but in classics of their day, such as an early production of *A View from the Bridge,* with Jon Voight in the cast and Dustin Hoffman as the assistant stage manager and understudy. Duvall was in *American Buffalo,* you'll remember. The man could do anything; my only charge against him is that he doesn't do enough.

Cardullo: Let's discuss a few other films that, in their way, are as good as *Tender Mercies.*

Kauffmann: I think that in 1982 we had the best farce since *Some Like It Hot*: *Victor/Victoria.* Blake Edwards is a talented man who swings very widely on the pendulum: he can be atrocious, he can be mediocre, and he can be excellent. He is for me the only person now directing in this country who has some feel for slapstick, who can make it vital and irresistible. That plus a finely honed sense of characterization and structure made *Victor/Victoria,* to me, a very successful film. Shall we stick to American films?

Cardullo: Yes, for now.
Kauffmann: Is *Sid and Nancy* an American film?

Cardullo: Hard to say. The director, Alex Cox, is British, as is the main character, Sid Vicious, but the film had lots of American money behind it.

Kauffmann: Well, the money doesn't matter as much to us as does the subject matter, and *Sid and Nancy* seems to be an American film because so much of it takes place in this country.

Cardullo: Yes, and so much of the pernicious influence on Sid and Nancy's relationship occurred here, in New York. He ate the music world up, and then it ate him.

Kauffmann: I know nothing about the kind of music Sid Vicious played—I'm not interested in that world. I went to see *Sid and Nancy* because I had to; I don't see everything, but there are certain films you feel you ought to see. My wife and I walked out afterwards and we looked at each other, amazed that it had been so good. It was a good film because it looked into certain darknesses, not with relish, not with exploitation, but with great empathy, I thought.

Cardullo: Yet it didn't try to make Sid and Nancy any more special than they were.

Kauffmann: Or heroic. It didn't try to make them victims in a bid for cheap sympathy.

Cardullo: I think we can all imagine what kind of film that would have been. I certainly expected that, but it's not what I got.

Kauffmann: Another recent American film that's meant something to me is *River's Edge,* a modest work based on an incident that happened in California. A teenaged boy kills his girlfriend for no particular reason and leaves her on a river bank.

Cardullo: Actually he does give a reason for killing her, but it's ridiculous: she said something bad about his mother.

Kauffmann: Right. He wasn't in a jealous rage or something comparable; she merely irritated him and he strangled her for it. That's a story in itself: that values should be so askew that one human being could kill another human being for so trifling a reason. And the killer is not an apparent psychotic. In fact, he's one of the most appealing people in the picture. That's only part of the mystery that's touched on in the film. The other, bigger mystery, and probably the reason the filmmakers made the picture, is that he tells his schoolmates of the killing in a somewhat offhand way. At first they don't believe him; they think he's bragging. Then when he takes some of them and shows them the body, they're impressed by what he's done, as if he'd won some kind of super-dangerous drag race, and they keep his secret.

Cardullo: Of course the film revolves around the fact that one of his friends eventually goes to the police.

Kauffmann: And is treated like a rat for doing so.

Cardullo: The police even try to implicate him in the crime.

Kauffmann: What horrified me about this film, in an important way, was that it showed what a breach there is between young people and society these days. Even the fact of murder (a) doesn't register as the horror to them that we would hope it would, and (b) if murder occurs, then it's their set's business, not society's—and within that set, it's almost a source of admiration.

Cardullo: I'd like to talk about a film that, in a wild way, is thematically related to *River's Edge*: Martin Scorsese's *Raging Bull,* which is not about the domestication of violence but, in the broadest sense, about the control or channeling of the violent impulse in American society.

Kauffmann: I myself think of *Raging Bull* as a picture about immigration. This is a film about Italians in America, also a film about the Irish in America—his wife is Irish. There have been plenty of films about poor men as such using boxing as a way out of the slums. This doesn't seem to be that kind of film. This man might have gotten out of the slum in some other way. There is something almost operatic about the character of Jake La Motta, something romantic about his behavior. I'm not referring to his dealing with women, but to his solitariness, his questing, his willingness to take the worst that can happen if by doing that he can gain selfhood and independence in America. For me the film was operatic right from the first shot, before the titles, when you see La Motta shadowboxing in slow motion to the strains of *Cavalleria Rusticana.* This showed at once that Scorsese had an idea, that he wasn't just going to give you another boxing film; and he "proved out" his idea very well. This picture's about an Italian—a first-generation one in this case—about the particular abrasions the Italians experienced as they confronted American society upon immigration. And I think that La Motta's violence comes from his cultural and social situation; it isn't just a question of psychological bent. He is the product of a certain ethnic group that feels it needs to make its way aggressively in America.

Cardullo: He even makes his way aggressively within his own circle: with his wife and friends.

Kauffmann: He is a fount of rage, outside the boxing ring as well as within it.

Cardullo: In my opinion *Raging Bull* is Scorsese's finest film, although I don't think a lot of people agree with me. Does it go beyond the ethnic boundaries to address the issue of violence per se in this country?

Kauffmann: I don't think it needs to, because America is made up of ethnic components and the American character consists of what ethnic groups have contributed to it. America *is* her ethnic groups, and in its violence, the Italian experience is just the quintessence of the immigrant's adversarial relationship with his new land.

Cardullo: And contact sports, among which boxing heads the list, are the quintessential outlet for American aggression, which expresses itself all too often, unfortunately, in actual everyday violence. Any other recent films that you'd like to single out for their quality?

Kauffmann: Certainly *Platoon. Platoon* has been lowered in general estimation ever since Stanley Kubrick's *Full Metal Jacket* came along. This is ridiculous, although *Platoon* is vulnerable on the grounds that its voice-over commentary—the protagonist's letters to his grandmother—is simply unbearable. This device seems to me—I don't know this, I'm speculating—the fee that Oliver Stone paid to the producer to get the film made. "Put some nice stuff on the soundtrack," I can hear the producer saying, "and then you can be as grim as you want to. If that isn't there, then the whole film's going to be grim, and it won't sell." And even within the picture that Stone wanted to make, there is some drastic differential character-drawing between the two sergeants, although I don't think it comes down to a battle between good and evil. These criticisms taken into account, you're still left with a film that is wonderfully made, wonderfully acted, and uncompromising once it gets to its real subject, which is what it is to be a human being who can sleep comfortably in the rain. When you see those soldiers sleeping in the jungle in pouring rain, and happy to have that sleep, you know what war can do to the human scale. Those shots said almost as much to me as the violent shots. Because it's harder to imagine that—sleeping in pouring rain—than it is to imagine fighting. We all have tempers; we've all wanted momentarily to kill people. So it's easy to put ourselves in the soldiers' place when they go out to engage the enemy. But to accept rain- and mud-soaked sleep as rest, and even bliss, really requires an extension of our experiential territory. I went to see the film again after I saw *Full Metal Jacket.*

Cardullo: There's no comparison.

Kauffmann: *Platoon* is the better film by far. On seeing it for the second time, I was especially struck by the beauty of its making, as when the protagonist is arriving in Vietnam. The first thing that happens is that the back of a transport plane comes down at you. Out come the soldiers and the camera moves with them, breaking its arc only to pick up the body bags.

Cardullo: Which are being transported in the other direction.

Kauffmann: The air is full of dust—the air itself looks strange to these newcomers.

Cardullo: It seems thick and colored.

Kauffmann: The rhythm created in this first, relatively short sequence at the airport assures you that you're in the hands of a man who's teeming with convictions and the ability to express them. This is not just another war film—you know that from the first ten seconds.

Cardullo: I thought the music in *Platoon* was very effective, especially Samuel Barber's *Adagio.*

Kauffmann: The use of the *Adagio* has been criticized for being arty and obtrusive, but to me this music carried forward ironically the Biblical epigraph of the film: "Rejoice, oh young man, in the days of thy youth." Before this war film begins, the epigraph sounds an elegiac note, and during the movie, Barber's music continues to sound this note in a context that is far from rejoicing.

Cardullo: Yes, I found it very moving.

Kauffmann: Whereas the music that was written especially for *Full Metal Jacket* seemed to me to be rather intellectually contrived.

Cardullo: I've seen *Full Metal Jacket* twice and I wish I hadn't gone the second time. I didn't miss anything: it's simplistic and labored, and without the redeeming features of either the sturdy characterization of *Paths of Glory,* Kubrick's film about World War I, or the black comedy of *Dr. Strangelove,* his film about a future nuclear war.

Kauffmann: People who admire *Full Metal Jacket,* and earlier films of Kubrick's like *2001: A Space Odyssey* and *Barry Lyndon,* seem to believe that he is succeeding in making art in a commercial world.

Cardullo: He tries. I'll give him that.

Kauffmann: In the whole time I've been writing film criticism for the *New Republic,* two reviews stand out in my mind as having elicited a flood of adverse letters. By a flood I mean thirty letters. One was an adverse review of Zeffirelli's *Romeo and Juliet.* I stepped on a lot of adolescent toes with that one, and all the adolescents weren't teenagers. The other was a review of *2001.* I got angry letters in response to my piece on *Romeo and Juliet*; in response to my piece on *2001* I got sorrowful letters. Two of them, I remember, from clergymen, who said more or less the same thing: "I pray for you, that in time you'll come to see the light about this film."

Cardullo: And now you're getting adverse letters in response to your review of *Full Metal Jacket.*

Kauffmann: A few so far. As in the case of *2001,* the writers seem to think that Kubrick is doing something important within the bounds of the programmed film.

Cardullo: One letter-writer even compared *Full Metal Jacket* with *Mother Courage* and *Les Carabiniers.* But it didn't seem to me that Kubrick was defamiliarizing war, was giving us a fresh look at it à la Brecht and Godard.

Kauffmann: No, he wasn't doing any such thing, and to say that he was is ridiculous.

Cardullo: On top of everything else, *Full Metal Jacket* doesn't end, it just stops—but I guess some would see this as yet another instance of Kubrick's (post)modernism.

Kauffmann: Kubrick, you know, sequestered himself on an estate in the English countryside after *2001,* and his work shows the effects of his insulation from the world. He makes his films in England, under his total control. He's a great chess player, and he likes to handle every component in a film the way he handles chess pieces. He creates what Leo Braudy calls "closed films." My first clue about what was going wrong in Kubrick's work came when I read that he was through with the actors in *2001* more than a year before the film was released. That meant that, for over a year, he was tinkering with every tiny piece, adding this sound, refining that effect, using the actors only as one component of a machine he was creating. Of course, literally, that's what actors are: one component. But this was, I felt, a deliberate equalization of all the components on Kubrick's part; it made him absolute Lord and God over everything in the movie. *Full Metal Jacket* is one more example of this little private game he's playing with film and the world. And like each of his films since *2001, Full Metal Jacket* has an air of smugness about it. It's as if Kubrick is saying, "What I give you, world, you must be satisfied with."

Cardullo: Which among the current generation of directors practicing throughout the world mean the most to you?

Kauffmann: If I were forced at gunpoint to select two, they'd both be German: Hans-Jürgen Syberberg and Margarethe von Trotta. A couple of

Sundays ago, I went to see *Parsifal* again—a difficult film, four-and-a-half hours long. It's Wagner's music drama, complete and in German, without subtitles. It's a film that was made, even in Germany, only for those who know and like *Parsifal*, or at least know it. But to me it's a triumph of creative imagination. Syberberg had a recording made of the music drama, and then he made a film, not just of *Parsifal*, but of what *Parsifal* evokes in him— about art and politics and history, about film and theater, about the possible exorcism of the demon Wagner himself. It's a prime example of what in the theater is called concept directing—a director's "statement" of a classic— and because of the fact that it's a film, it points, for me, to something in the future that you might call theater-film. Syberberg's *Parsifal* is far less pure cinema than a superb television film of a production in a hypothetical theater. As such, it is a thrilling conjunction of tradition and innovation.

Cardullo: I didn't dislike von Trotta's *Rosa Luxemburg,* although I wouldn't rate it as highly as you seemed to in your review.

Kauffmann: Well, I think it has severe faults. The subject is an impossible one for a film. That doesn't mean one has to admire her for tackling it, but still it is an impossible subject and I won't even say she came up with the best possible script. I don't think she did. Nevertheless, once the script be-came a given, what happened thereafter was enormously impressive: her cast-ing of the roles, the performances she elicited, every aspect of the film's making. Her best film for me to date, though, is *Marianne and Juliane.* To me it's one of the most important films of, let's call it, the post-Antonioni period. You can now call it the post-Bergman period, since he's retired. It's a film about the difficulty of being a liberal these days, the crisis and the drama entailed in being one.

Cardullo: In Germany.

Kauffmann: Anywhere. But especially in Germany, because they have terrorism and as yet, thank heaven, we don't. And they have a different past; intelligent young people have a quite different past to remember in that country.

Cardullo: I'd like to talk briefly about two other German filmmakers, Werner Herzog and Rainer Werner Fassbinder, whom I would rate one and two ahead of Syberberg and von Trotta.

Kauffmann: Well, Herzog and Fassbinder are the next names on my list. Herzog is a major adventurer in film, and not just physically in the sense that he goes into the South American jungle to make *Aguirre, the Wrath of God,* although that's part of it. He's a magnificent talent, but there's no one film of his that, in my opinion, ranks as high as two films of von Trotta's: *Marianne and Juliane* and a film made just before it called *Sisters.*

Cardullo: I couldn't disagree with you more, so let's move on to Fassbinder. What's that film of his where a teenaged girl and her slightly older lover kill her father?

Kauffmann: *Jail Bait.* It's based on a play by Franz Xaver Kroetz.

Cardullo: A wonderful film.

Kauffmann: Fassbinder is such a wild farrago of talent and insanity that it's very hard to talk about his work as a whole. After all, he made forty-one feature-length films, and he was only thirty-six when he died in 1982! For me the two best Fassbinder films are *Effi Briest* and *Berlin Alexanderplatz,* which is a staggering piece of work. If you prefer Fassbinder and Herzog to Syberberg and von Trotta, I can't argue with you: that's just a matter of taste. There's no question that the most fertile source of good films in the last fifteen years has been Germany. In addition to the films of the four directors we've been discussing, there are, to name just two, Wim Wenders's *The Goalie's Anxiety at the Penalty Kick,* from a novel by Peter Handke, and Handke's own *Left-Handed Woman,* also from a novel by him. There's at least one reason for all this German fertility, and it's related to something we talked about earlier: finances.

Cardullo: Yes, Germany subsidizes the theater and it subsidizes film, directly and through television. It's important to realize that the Germans are preeminent in theater and film partly because of the money the German government puts into both these enterprises.

Kauffmann: For four years in the early 1970s, I was on the Theater Advisory Panel of the National Endowment for the Arts, and if I'm remembering correctly, we met six times a year and read long reports and applications and worked very hard to apportion justly a total budget of about three-and-a-half million dollars. The city of Hamburg at the time was giving about six million dollars to its opera house alone.

Cardullo: And people fill that opera house, they fill theaters throughout Germany—they have to, or the government wouldn't put up the money. There's a demand for art in that country, and the government helps to satisfy it.

Kauffmann: But to talk about subsidy for film in this country is ridiculous, because films are so very expensive to make here. To help a filmmaker, you'd have to give him, and all like him, many millions.

Cardullo: What costs so much? Is it artificial cost—created by the unions, for example—or is it genuine?

Kauffmann: Are union expenses artificial?

Cardullo: They are and they aren't. They're artificial when, to use the example of the New York theater, you have to pay people in a band who aren't needed simply because their union contract says that, if you use a band, you have to employ so many band members. I'm sure that this occurs in film also.

Kauffmann: Featherbedding, they used to call it, and I'm certain that it goes on a great deal in films. Even if artificial costs such as this represented 50 percent of the budget, which they don't, and you got rid of them, you'd still be left with a budget for an average feature film these days of around ten million dollars. How could a subsidy possibly defray that amount in any significant way?

Cardullo: German subsidies seem to defray the cost of German films.

Kauffmann: That's because the budgets for those films are so much smaller than ours.

Cardullo: You see, you're making my point for me: the costs are largely artificial in this country. Werner Herzog did not spend as much money to make *Aguirre* as Steve Martin and company spent to make *Roxanne.* A good example of an American film that, relatively speaking, did not cost a lot to make is *Gal Young 'Un,* directed by Victor Nuñez. Yet the production values were very high. How did they do it?

Kauffmann: You know very well that they had no actors of any renown in *Gal Young 'Un,* no union costs of any kind, no studio rental charges, etc.

Cardullo: Well, this is what I'm talking about. Your definition of featherbedding, it turns out, is much less inclusive than mine.

Kauffmann: But you can't monkey too much with the conditions of Hollywood filmmaking or you're killing what you're trying to help. Hollywood itself, if the term still means anything, means a certain level of technical proficiency, and you won't help film in this country, or American film in the world, if Hollywood is threatened. We're talking about subsidizing filmmaking at its highest technical level, not about subsidizing so-called independent productions like *Gal Young 'Un*. Which isn't to say that they don't have a place, a very necessary place, but that's not what we're talking about. When we talk about German directors such as Herzog and von Trotta, we're not talking about what we would call independent production. We're talking about central productions in the filmmaking of that country.

Cardullo: Why not subsidize independent productions to the point that they could compete technically with Hollywood and thus become central to the filmmaking of our country? Film is going to continue to scare away potentially great artists if more independent avenues aren't opened to them.

Kauffmann: Or it scares them away from independent filmmaking, toward trying to get into the mainstream.

Cardullo: Yes, that happened to Nuñez, I believe. He made a big-budget, Hollywood film after *Gal Young 'Un* and it went nowhere.

Kauffmann: It also happened to a woman named Claudia Weill. She made a good film called *Girlfriends* on her own, so to speak, and then was taken to Hollywood, where she made the dreadful *It's My Turn*.

Cardullo: And what about Susan Seidelman?

Kauffmann: Susan Seidelman made a very good first film called *Smithereens*. Then she made, intentionally or not I don't know, a commercial caricature of *Smithereens* entitled *Desperately Seeking Susan*. And she's gone on to make an even worse film, *Making Mr. Right*.

Cardullo: Jim Jarmusch shows some desire to remain independent.

Kauffmann: He will not make anything but his own films, and he knows that in order to do this he must work very cheaply. So far he's delivered handsomely with *Stranger than Paradise* and *Down by Law*.

Cardullo: I wish there were more like him. I'd like now to take our discussion to an abstract level. What is it that film can do that other art forms can't? Why should film be as important as we say it should? Why should more potential young artists be drawn to film, costs aside for the moment? Why should they be drawn to it as art?

Kauffmann: Now what can the film do? We both know that Grotowski's theatrical mission was to strip away the trappings of the theater, to tread a *via negativa* in order to discover what it is quintessentially the theater can do that nothing else can do, and of course he was thinking specifically of film as the opponent. What is it, he asked, that the theater can do that film cannot do? We're now trying to consider, you and I, what the film can do that neither the theater nor the novel, nor radio nor television can do. Television is a subject complicated by the commerce of the world. It is intrinsically different from film, but it shares so much of the vocabulary and syntax that some of the things I'm going to say now about film could also be applied to television. One thing that film, as a performance art, can do that no other performance art—like a play—can do is get inside human beings, get inside their minds and explore interiority.

Cardullo: How?

Kauffmann: Through voice-over, the close-up, and through the camera-narrator's ability to shift consciousness, as Fellini does in *8 1/2*: between present awareness and the realm of memory, (day)dream, fantasy, or subconsciousness. I don't know any other art form that could do that. A novel could do it, of course, but the words wouldn't have the immediacy and effect of film, the power of the image.

Cardullo: But some have said that filmic images cannot mean complexly in the way that the words of a novel can. Can you respond to that?

Kauffmann: No, because it's not a provable point one way or the other. For me, images have meant as much as words.

Cardullo: A good example of such an image is that close-up from *Persona* in which Liv Ullmann is kissing Bibi Andersson's neck, both of them with their eyes closed.

Kauffmann: Think of the next-to-last moment of *Wild Strawberries,* where Victor Sjöström waves across the inlet to his parents, who see him as a boy.

Cardullo: I would counter the argument that images cannot mean as complexly as words by saying that images can almost mean more deeply and more ambiguously because they're not as explicit.

Kauffmann: That's true, but they can also be more facile than words. Film has a built-in power that is a built-in danger: it's immediately strong in a way that no other art is except music. You often feel that you have to fight your way out of a film when you're not liking it because the images are so strong, so overpowering.

Cardullo: I think that Robert Altman is the filmmaker most often guilty of trying to make images mean what they don't. He even directed a film with that very title, *Images,* and it's terrible.

Kauffmann: He and the Taviani brothers are among the worst offenders in this area.

Cardullo: Yes, the Tavianis' *Padre Padrone* suffers from this defect.

Kauffmann: But if we agree that images have an authenticity of their own, then the images of *8 1/2* do for interiority what no other art could duplicate.

Cardullo: Some surrealist painting does it.

Kauffmann: Doesn't do it in motion, doesn't do it serially and cumulatively.

Cardullo: Right, think of the surrealist films *Un Chien Andalou* and *L'Age d'Or,* on which Salvador Dali and Luis Buñuel collaborated.

Kauffmann: Then there's the aspect of, let's call it, isolation: the ability of film to isolate factors in a work. I'll give you an example, a negative example. I once saw a production of *'Tis Pity She's a Whore,* which is a fascinating play. In the last scene the brother, Giovanni, comes in with his sister's heart impaled on a dagger and stands there with it almost until the end of the play. Now that is simply impossible to play these days. There's no way that he can stand onstage with his sister's heart on the end of a dagger and play a long scene with a lot of other people. Everyone in the audience was tittering. First, they knew that it was a fake heart, and second, even if it had been a real heart, the scene wouldn't have held, because obviously the distraction would have been too great. We're conditioned by film now to want what's important to be selected and isolated. The film director could have cut away from that damned heart and dagger so that you wouldn't have to see them through the whole scene; you would have seen only the face of the brother or the faces of the other people. That's more than a convenience: it's in the nature of the medium to allow you to arrange space and assign prominence. This gives film great power.

Cardullo: Someone like André Bazin would argue that this power is the dangerous one of manipulation.

Kauffmann: Anything can be manipulative. Harmony and counterpoint can be soppy and manipulative. It's true, nevertheless, that film is more powerful in this way than any other art form. The question is, to what use does it put its power? In Bergman's exquisite, strange last film, *After the Rehearsal,* it's the film's power to concentrate on an individual or two individuals, to isolate him or them from context, that makes the drama of the piece—not drama in the conventional sense, but internal drama. I would say that the attributes of film that are most important to me are not the ones of spectacle and motion—the ability to move anywhere and show anything—but the ones of selectivity and interiority.

Cardullo: Let's talk for a minute about Kracauer's description of film as "the redemption of physical reality." Bazin said something similar, except that, with his Catholic sensibility, he probably put the emphasis on "human reality" rather than "physical reality." How would you characterize this use of the word "redemption"? What are these men talking about?

Kauffmann: They're talking about making God's creation more marvelous to us than it is.

Cardullo: Through the process of framing, which confers a special importance on it.

Kauffmann: Yes, through the process of photographing this creation in motion. It's the filmmaker's function, Bazin believed—and I'm putting this very baldly—to celebrate God's miracle—the miracle of the world and human existence in it—by presenting it to us. Merely by reverently presenting it to us whole, in all its mystery and splendor. That's one of the two major options available in film, the other being the "interfering" option, as espoused by Sergei Eisenstein.

Cardullo: The manipulative one, which uses editing and montage to reconstruct reality.

Kauffmann: For example, Margarethe von Trotta could be called a Bazinian and Hans-Jürgen Syberberg an Eisensteinian. There's a historical antecedent for this opposition in the opposed theater views of Stanislavsky and Meyerhold. And one can see all of twentieth-century theater and film—by theater I mean not only the plays themselves but also their theatrical production—falling into one category or the other. Of course, there are some admixtures—*8 1/2* is one example in film—but mostly there's a bias one way or the other.

Cardullo: I'd like to get back to national cinema for a bit. There has been a resurgence in British filmmaking recently. Some titles: *My Beautiful Laundrette, Prick Up Your Ears, Withnail and I, Rita, Sue and Bob Too, Wish You Were Here, The Whistle Blower.* Historically, why hasn't British cinema been able to compete with that of other nations? Is it because of the predominance of theater in England, the existence of so long and rich a theatrical tradition that there hasn't been room for film alongside it?

Kauffmann: I don't think it's that so much as two other things. First, there was considerable censorship in Britain before World War II—Eisenstein's *Battleship Potemkin,* for example, couldn't be shown there. Second, American films swamped the market. There was hardly room, figuratively speaking, for British film to breathe. I know that there are volumes of British film history. But look through them and what do you find that's of any significance? I'm not talking about the technological side—Britain had a lot to do with the invention and perfection of the equipment of filmmaking. But it has not had a lot to do with film artistry. The best directing talent it has ever produced, Lindsay Anderson, has in my opinion had a thoroughly unfulfilled career.

Cardullo: What happened right after the war?

Kauffmann: There was a lack of Hollywood films, and for a moment the British were all by themselves. But instead of going on to develop an indigenous cinema of quality, they very soon aped Hollywood and then again became predominantly an American market.

Cardullo: What happened in the late 1950s to cause a blossoming in British film that coincided with a rebirth of its drama?

Kauffmann: Their society was undergoing radical changes that led, in drama, to the plays of the "Angry Young Men," and in cinema to the so-called social realist films of the 1950s and early 1960s: *Room at the Top, Saturday Night and Sunday Morning, The Loneliness of the Long-Distance Runner,* etc. But this movement played itself out fairly quickly: the substance of the films became thin and their aims were sometimes less than large. For me, some of the films from this period—they come right before it, actually—that stand up best are the Ealing Studio comedies.

Cardullo: Yes, *Kind Hearts and Coronets, The Man in the White Suit,* and *The Lavender Hill Mob* come to mind. What's responsible for the recent flurry of good British films?

Kauffmann: I think it's a matter of new talent and opportunities for older talent. Alan Clarke, who has been active in British television for twenty years or so and has a very good reputation as a director, finally got the chance to make *Rita, Sue and Bob Too.* The script has some faults, but this is quite plainly a vigorously directed film by a man who knows what he's doing and knows what he wants. What has helped this recent resurgence is the sponsorship of Channel 4 on British television, for which a lot of these new films were made.

Cardullo: Australian film has been thriving for some time now. We've had, just to name a few items, Fred Schepisi's *The Chant of Jimmie Black-smith,* Gillian Armstrong's *My Brilliant Career,* and Bruce Beresford's *Breaker Morant.*

Kauffmann: Yes, but what's happening—and I suppose this is inevitable in the world as it is—is that Australia's becoming the source of talent for other countries' films. David Lean used Judy Davis, the star of *My Brilliant Career,* in *A Passage to India.* Schepisi made *Roxanne* over here, Beresford did *Tender Mercies.* And Peter Weir, most familiar as the director of *Picnic at Hanging Rock,* made his best film that I know in this country: *Witness.*

Cardullo: In conclusion, two related questions. How do you feel, after thirty years on the job, about writing for the *New Republic,* and whom are you addressing in your reviews? That is, who's your ideal reader?

Kauffmann: I can't imagine a better critical post than the one I have at a respected weekly magazine whose readership is in the hundreds of thousands and is at a certain general intellectual level. *Time* magazine has, what, twenty-five million readers a week in all of its editions, but its readership comprises a vertical slice of the population. The *New Republic* gets a horizontal slice, and those readers are a wonderful audience. And after thirty years, the effect is cumulative, almost familial: I started writing for a certain group of people and now I'm writing for their children. At least this is the feeling I get—I hope I'm not under any illusions. I must note how wonderfully I've always been treated by the people at the *New Republic.* The situation was good under the first owner I worked for, Gilbert Harrison, and it's become even better under his successor, Martin Peretz. Peretz and his staff couldn't possibly be more congenial and helpful. Everything about what I do is left entirely to my discretion. I choose my own material, and there is no interference in what I say or how I say it. Writing for the *New Republic* suits me because I'm much more interested in writing for the most intelligent non-specialist in film than for film people—this is a matter of temperament, not of intellectual decision. And that's the readership that, by and large, the *New Republic* affords me. In a word, I have a dream job. Perhaps I shouldn't admit this, but it's certainly true that I have found my experience in writing for the *New Republic* to be a golden proof of Oscar Wilde's dictum that criticism is the best form of auto-biography.

Cardullo: One last question. How in fact did you become a film critic? What led up to your assuming the film critic's post at the *New Republic* in 1958?

Kauffmann: The Mafia. I had been educated for the theater, had worked in it, had always loved films but had never, in a certain sense, concentrated on them. In late 1957 I was a juror in a Mafia trial in New York, a trial that lasted nine weeks, and a practicing film critic, Arthur Knight, was a fellow juror. We lunched together almost every day for those nine weeks, and by conversing with him, I realized how much I'd absorbed about film through the years. Then, while that trial was still on, a writer I knew came around one evening to say goodbye—he was moving to England. He said he had been approached by a magazine called the *Reporter*—now long defunct—to be their film critic, had told them he was moving to England, and had recommended me. I told my friend about my film discoveries during those jury lunches. In a few days the *Reporter* called, and I wrote three or four reviews for them. But we didn't get on. It ended with my having an unpublished review on my hands. I sent it, by some divinely lucky fluke, to the *New Republic,* and the then arts editor, Robert Evett, who became a dear friend, welcomed me immediately, lastingly. But if it hadn't been for those lunches prompted by the Mafia, it might never have happened. An ill wind blew tremendous good my way.

Stanley Kauffmann Talks about Forty Years of Film Reviews

Charlie Rose / 1998

From the *Charlie Rose Show* no. 2200, New York, New York, 9 July 1998.

Charlie Rose: There are few things that Stanley Kauffmann loves more than going to the movies. At the age of eighty-two, he is currently celebrating his fortieth year as the film critic for the *New Republic* magazine. Each week he delivers an intelligent and entertaining look at the current releases. He joins me tonight to take a look at a long career and give his opinion on the current state of movie-making. And I am pleased, very pleased to have him at this table. Welcome, sir.

Stanley Kauffmann: Thanks very much.

Charlie Rose: Great to have you here.

Stanley Kauffmann: Thank you.

Charlie Rose: Leon Wieseltier, one of your editors, said, "If there's one person that you cannot afford *not* to have on your show," it's you, and I'm thankful for the advice.

Stanley Kauffmann: Good. That's a friend.

Charlie Rose: You love movies?

Stanley Kauffmann: Yes.

Charlie Rose: Good movies.

Stanley Kauffmann: I love the idea of movies. I love the excitement of going. I love—I've never been bored with the idea of going to films. Of course, obviously many films are boring.

Charlie Rose: Sure.

Stanley Kauffmann: That goes without saying.

Charlie Rose: Is it any different than any other art form, in that there are few really good ones?

Stanley Kauffmann: There are more good films than there are good plays.

195

Charlie Rose: Yeah?

Stanley Kauffmann: And, if I were to go over the forty years of my film-writing career and make a list of the films I've liked, just numerically it would far outnumber the number of novels that I've liked in that period of time, although we all know there have been some good and some great novels written in that time.

Charlie Rose: Sure. But you've seen more films than—

Stanley Kauffmann: I'm talking about numbers—

Charlie Rose: —novels you liked.

Stanley Kauffmann: Yes. I've been very fortunate in a way. A lot of very fine films have been made, and a number of very reputable ones have been made during my time with the *New Republic,* during the time I've been writing. Coleridge said that a critic depends on the artists who work at the time that he is writing.

Charlie Rose: Yeah.

Stanley Kauffmann: And good luck has been mine in this regard.

Charlie Rose: A lot of good artists working at the time you're writing.

Stanley Kauffmann: Yes.

Charlie Rose: What is it about the film as an art form that you like so much?

Stanley Kauffmann: Surprise and familiarity. The sense of being embraced by something that I have known for a long time very well and the knowledge that that embrace may contain something pleasantly novel for me, something expanding. I'm not talking about thrills necessarily or plot twists. I'm talking about extended experience, extended knowledge of my own experience that comes to me through films. Film is in a sense a rather meretricious form, I've always thought, because it's so easily powerful. I mean, there's nothing easier than to sink into a chair in a film theater and be seduced, be overwhelmed.

Charlie Rose: Right.

Stanley Kauffmann: But beneath that ease, that facileness, there's a tremendous strength, a tremendous imaginative tickle that I get—everyone gets—

Charlie Rose: Yeah.

Stanley Kauffmann: —from film.

Charlie Rose: And there are just so many things you can do. I mean, it's the combination, for me, of the eye and the ear and music and dialogue and visual—breathtaking visual penetration.

Stanley Kauffmann: Once I went to *Citizen Kane*—and this was long before the days of videotape—and tried to keep my eyes shut, just so I could listen to Bernard Herrmann's wonderful score. Just one component of a great work. I was taught when I was a theater student, which I was at one time, that the theater drew on all the other arts around it and before it. Film is one step—in that—in the historical sense—one step higher because it draws on the theater and all the other arts.

Charlie Rose: It's the next logical extension of drawing on everything.
Stanley Kauffmann: Yes.

Charlie Rose: How has the movie business—as you have watched its evolution—how has it changed? How has film changed?
Stanley Kauffmann: Well, in lots of ways. First of all, obviously in content, in permissiveness—if you are talking about my brief forty-year span—

Charlie Rose: Forty years, from 1958 to '98.
Stanley Kauffmann: Permissiveness has changed tremendously, which is simply a corollary to what's happening in society generally. Here's one example. In 1966, I reviewed the film *Who's Afraid of Virginia Woolf?,* and I made a point of noting that "Hollywood star Elizabeth Taylor actually used on screen the phrase 'son of a bitch.'" Now there's a quaint if you—

Charlie Rose: You took note at the time that S.O.B. was used.
Stanley Kauffmann: It was extraordinary, and that's simply a marker in a—in a lexicon of permissiveness that's grown since then. Lots of other things have changed, too.

Charlie Rose: Well, permissiveness is good, isn't it? Because in effect it's more a reflection of reality.
Stanley Kauffmann: Permissiveness is necessary, but permissiveness—as in the theater, as in novels and any art form—is an open door to those who exploit it as well.

Charlie Rose: Right. Do you ever go on the set of a movie?
Stanley Kauffmann: I have done—I haven't lately, but I have done so a number of times. But once in particular I spent a day with Fellini in Rome—a whole day while he was shooting material from *Juliet of the Spirits.* That's

one aspect of the film business in a nutshell. He spent a whole day waiting for the right light and so on and so forth and fussing and lunch intervened—a wonderful lunch with his favorite meatballs—

Charlie Rose: Yeah?

Stanley Kauffmann: —and when the film came out that scene wasn't in it. He'd cut that scene.

Charlie Rose: But he waited all day for the right light.

Stanley Kauffmann: But that's just part—

Charlie Rose: Where do you put him?

Stanley Kauffmann: Fellini?

Charlie Rose: Yes.

Stanley Kauffmann: High.

Charlie Rose: Very.

Stanley Kauffmann: High. It's an interesting career if you want to talk about Fellini.

Charlie Rose: Sure.

Stanley Kauffmann: He began as a—in the neorealist vein that took over Italy immediately after World War II and he made some beautiful films in that vein—most notably the one in Italian that is called *I vitelloni,* which was called here *The Young and the Passionate,* about youth, young people in a small Italian city. And midway in his career there came a caesura, a pause of about four or five years, after which he changed completely. He became a director—he moved from the nitty-gritty to the fancy, the elegant, the baroque. If you saw for example *La dolce vita* right after you saw *The Young and the Passionate,* you wouldn't believe the same director—

Charlie Rose: Not the same filmmaker?

Stanley Kauffmann: No. And he has made, I think, at least one film that's not just a first-class film. It's one of the important artworks of the twentieth century. And that's *8½*—

Charlie Rose: Why is that?

Stanley Kauffmann: —a film about—a film about the artist's dilemma in our century, the difficulty of knowing why you're making art in a—in civilization, in a culture that has lost so many of its compass points that guided its artists of the past in so many different ways.

Charlie Rose: I'm jumping around, but you lead me there—
Stanley Kauffmann: With me.

Charlie Rose: Could *8½*, with today's financial structure in place in Hollywood, be made today? With a filmmaker as good as Fellini.
Stanley Kauffmann: I—it's hard to answer that question. It's purely supposition.

Charlie Rose: Right.
Stanley Kauffmann: But I think that, in those circumstances, given his material, his talent, and his reputation at the time, probably it could be made. Prices, costs have risen tremendously, but so have receipts. And I'm not sure—I don't even know if that film was a financial success, but I think there would probably have been someone who would have—some group that would have backed that film. One reason for saying so is that, although we don't exactly have a Fellini working today in Italian film or any other film— any other country—there are lots and lots of very gifted people making films in the world today that are not what you would call "sure-fire commercial items." And they're coming to us from all over the world, including from America. And someone is taking chances on these films.

Charlie Rose: Is Woody Allen one of those people?
Stanley Kauffmann: Woody Allen is a—is *sui generis.* He's himself. He's not a commercial hotshot, but nevertheless he's backed by people with money. But I'm talking about directors from Taiwan, from China, from Burkina Faso, from Senegal, from America who are making films that are of genuine merit, real worth.

Charlie Rose: And they find an audience?
Stanley Kauffmann: That's another question. That's a really difficult question. As you know there's been much talk lately about the death of cinephilia. Some very intelligent people have written articles on that subject. And, as a matter of fact, in 1986 I wrote such an article. I've done considerable teaching in my life, including film courses. And I noted in 1986 that the knowledge and appetite and hunger for films, which was evident when I began teaching years before, had filtered, diminished, dwindled. We're faced now in the film world with a contradictory situation. On the one hand, there are these films of genuine worth and interest, worth any intelligent person's time, that are being made and coming here—coming at least to New York— from all over the world. And, on the other hand, there are young people—the

equivalent of that film generation of 1966—intelligent, alert, motivated people who aren't as hungry for films as they were then, don't care as much about them. I don't know exactly why that's the case—though I've written about it. I sometimes write about things I don't know, exploring them.

Charlie Rose: Using the essay as a point of departure for your own exploration of an idea or a—
Stanley Kauffmann: Trying to find out what I think about something.

Charlie Rose: Exactly. Exactly.
Stanley Kauffmann: I make some guesses about it, I think—

Charlie Rose: Was it Auden or somebody who once said, "I don't know what I think until I see what I've written."
Stanley Kauffmann: Until I write it.

Charlie Rose: Yeah.
Stanley Kauffmann: But it's a puzzle. I've—May I tell you this story?

Charlie Rose: Sure, of course.
Stanley Kauffmann: Last fall I did a film course at a place where I had taught for seventeen years—the Yale School of Drama, which is a graduate school. A wonderful group of intelligent, mature, alert people, literate, highly literate, well-versed in music, et cetera, et cetera. I showed nine films in the course of the course, that are accepted as "classics"—a tired word, but nonetheless true of these films.

Charlie Rose: Masterpieces.
Stanley Kauffmann: Yes. Without much question. And these people reacted as if a new world were being opened up to them.

Charlie Rose: They hadn't seen them?
Stanley Kauffmann: Hadn't seen them. Most—once in a while in the course of those nine weeks—oh, three or four people had seen the film. I remember once on an earlier occasion, I showed a masterpiece—Dreyer's film *The Passion of Joan of Arc.*

Charlie Rose: Yeah.
Stanley Kauffmann: And, after the class, I was walking away, and a young woman—a very intelligent young woman—came up to me angry. Angry. And she says, "Why didn't they tell me there were films like this?" And I was angry with her.

Charlie Rose: Angry with her because she hadn't gone out to find them on her own, and she should have.

Stanley Kauffmann: She had been, she felt, deliberately deprived of—

Charlie Rose: Sure.

Stanley Kauffmann: —of access to these wonderful films that are there now more than ever because of videotape.

Charlie Rose: Yeah.

Stanley Kauffmann: One fact—

Charlie Rose: And we're soon to have interactivity so you can just order them up.

Stanley Kauffmann: Yes, yes. You can—you—I mean, it's a dream situation.

Charlie Rose: Exactly.

Stanley Kauffmann: Anyone who wrote about films before videotape always made mistakes because he had to write from memory. Now, in many cases, you can have the thing itself to deal with.

Charlie Rose: Before I forget this thought—

Stanley Kauffmann: Yeah.

Charlie Rose: What were the nine films that were the masterpieces?

Stanley Kauffmann: I can't remember them all, but—

Charlie Rose: Give me just what you remember.

Stanley Kauffmann: Well, *Grand Illusion.*

Charlie Rose: Right.

Stanley Kauffmann: A wonderful German film called *Marianne and Juliane,* which is a political classic. There was, of course, *Citizen*—I ended with *Citizen Kane.*

Charlie Rose: What'd you think of the American Film Institute's Top 100 Films?

Stanley Kauffmann: I was invited to vote in the initial—not in the "ten best" contest but in the initial go-around.

Charlie Rose: Right.

Stanley Kauffmann: And I didn't because I didn't want to be trampled under the thundering herd of opinions that I didn't agree with. Obviously there are some—well, anyone—whoever he or she might be—who would disagree with—

Charlie Rose: Of course they would. And they'd have something—there's an omission here or there's an addition—
Stanley Kauffmann: But—

Charlie Rose: Mainly omissions.
Stanley Kauffmann: But I thought there were some on the list that were just ludicrous.

Charlie Rose: All right, let me just go through the top ten and tell me if you like—which ones you would disagree with—
Stanley Kauffmann: O.K.

Charlie Rose: *Citizen Kane.*
Stanley Kauffmann: Fine.

Charlie Rose: *Casablanca?*
Stanley Kauffmann: No. *Casablanca* is not one of the best American films by any means. It's one of the most endearing American films. It's one of the most memorable American films. But a lot of it—it's really—the fact that it was made then, when it was—in the 1940s, is lucky for it in a way because it's really a slushy romance, and we can watch it now and indulge in old-fashioned romance without feeling soppy.

Charlie Rose: All right.
Stanley Kauffmann: We can feel sophisticated about it.

Charlie Rose: You sometimes like slushy romance?
Stanley Kauffmann: Yes.

Charlie Rose: *The Godfather?*
Stanley Kauffmann: *The Godfather,* I had reservations about. It's certainly a well-made film, but I think it's merely an aggrandized gangster film of—I think the best performance in it for me is not—

Charlie Rose: Brando.
Stanley Kauffmann: Not Brando, and not Al Pacino. It's James Caan.

Charlie Rose: Jimmy Caan. Yeah. I thought you'd say either that or Duvall. *Gone With the Wind?*

Stanley Kauffmann: *Gone With the Wind* is—you know, it's a sacred monster. It's not a—

Charlie Rose: *Lawrence of Arabia*?

Stanley Kauffmann: *Lawrence of Arabia* is a wonder. A wonder. It's a marvelous film. The screenplay—the screenplay wiggles and waggles a little in the second half of the film. They sort-of lost direction. I mean—I don't mean "directing," I mean "direction" in the script, but O'Toole's performance and David Lean's directing and Freddie Young's cinematography and Anne V. Coates's editing—You know she edited *Out of Sight*?

Charlie Rose: She did what?

Stanley Kauffmann: She edited this new film, *Out of Sight.*

Charlie Rose: Oh, she did?

Stanley Kauffmann: She's seventy-three—

Charlie Rose: I was going to ask about that.

Stanley Kauffmann: —seventy-three years old.

Charlie Rose: It's a terrific film. Did you like it?

Stanley Kauffmann: Very much. Do you know? It's another paradox. What I would call "good rewarding serious films"—whether they're comedies or dramas—are more frequent these days than good entertainment films in my— You're supposed to assume the reverse is true.

Charlie Rose: Yeah.

Stanley Kauffmann: That the good serious films are the exceptions. In my opinion—

Charlie Rose: There are more good serious films.

Stanley Kauffmann: —there are more good serious films. They're not— you don't get double-page-spread ads about them, and a lot of hoopla.

Charlie Rose: But you consider this simply an entertainment film.

Stanley Kauffmann: Yes.

Charlie Rose: Right, that's what I did, too. So, there are not many of those, and so when you see one that's advertised as good entertainment—

Stanley Kauffmann: They're not going to entertain me.

Charlie Rose: Exactly. And that does it.

Stanley Kauffmann: But this one certainly did.

Charlie Rose: What's the best serious film you've seen recently?

Stanley Kauffmann: Probably one from Iran by a man named Abbas Kiarostami, called *A Taste of Cherry*—a perfect example of what I'm talking about. In Iran, of all the unlikely countries, arises a group of filmmakers headed by this man who's now in his sixties, who are subtle, discreet, penetrating artists. His films, I've seen four or five of them, are contemplative, deep, ruminative, moving works full, first of all, of love for his people—the people of Iran—and knowledge of them. And also what's most interesting to me in his work is that he is entranced by the mysteries of film, of filmmaking.

Filmmaking is part of many of his films. A beautiful, beautiful artist. And his happens to be the last film I saw that meant so much to me.

Charlie Rose: You had a lot to do with *The Moviegoer,* didn't you?

Stanley Kauffmann: Yes. You mean the novel?

Charlie Rose: Yes, the novel.

Stanley Kauffmann: Walker Percy's novel. I was in publishing—

Charlie Rose: It was as an editor, weren't you? Or what?

Stanley Kauffmann: Yes. I found the novel. And worked on it for, oh, a year-and-a-half or more before it was published. He rewrote it three times. Every word is his, but I made some suggestions along the way that enabled him to do a beautiful book. You've read it, I'm sure.

Charlie Rose: Yes, yes.

Stanley Kauffmann: I was in book publishing for about ten years.

Charlie Rose: There is so much we can talk about. I want to invite you back and talk much more about movies—

Stanley Kauffmann: Thank you. I'd be delighted.

Charlie Rose: This summer we'll come back for several visits and talk more. I want to talk about how criticism has changed. I want to talk about some other subjects. But, if I talk longer tonight, we won't be able to get it into the program. So, I want to make sure we get this first installment. Thank you, Stanley.

Stanley Kauffmann: Thank you.

Charlie Rose: A pleasure to have you on the broadcast. Congratulations—forty years of writing for the *New Republic*. My thanks to Stanley Kauffmann. We will indeed do this again soon.

Index